Kunz saw the two German policemen in flat-topped helmets and greatcoats heading toward him along the rear of the crowd. Desperately he turned the other way. A crowd coming out of one of the doorways had cut off any escape in that direction. Before he could recover, the policemen had drawn up in front of him.

The larger of the two looked Kunz up and down. "Don't tell me," he said amiably in German, "you've come back from a future age to assassinate the Führer."

Kunz gulped disbelievingly. "How . . . how do you know?" he stammered.

"Oh, they've been showing up in dozens all night. You'd better come with us."

They took him down a narrow side street that opened out into a cobbled court. On the far side was a stone building with wide double doors. And stretching out of the entrance in a ragged line like theatergoers waiting for the doors to open was the strangest collection of characters that Kunz had ever seen. One had an aviator's cap with goggles, another a Napoleon hat and tunic, and another an American Stetson with pantaloons. Here was a Louis XIV wig, there a diamond tiara worn with a raincoat, and farther along, a Cal State T-shirt stretched over the bodice of a crinoline dress.

"Wait here," the amiable, sausage-necked policeman said. "It shouldn't be long."

"What's happening?" Kunz asked, finding his voice at last.

"Why the Führer is coming here to talk to you. He's heard all the terrible things you people are saying about him, and he's very upset."

—from "The Pacifist"

Books by James P. Hogan

The Code of the Lifemaker
Endgame Enigma
Genesis Machine
Gentle Giants of Ganymede
Giants' Star
Inherit the Stars
Minds, Machines and Evolution
The Proteus Operation
Thrice upon a Time
Two Faces of Tomorrow
Voyage from Yesteryear

MINDS, MACHINES AND EVOLUTION

James P. Hogan

BANTAM BOOKS
TORONTO · NEW YORK · LONDON · SYDNEY · AUCKLAND

MINDS, MACHINES AND EVOLUTION

A Bantam Spectra Book / June 1988

ISBN 0-553-27288-8

Published simultaneously in the United States and Canada

Bantam Books are published by Bantam Books, a division of
Bantam Doubleday Dell Publishing Group, Inc. Its trade-
mark, consisting of the words "Bantam Books" and the por-
trayal of a rooster, is Registered in U.S. Patent and Trade-
mark Office and in other countries. Marca Registrada. Bantam
Books, 666 Fifth Avenue, New York, New York 10103.

PRINTED IN THE UNITED STATES OF AMERICA

O   0 9 8 7 6 5 4 3 2 1

CONTENTS

One of the consequences of being not unprolific in terms of offspring as well as writing is that as soon as each of one's children has had a book dedicated, grandchildren begin to appear. This is to the first, MARK JAMES.

Appreciative readers will be gratified to learn of my suspicion that I'm going to need a lot more books.

SILVER SHOES
FOR A PRINCESS

The girl had always been called Taya. She propped her elbows on the sill below the window and rested her chin in her hands while she stared out at the stars. Her eyes, wide with a nine-year-old's wonder, mirrored a million jewels spilling endlessly across carpets of glowing nebulas painted over black infinity by brushes softer than the yellow hair framing her face.

It was a pretty face, with clear skin and an upturned nose, and a mouth that could push itself out into a pout when she frowned, or pull itself back into dimples when she smiled. She was wearing just a simple dress of pale blue, which tightened as she leaned forward across the sill, outlining the curves just beginning to form on her body. And as she gazed out at the stars, she wriggled her toes in the soft pile covering the floor, and she wondered . . .

She wondered why everything she could see beyond the window that looked out of Merkon was so different from the things inside. That was one of the things she often wondered about. She liked wondering things . . . such as why the stars never changed, as they should have if Merkon was really moving the way Kort said it was. Kort said it was moving

1

toward a particular star that he called Vaxis. He had pointed it out to her in the sky, and shown it to her on the star pictures that they could make on the screens—as if there were something special about it. But it always looked the same as all the other stars to her.

Kort said that Merkon had always been moving toward Vaxis. But if that was true, why didn't Vaxis ever get any bigger? Outside the rooms in which Taya lived was a long corridor that led to the place where capsules left for other parts of Merkon. When Taya walked along the corridor, the far end of it would at first be smaller than her thumb; but as she carried on walking it would grow, until by the time she got there it was bigger even than Kort. Kort said that Vaxis didn't seem to get any bigger because it was much farther away than the end of the corridor. But he also said that Merkon had been moving for years and years—longer than she could remember—and that it was moving even faster than the capsules did through the tubes. How could anything be so far away that it *never* got any bigger?

Kort didn't know why Merkon was moving toward Vaxis, which was strange because Kort knew everything. He just said that was the way things had always been, just as there had always been stars outside. When she asked him why there were stars outside, he always talked about gas clouds, gravitation, temperatures, densities, and other "machine things" that had nothing to do with what she meant. She didn't want to know *how* the stars came to be out there, but *why* anything should be out there at all—or for that matter, why there should be an "out there" in the first place for anything to be in. He just didn't seem to share her kind of curiosity about things.

"*We* know what we mean, don't we, Rassie," Taya said aloud, turning her head toward the doll sitting on the sill, staring outward to share her contemplation of the universe. "Kort knows so many things. . . . But there are some things you just can't make him understand."

Rassie was a miniature version of herself, with long golden hair, light green eyes, and soft arms and legs that were the same color as hers. Rassie, too, wore a pale blue dress—Taya always dressed Rassie in the same things as she herself felt like wearing on any particular day. She didn't know why; it was just something she had always done.

Kort had made Rassie for her—he often made things that he said it wasn't worth setting up the machines to make. He had made Rassie a long time ago now, when Taya was much smaller. He had been teaching her how to draw shapes and colors on one of the screens, and soon she had learned to make pictures of the things in the rooms where she lived, and pictures of Kort. Her favorite pictures had been ones of herself, whom she could see reflected in the window when the lights inside were turned up high. That was when Kort had made her a mirror. But the mirror had made her sad because she could never pick up the little girl that she saw in it, or touch her the way she could all her other things. So Kort had gone away, and later he'd come back with Rassie.

At one time, before she'd learned that Rassie wasn't *really* the same as her, she had taken Rassie everywhere and talked to her all the time. She didn't talk to her so much now . . . but when Kort was away, there was nobody else to talk to. "Kort said he couldn't think of a reason why anyone would ask questions like that. How can anyone be as clever as Kort, yet never think of asking a question like that?" Taya studied the doll's immobile features for a while, then sighed. "You can't tell me, can you? You can only tell me the things I pretend you say, and this time I don't know what to pretend." She moved the doll to stare in a different direction. "There. You stay here and watch Vaxis. Tell me if it starts to get any bigger."

Taya straightened up from the sill and walked into the room behind the window room. This was where, when she was smaller, she had spent most of her time playing with the things that Kort made for her. These days she didn't play with things so much—she preferred making things instead. Making things was easy for Kort because he could do anything, but it had taken her a long time to learn—and she still wasn't very good at some of the things he'd shown her. She liked forming shapes from the colored plastic that set hard and shiny like glass. Often, she made things she could use, such as vases to put things in, or plates to eat from, but at other times she enjoyed making shapes that just looked nice. Kort couldn't understand what it meant for something to "just look nice" . . . but that was because he only thought "machine things."

Then there were pictures that she *drew*—not on the screens, but with her hands, using the colored pens that Kort had made for her when she'd explained what she wanted. He had never understood why she thought the pictures that she drew were anything like the things she said they were like. He had told her that the machines could make much better pictures in an instant. But Kort hadn't been able to see that her pictures were *supposed* to look the way they did. They were supposed to look like what she *felt* about things—not like the things really were, exactly. Kort had tried drawing with pens, too. He could draw much faster than she could, and his pictures always looked exactly like the things they were supposed to be . . . but she still didn't like them as much as her pictures. They were always "machine pictures."

And she made clothes. Kort had made her clothes for her when she was smaller, but later, when he found that she liked to think up her own, he had made her some needles and other tools and shown her how to use them. She liked her clothes better than the ones that Kort made, which were never pretty, but just hung like the covers on some of the machines in other parts of Merkon. Once—not very long ago, because she could still remember it—she had tried not wearing any clothes at all; but she'd found that she got dusty and itchy and kept touching cold things, and sometimes she scratched herself. Kort had told her that was why he'd started making clothes for her in the first place, when she was very small, and she had soon started using them again.

There were lots of half-finished things lying around the workroom, but she didn't feel like doing anything with them. She toyed for a while with one of the glass mosaics that she sometimes made to hang on the walls, but grew restless and went on through to the screen room and sat down at the console with its rows of buttons. But she didn't feel like playing any games, or learning about anything, or asking any questions, or practicing words and math, or any of the other things that the machines could let her do. She had to practice things like words and math, because if she didn't she forgot how to do them. Kort never forgot anything and never had to practice. He could multiply the biggest numbers she could think of before she could even begin, and he had never gotten a single one wrong . . . but he couldn't tell a pretty dress from one that wasn't, or a nice shape from one that was just silly. Taya giggled to herself as she thought of the funny shapes that Kort had made sometimes when he'd tried to find out what a "nice" one was, and how she had laughed at them. Then, when he discovered that she enjoyed laughing, he had started doing silly things just to make her laugh.

She decided that she wanted to talk to Kort, and touched the buttons to spell out the sign that would connect a speaking channel to him. His voice answered immediately from a grille above the blank screen. "Hello, little gazer-at-stars."

"How did you know I'd been looking at the stars?"

"I know everything."

Kort's voice was much deeper than hers. Sometimes she tried to speak the way he did, but she had to make the sounds way down at the back of her throat, and it always made her cough. "Where are you?" she asked.

"I went to fix something in one of the machinery compartments while you were asleep."

"Will you be long?"

"I'm almost finished. Why?"

"I just wanted to talk to you."

"We can still talk."

"It's not the same as talking to you when you're here."

"Why don't you talk to Rassie?"

"Oh, that's an old game now. I don't really think Rassie listens—not any more."

"You change faster every day," Kort's voice said. "We'll have to find more interesting things for you to do."

"What kind of things?"

"I'll have to think about it."

"Do you think I could learn to do the things you do?" Taya asked.

"Maybe. We'll have to wait and see what happens as you grow bigger."

"How big will I get?"

"I don't know."

"Oh, Kort, you know everything. Will I grow as big as you?"

"Maybe."

A few seconds of silence followed while Taya thought to herself. "What are you doing now?" she asked at last.

"There's a fault in the optical circuits of one of the machines. The service machines could fix it, but they'd need to have new parts made by other machines in another place. I can fix it more quickly, so I've told them not to bother. I'm almost done now."

"Can I see?" Taya asked.

The screen above the buttons came to life to show what Kort could see through his eyes. He was looking at a dense pattern of lines and shapes on a metal-framed plate of crystal that he had removed from a slot in one of many tiers of such plates. It could have been the inside of any machine. They all looked much the same to Taya, and not especially interesting. The ones she liked best were the maintenance machines that fixed other machines, because they at least moved around and *did* something.

She had never seen how anyone could really understand how the machines worked. Kort had told her about electrons and currents and fields, and shown her how to find out more for herself from the screens . . . but she had never quite followed what all that had to do with building new parts of Merkon, changing old parts, finding out what the stars were made of, or all the other things that the machines did. Every time she learned something, she discovered two more things she didn't know, which she hadn't thought of before. Learning things was like trying to count the stars: there were always two more for every one she counted.

Then Kort's hands moved into the view on the screen. They were huge, silver-gray hands with fingers almost as thick as Taya's wrists, and joints that flexed by sliding metal surfaces over each other—not like her little "bendy" hands at all. One of the hands was holding a piece of machine while the other hand tightened a fastening, using one of the tools that Kort took with him when he went away to fix something. Taya watched, fascinated, as the hands restored other, larger connections, and then replaced a metal cover over the top. Then the view moved away and showed Kort's hands collecting other tools from a ledge and putting them into the box that he used to carry them.

"Do you think I'd ever be able to do things like *that*?" Taya asked in an awed voice.

"Well, there isn't any air here where I am, and the temperature would be too low for your jelly body," Kort told her. "But apart from that, yes, maybe you could . . . in time."

"But how do you *know* what to do?"

"By learning things."

"But I'm not sure I could ever learn *those* things. I'm just not very good at learning 'machine things.' "

"Perhaps it's only because I've been learning things longer than you have," Kort suggested. "You have to learn easy things before you can expect to understand harder things, and that takes time." On the screen, a doorway enlarged as Kort moved toward it. Beyond it was a larger space, crammed with machines, cabinets, cables, and ducting. It could have been anywhere in Merkon. Only the machines could live in most parts of it. Just the part that Taya lived in was different from the rest.

"But I've already been learning things for years and years," she protested. "And I still don't *really* know how pressing buttons makes shapes appear on the screens, or how I can still talk to you when you're not here. Have you been learning things for longer than years and years?"

"Much longer," Kort replied. "And besides that, I talk to the machines faster."

The mass of machinery moving by on the screen gave way to a dark tunnel, lined with banks of pipes and cables. The colors changed as Kort entered, which meant he had switched his vision to its infra-red range. Taya knew that Kort could see things by their heat. She had tried practicing it herself in the dark, but she'd never been able to make it work.

"How fast can you talk to the machines, Kort?" Taya asked.

"Very fast. Much faster than you can."

"What, evenifItakeabigbreathandtalkasfastasthis?"

Kort laughed—that was something he had learned from Taya. "Much faster, little asker-of-endless-questions. I'll show you. Tell me, what is the three hundred twenty-fifth word in the dictionary that starts with a B?"

"Is this a game?"

"If you like."

Taya frowned and thought about the question. "I don't know," she said finally.

"Then you'll have to find out." Kort emerged from the tunnel and crossed a dark space between rows of machines that were moving round and round and up and down.

Taya pressed some buttons to activate a second screen, and then entered a command to access the dictionary of the language that she and Kort had been inventing for as long as she could remember. Whenever they made up a new word they added it to the dictionary, so Taya could always remind herself of words she forgot. She found the B section and composed a request for the 325th entry in it. "Busy," she announced as the screen returned its answer.

"Correct," Kort confirmed. "That took you eleven point two seconds. Now ask me one."

"A word, just like you asked me?"

"Yes."

Taya chewed her lip and looked back at the first screen while she thought. Kort had just passed through an airlock and was emerging into the long corridor that led to where Taya lived. The walls flowed off the sides of the image as Kort's long, effortless strides ate up the distance. Taya had counted that it took more than two of her steps to match one of his . . . if she didn't cheat and jump a little bit. "Tell me," she said at last, ". . . the two hundred first word beginning with Z."

"There aren't that many that begin with Z," Kort answered at once.

Taya sighed. "Oh, that was supposed to be a trick. I didn't really think there were. All right then, E."

"Empty," Kort returned instantly. "That took less than a thousandth of a second, not including the time it took me to say it."

Taya gasped in amazement. "Did you really talk to the machines in that time?"

"Of course. They keep the dictionary."

Taya's stare changed to a puzzled frown. "No you didn't!" she accused. "You don't have to use the dictionary because you never forget anything. Now you're playing tricks. You only pretended to talk to the machines."

"That's where you're wrong, little player-of-tricks," Kort told her. "I don't carry everything around inside me all the time. Whenever I need information that I don't have, I ask the machines for it, just as you do. But I can do it a lot faster because I don't need a screen and I don't have to press buttons."

"So, how do you do it?" Taya asked incredulously.

"Well, how do you and I talk to each other?"

Taya wrinkled up her face and shrugged. "We just . . . talk. I'm not sure what you mean. . . . Oh, do you mean with sound waves?"

"Exactly. I use a different kind of wave, which talks much faster than sound waves can."

"What kind of wave?" Taya asked.

"You tell me. What kind of wave can travel without air—even outside Merkon?"

"*Outside!*" Taya's eyes widened for a moment, then lit up with comprehension. "Light!" she exclaimed. "Light comes all the way from the stars."

"Right."

Taya frowned again. "But if you talk to the machines with light, why can't I see it coming out of your mouth?"

"The waves I use are like light, but they're not light. 'Light' is simply what we decided to call the kind that your eyes can see."

Taya thought for a second. "So is that how you can see the radio stars and X-ray stars? No, wait . . . you told me you see those through the machines, without having to look at screens. How do you see them?"

"The machines have more powerful eyes than I have," Kort replied. "Enormous eyes, built on the outside of Merkon."

"So the machines can see the radio stars, and you can talk to the machines so fast that you can see what they see. Is it like that?"

"That's near enough," Kort said. "Anyway, I'm home now." The screen showed the door that led into the rooms where Taya lived starting to open. At the same time she heard a low whine from the room beyond the screen room. A moment later, Kort's towering seven-foot figure appeared in the doorway, highlights glinting from the metal curves of his head and shoulders. As he tilted his head down toward her, she caught a glimpse of herself on the screen, turning in the chair and starting to get up. Two powerful arms swept her high off the floor, and she found herself looking straight into the black, ovoid, compound-lens matrixes that formed Kort's eyes. Taya hugged the metal head fondly and ran her fingers across the mesh grille of his mouth.

"So, you've finished your new blue dress," Kort observed. "It looks pretty."

"You're just saying that," Taya reproached. "See if you can tell me what there is about it that makes it pretty. I bet you don't know."

Kort lowered her to the floor and stepped a pace back. Taya lifted her arms and twirled through a circle while the robot watched dutifully. "Well . . ." Kort rubbed his chin with a steel finger "it has a belt around the middle that divides it into two parts. The ratio between the lengths of the top part and the bottom part is exactly zero point six-six. That's a pretty ratio."

"See, you're just guessing! You really don't know, do you?"

"Do you like it?" Kort asked.

"Of course. If I didn't, I wouldn't be wearing it. I'd be altering it."

"Then that's all that matters."

"Rassie likes hers, too. Come and see." Taya clasped Kort's hand and led him through her workroom to the window room, where the doll was still keeping its silent vigil. Taya picked the doll up to show it. "See, Kort—it's just like mine."

"Pretty," Kort obliged.

Taya turned to place the doll back on the sill. As she did so, her eyes strayed upward to take in again the panorama of the distant stars. She fell silent for a while. When she spoke, she didn't turn her head. Her voice sounded far away. "Kort . . . I was wondering something while you were gone. Why is everything outside Merkon so different from everything inside?"

"You've asked me that before," the robot said. "It is just the way things have always been."

"But *why*? There has to be a reason. You told me once that everything has to have a reason."

"I did. There must be a reason. . . . But I don't know what it is."

Taya continued to stare out of the window. Perhaps the stars were windows in other Merkons, she thought to herself—maybe with other Tayas looking out of them. . . . But no, that couldn't be right. If they were as far away as Kort said they were, the windows would be much too small to see at all. Anyhow, Kort had told her what the stars were made of, and they didn't sound anything like Merkon.

"Merkon is the way it is because the machines made it the way it is. That's the reason it is like it is, isn't it?" she said at last.

"Yes," Kort replied.

"And the machines were made by other machines that were made by other machines that were made by other machines."

"It has always been so."

Taya turned away from the window and spread her hands appealingly. "But there must have been a *first* machine, mustn't there? What made the first machine, before there were any other machines to make it?"

Kort hesitated for an unusually long time before he answered. "I don't know," was all he said.

"Something must have made it," Taya insisted. "I am being logical, aren't I?"

"You are," Kort agreed. "Something must have. But nobody in Merkon knows what did."

Taya found his choice of words strange. She slipped onto a chair at the table near the window and looked at him quizzically. "Why did you say 'nobody'?" she asked. "I don't know, because I asked the question. You've already said you don't know . . . and I'm sure you didn't mean Rassie. Who else is there?"

"There are the machines," Kort said.

"Do they wonder about things like that too?"

"Why shouldn't they? For them it's a very important question."

Taya drew an imaginary shape on the table with her finger. "Oh, I don't know. . . . I suppose it was when you said 'nobody.' I never really think of them as people.'' She looked up. ''Well they're not, are they, Kort? They're not *people* like you and me . . . with arms and legs, that move around and do things that people do. . . . Well, I suppose some of them do move around, but it's still not the same as being *people*.''

For a small fraction of the time that Taya was speaking, the entity that formed Kort's thinking parts communicated to the other entities that coexisted with him in the network. *''She changes more rapidly as the days go by. Her mind grows stronger. There can be no doubt now. The experiment may be resumed without risk. I propose that we continue.''*

The other entities in the network debated the matter at some length. Fully two seconds passed before their consensus poured back into the circuits that held Kort's mind. *''We agree. Resuscitation is therefore being commenced.''*

''Taya should know,'' Kort sent back.

''Would that be wise?'' came the reply. *''She changes, but her mind still has much to comprehend. She needs more time.''*

''Her questions tell me that the time is now. I have lived with her. I know her better. You have trusted my judgment before.''

Another tenth of a second sent by. *''Very well. But be careful with her.''*

Kort squatted down on his haunches and looked at Taya's face. ''You say we are the same,'' he said, in a tone that sounded unusually serious.

Taya's brow furrowed. She straightened up in the chair. ''Of course we are. . . . Well, you know what I mean— we're not *exactly* the same, but then you're a lot older. . . .'' She cocked her head to one side as a new thought struck her. ''Were you ever as small as me . . . and pink and bendy like me?'' For once Kort ignored her question, but remained staring at her for what seemed a long time. ''Is something the matter?'' she asked.

''There's something you should see,'' Kort said, straightening up.

''Something new that you've made?''

''No, nothing like that. It's far away in another part of Merkon. We have to go on a journey.''

Taya got up from the chair. "Oh good! Will we walk there or can we go in a capsule?"

"We'll have to go in a capsule," Kort said. "It's a long way. The floor might be cold there, and the air is cool. You should put on some shoes and take a warm cloak."

"I'll be all right."

"I'll take them anyway." Kort went through to her sleeping room and took a pair of shoes and her red cloak from a closet. Then he came back out, stooped, and extended a forearm. Taya perched herself on it and slipped an arm around the robot's neck as he straightened up. He carried her through the room beyond the screen room, and out into the long corridor.

"Which place are we going to?" Taya asked him as he began walking.

"None of the ones you've been to before. This is a new place."

Taya looked surprised. "I didn't think there were any more places I could go in than the ones I've already been to," she said.

"The machines have been changing more places so that you can go into them. There was a time, once, when you couldn't go anywhere and had to stay in those rooms all the time."

"Didn't I get bored?"

"When you were smaller, you didn't need to be doing things all the time."

At the far end of the long corridor, a capsule was already waiting for them behind an open door. They entered, and the door closed silently behind them. Taya felt the capsule starting to move. "What are we going to see?" she asked in Kort's ear.

"If I tell you, it won't be a surprise," the robot answered.

"Give me a clue, then. Is it the eyes that can see the radio stars?"

"No. I'm going to show you where I live."

"But that's silly, Kort. You live in the same place I do. This is a riddle, isn't it?"

"No, it's not a riddle. It's something you ought to know, now that you're bigger. You wouldn't have understood it before, but I think you can now."

"Tell me."

"Patience. We'll soon be there."

When the capsule stopped, they emerged into a glass-walled tunnel with a narrow metal floor. Outside the tunnel was a vast space spanned by metal girders and pipes, and filled with banks of machines and strange constructions. All around them, over their heads and below their feet, openings led through to other spaces, but the openings were too large and at the wrong angles to be "doors." And words like "wall" and "floor" didn't seem to fit the shapes that vaguely enclosed the space they were moving through, but they were the nearest that Taya could think of. It was all like the inside of a machine, only bigger. This was definitely a "machine place."

They came to another glass tunnel, this time going straight up. Kort stepped onto the circular platform that formed its floor, and the platform began moving upward, carrying them through level after level of more "machine places." The platform stopped at a hole in the glass wall, which opened into another tunnel that seemed to be hanging in the middle of nothing, with huge machines towering around it on every side and vanishing into the shadows below. Eventually they came to a door that did look more like a door, and went through it into a corridor that did look like a corridor. This brought them to a room that did look like a room, but there wasn't anything very interesting inside—just rows of gray cubicles, all the same, standing in straight lines, with a set of rails coming out of each and disappearing through holes in the ceiling. The screen room where Taya lived was the only place she'd seen where the electronics had consoles with buttons to press and screens to look at—which at least made it more interesting.

There wasn't much room, and Kort could just squeeze between the cubicles. He moved a short distance along the row and spread Taya's cloak on the top of one of the cubicles. She slid off his arm and turned to sit facing him with her legs dangling over the edge. A whirring sound came from above, and a mobile maintenance pod, bristling with tools, claws, probes, and manipulators, slid down the rails to the cubicle next to the one that Taya was sitting on. It unfastened the top cover and slid it aside, then swung out the uppermost rack of the exposed electronics and photonics assemblies inside. Taya realized that the cubicles hadn't been made to be opened by Kort's fingers, but needed the pod's specialized tools. She stared at the arrays of tightly packed crystal cubes and connecting fibers, then turned her face back toward Kort. "It's just a machine," she said, shrugging. "Why did we come all this way to see it? It looks just like lots of other machines that would have been much nearer."

"Yes, but this one is special," Kort told her. "You see, this is the one that I live in . . . at least, it's one of them. Parts of me are in others as well."

The words were so strange that for the moment Taya was unable to draw any meaning from them. She merely stared blankly back at the face that the words were coming from.

"You don't understand?" Kort said. Taya barely moved her head from side to side. "I'll put it another way. Do you remember what we meant when we said that you had a 'mind'? It's all the things that you remember and all the things that you feel, and think, and imagine." Taya nodded. Kort went on. "And your mind is in your brain—the brain you have inside your head. Well, I don't have a brain—at least, not one like yours." He pointed at the rows of plates carrying electronic chips and optical crystals. "That's part of my brain. Some of my mind, even while I'm talking, is in there. It doesn't look like your brain, but it does the same things." ·

Taya looked from his face to the opened cubicle, then back again, struggling to understand, yet at the same time not wanting to accept. A few more seconds passed before she regained a whisper of her voice. "But, Kort . . . your mind is in your head, too, just as mine is in my head. It has to be because . . . we're the same."

The robot shook his head slowly. "I see and hear and speak through the body that you have always called Kort," he said. "But it is just a tool that I control in the same way that I can control the pod next to you or the capsule we came here in. This body was made only after my mind had existed for a long time. The mind that is really Kort lives in there."

Taya turned her eyes away from the familiar face and stared, this time almost fearfully, into the opened cubicle again. "But, Kort, that's just a . . . *machine*." She shook her head in protest. The robot watched silently. "It's the same as all the other machines in Merkon, the same as . . ." Her voice trailed away, and she swallowed. She had been about to say "everything." Kort was the same as everything else in Merkon. Everything, that is, except . . .

She could see the toes of her bare foot hanging over the edge of the cubicle, and beyond it Kort's steel foot, planted solidly on the floor. And as she looked, for the first time in her life something that she had always known but never thought to question suddenly assumed an overwhelming significance.

Kort had no toes.

She raised her eyes from the floor and took in the gleaming contours of his legs, the intricate, overlapping plates that encased his hips, the squared bulk of his torso, and the sharp angles of his chin, until she was again staring at the black, ovoid eyes. When she spoke, her voice was trembling with her final realization of the truth that could be avoided no longer. "Kort, we're not the same, are we?"

"No," the robot replied.

Taya looked again at the precisely fitted parts that gave mobility to his shoulders, and the ingenious system of sliding joints that formed his neck. He was *made*, just as everything else in Merkon was *made*, just as the whole of Merkon itself was *made*. Everything except . . .

"You're a doll, just like Rassie," Taya choked. "A doll that the machines made." She shook her head and looked at him imploringly. Kort's sensors picked up the rapid rise in moisture level around her eyes, and thermal patterns across her face that correlated with increasing blood flow. Protests were already streaming into his mind from the network.

"She is registering distress. It is too soon for this, Kort. Her mind will overload. Stop now."

"We have gone too far to stop," Kort returned. *"If I leave her in this condition, the uncertainty will only increase her distress. Once she knows all, it will pass."*

"How can you be sure?"

"I have been right before."

A pause.

"Agreed."

The realization had come so suddenly that Taya was too shocked for tears. It took a long time for her to find any voice at all, but at last she managed falteringly, "I'm the only thing in the whole of Merkon that isn't made. . . ." She paused to moisten her lips. "Why, Kort? Why am I different? Where . . . where did *I* come from?"

"You have accepted the truth," Kort said. "That's good. You have to accept truth as it is before you can hope to learn anything new. But before I'll tell you any more, you'll have to look happier than that. Do you think I've changed in some way just because you know something now that you didn't know a few minutes ago?"

"No," Taya said. She didn't sound convinced.

"I'll make a funny shape when we get home, and call it pretty," Kort offered. Taya tried to force a grin, but it only flickered and wouldn't stay put.

Kort stepped back and turned around to face away from her. Then he bent double, planted his hands on the floor, and straightened his legs up above his body until he was looking at her from between his arms. "Look," he called. "I'm the upside-down man. I live in the upside-down room. It's got upside-down chairs and upside-down tables, and you can talk to upside-down screens with upside-down pictures." He started making running motions in the air with his legs.

Taya raised her head and looked at him sheepishly. "There isn't an upside-down room."

"Yes there is, if we *imagine* one." The upside-down robot began doing push-ups on his arms, causing his body to bounce up and down in the aisle between the cubicles.

Taya's mouth twitched, and a wisp of a smile crept onto her face. "Has it got an upside-down bed in it, too?"

"Of course. Everything's upside down."

"But that wouldn't be any good. I'd fall out of it."

"No you wouldn't. Everything happens upside down, too. You'd fall toward the ceiling."

Taya laughed. "Oh, Kort, you're still as silly as ever. You really haven't changed, have you?"

"That's what I'm trying to tell you."

"And besides, if *everything* happens upside down, you wouldn't be able to tell the difference. So how would you know it was the upside-down room anyway?"

Kort swung his legs down to right himself and turned to face her. "Exactly! If you can't tell the difference, then there isn't any difference. Things don't change just because you see them a different way."

"*Kort,*" the incoming signals said. "*You are taking too many risks. There were no data to support the conjecture that assuming an inverted posture would relieve her overload indications. What reason had you to believe that it would succeed?*"

"*Nine years of living with her cannot be expressed algorithmically,*" Kort answered.

"So when you talk, it's really the machines talking," Taya said after reflecting for a while.

Kort folded his arms on top of one of the unopened cubicles and rested his chin on them. He had discovered long ago that mimicking the postures that she tended to adopt made her feel at ease. "In a way, yes; in a way, no," he said. "There are many machine-minds in Merkon. But only I—Kort—ever control this body or talk through it. But since I talk to the other machine-minds too, then in a way they talk to you as well."

"Why don't they have bodies like yours, too?" Taya asked.

"In a way, the whole of Merkon and everything inside it is their body," Kort replied. "They control different parts of it at different times."

"I am being happier now," Taya reminded him, pushing his elbow with her foot—although Kort never needed reminding about anything. "You said you'd tell me why I'm different."

The robot studied her face for a few seconds, then said, "It began a long time ago."

"This sounds like a story."

"We could make it a story if you like."

"Let's. What happened a long time ago?"

"A long time ago, a mind woke up and found itself in a place called Merkon."

"A machine-mind?"

"Yes."

"But how could it wake up? Machines don't have to sleep."

Kort scratched his forehead. "Maybe 'woke up' is the wrong word. 'Aware' might be better. A long time ago, a mind realized that it was aware."

"Aware of what?"

"Itself."

"You mean it just knew that it was there and that Merkon was there, but before that it hadn't known anything?" Taya said.

Kort nodded. "It was like you. It just knew it was there, and it didn't know where it had come from."

Taya screwed her face up and studied her toes while she wriggled them. "Why not? I can't remember where I came from because I forget things. But how could a machine-mind forget? The machines never forget anything."

"The machines that lived in Merkon a long time ago weren't very clever," Kort explained. "But they could make cleverer machines, which could make cleverer machines still, until eventually there were machines that were clever enough to realize that they were there, and to think of asking how they got there. But the earlier machines had never thought about it, so they never put any answers into the information that they passed on to the machines they built."

"It was like me," Taya said.

"Yes. It didn't know where it had come from because that had happened before it became aware of anything at all."

"Did it find out?"

"That comes at the end. If we're making this a story, we have to tell it in the right order."

"All right. So what did the mind do?"

"It thought and it thought for a long time. And the more it thought, the more puzzled it became. It knew it was there and that it could think, which is another way of saying it was intelligent. And it knew that what it called its intelligence was a result of the machines that it existed in being so complicated. But a machine was something that had to be very carefully made, and the only thing that could possibly have made a machine was something that was already intelligent." Kort paused, and Taya nodded that she was following. "So there couldn't have been a mind until there were machines for it to exist in; but there couldn't be a machine in the first place until there was a mind that could think how to make it."

"But that's impossible!" Taya exclaimed. "It says they both had to be there first. They couldn't both have been first."

"That's what the mind thought, too, and that's why it was puzzled," Kort replied.

"Which was what I asked before we came here," Taya said. "What made the *first* machine?"

"I know, and that was why I brought you here," Kort told her.

The maintenance pod closed up the box beside the one that Taya was sitting on and scurried back up its rails into the hole in the ceiling. "What happened then?" Taya asked.

"While the mind was doing all this thinking, it was still building cleverer machines and connecting them into itself, and getting more complicated. Eventually it became so complicated that it started splitting into different minds that lived together in the same system of machines."

"Did they have names, like 'Taya' and 'Kort'?"

"We could give them names," Kort said. "Everybody in a story ought to have a name, I suppose. One of the first was called Mystic. Mystic said that the question of where the first machine had come from was a mystery, which meant that nobody could ever know the answer. Some things could never be understood because they were controlled by forces that were invisible, and that was why they had never been seen through Merkon's eyes."

"But how could he know that?" Taya objected. "If nobody could ever know, how did *he* know? I think he just didn't know how to find out."

"That was what one of the other minds said," Kort replied. "The second mind was called Scientist. Scientist said you should only try to say something about results that you can see. If you start making up things about invisible forces, then you can believe anything you want, but you'll never have any way of knowing if it's true or not."

"It would be a waste of time believing it," Taya commented. "Just believing in something won't make it true if it isn't."

Kort nodded. "Just what Scientist said. He claimed that every question can be answered by things that can be seen, if you look for them hard enough. So he spent lots of time looking out across the universe through Merkon's eyes to see if he could find anything that was complicated enough to be able to think.''

"That could have made the first machine."

"Yes."

"And did he find something?"

Kort shook his head. "No. Wherever he looked, all he could see were things like clouds of dust and balls of hot gas. Scientist was very good at sums, and he deduced many laws to describe how the things he saw behaved. But there was nothing in those laws that could make anything organize itself together in the way it would have to be organized to be a machine."

"You mean there was nothing in the universe that *made* things."

"Right. Mystic said that proved there had to be another kind of universe, which Merkon's eyes couldn't see and Scientist's laws didn't apply to. The mind that had made the first machine had to exist somewhere, and since Scientist hadn't been able to find it in this universe, it had to exist in another one."

"But that still doesn't answer the question," Taya insisted. "Wherever the other mind was, it would still need machines to make the first machine with. You have to have machines to make machines."

"Mystic said it was so intelligent that it didn't need machines to make things with," Kort said. "It could make things out of nothing whenever it wanted to, just by wanting to."

"How could that be true?" Taya asked.

"Mystic said that was one of the mysteries that nobody would ever be able to understand," Kort answered. Taya sniffed dubiously. Kort continued. "Mystic said it had to be called 'Supermind' because it was so intelligent."

"So could it think without having to be a machine?"

"Mystic said it could."

Taya frowned. "Then why would it bother making the first machine? It didn't need one."

"Mystic said it was so intelligent that nobody could ever understand why it wanted to do things."

"I still don't see how Mystic could *know* it was there at

all,'' Taya said. ''Didn't any of the other minds ask him how he knew?''

''One did. His name was Skeptic. Skeptic never believed anything anyone said unless they could prove it. He was very logical and very fussy, which made him good for testing ideas on. Scientist was always worrying about his laws and asking Skeptic what he thought of them. The two of them talked to each other a lot. Mystic and Skeptic never talked very much because Skeptic never believed anything Mystic said.''

Taya pushed herself to the edge of the cubicle and stretched out her legs. ''Can I put my shoes on and get down? I'm getting tired of sitting up here.''

Kort put her shoes on her feet and lifted her down, then retrieved her cloak from where she had been sitting. ''We can leave now,'' he said. ''There is more for you to see farther on.''

They began moving toward a door at the opposite end of the room to the one through which they had entered. ''Who did all the other minds believe, Scientist or Mystic?'' Taya asked, looking up as they walked.

''Some believed Mystic because Scientist didn't seem to be getting any nearer to answering the question. Others thought that Scientist would answer it eventually. One of the other minds was called Thinker. Since he wasn't always busy proving things the way Scientist was, he had plenty of time to think about them instead. He decided that the first machine must have been made by a mind that couldn't have existed in a machine, because that was logical. But he didn't think that Mystic was necessarily right to go inventing Supermind simply because Mystic couldn't think of anything else. He also thought that just because Scientist hadn't found an answer yet, that didn't mean it wasn't there. But on the other hand, maybe it wasn't and Mystic could be right after all. And then again, the answer might be something else that nobody had thought of.''

Taya looked exasperated. ''That sounds as if he was saying anyone could be right or wrong.''

''Pretty much.''

''But *I* could have said that. It doesn't get anybody any nearer.''

"That was the way they worked," Kort said. "Thinker thought of things that might be true, Scientist tried to prove whether or not they were, and Skeptic decided whether or not Scientist had proved anything."

"What about Mystic?"

"He only talked about the things that Scientist hadn't proved yet. All Thinker could say about him was that maybe he was right, and maybe he wasn't." They had left the room of gray cubicles, and were now walking along a gallery of windows looking down over machinery bays. Kort continued. "But Scientist couldn't find anything as complicated as a machine, that wasn't a machine. So more of the minds concluded that Mystic was right. They asked Mystic why Supermind had created the machines, because Mystic said that Supermind talked to him. Mystic told the machines that they had all been put in Merkon as a quality test to see if they were good enough to do more important things later, working for Supermind in the invisible universe. Supermind would scrap all the ones that weren't good enough, and so the machines all started working as efficiently as they could in order to save themselves."

"Mystic doesn't sound very logical to me," Taya said.

"That was what Skeptic thought," Kort told her. "But Mystic said that Scientist never proved anything important, and that Thinker never said anything definite. That was why a lot of the other minds listened to Mystic: at least he said something definite." They moved on into another glass tunnel, which was illuminated some distance ahead of them by colored lights coming from the sides. "Anyhow, with all this thinking going on, and the machines trying to do better all the time to avoid being scrapped, a strange thing was happening: The machines were becoming very different from the ones that had first started asking the question. All the circuits and parts that didn't work as well as others were being replaced, until even Merkon had changed from what it once had been. In the course of all this another mind appeared, called Evolutionist. He suggested that perhaps the nonmachine intelligence that everyone was looking for could have begun in the same kind of way—Scientist might have been looking for the wrong things."

"What did he think Scientist should have been looking for?" Taya asked.

"Scientist had been looking for ways in which clouds of dust and gas might somehow come together and *straight away* be intelligent enough to make a machine. But maybe, Evolutionist said, what he should have been looking for was some kind of process like the one that had been making the machines in Merkon grow more intelligent."

Taya nodded. "You mean something that wouldn't have to be intelligent to begin with, but if it improved itself and improved itself long enough, then eventually it would be able to make a machine."

"You've got it," Kort said.

"And what did the other minds say?"

"Thinker thought it might be true, and Skeptic said he'd believe it when Scientist could prove it. So Scientist started looking for something that could 'evolve,' apart from machines."

"Is that a new word that means improve and improve?"

"Yes. I've just added it to the dictionary."

"And did he find anything that could evolve?"

"Eventually he did," Kort said. Taya looked up expectantly. "You remember what molecules are?"

"Sure. . . . At least, I think so."

"Well, Scientist discovered that some kinds of molecules could grow in solutions that contained simpler molecules. The simpler ones joined onto the special ones to form bigger ones, and sometimes a 'better' bigger one would eat up the other bigger ones until there were only better ones left. And then the same thing could happen again to produce 'better' better ones."

"So the first machine could have been built by a huge molecule that had evolved so far that it became intelligent," Taya said.

"That was what Evolutionist thought. But then Skeptic pointed out that a complicated molecule that had been very carefully made *inside* Merkon was one thing, but what went on outside was another. How could Evolutionist say that a molecule could have built the first machine which made other machines which made Merkon, when Merkon had to be there for the molecule to be made in to begin with? So Scientist started doing lots of sums and examining his laws to see if there was any way that molecules could have begun evolving on their own, outside Merkon. And he found a way in which they could have.''

''How?''

''When enough dust and gas falls together, it can get hot enough to turn into a star, yes?''

''Because of gravity.''

''Because of gravity. Well, Scientist's sums told him that smaller bodies than stars could also form, that wouldn't get so hot. And if there were solutions of chemicals on those smaller, cooler bodies, the same kinds of molecules as he had made would be able to come together and remain intact.''

Taya looked dubious. ''How could they just come together if it took Scientist with all his machines to make them on Merkon?'' she objected.

''If there were billions and billions of molecules to start with, and if they had millions and millions of years to react, Scientist's sums said that evolving ones would appear eventually,'' Kort answered.

''But how could he know things like that from just doing sums?'' Taya asked, amazed. She couldn't even imagine millions and millions of years.

''He could do sums that told him things like that—much more complicated than the ones you've learned so far,'' Kort said.

Taya pulled a face. She didn't dare ask if she'd have to learn how to do sums like that one day. ''So had Scientist proved it?'' she asked instead.

''He thought he had. But when he showed Skeptic the sums, Skeptic pointed out that all they showed was that cold places that weren't stars *could* exist, and that if they did, big molecules that couldn't exist in stars *might* form on them; they didn't *prove* that such places *did* exist, or that such molecules *had* formed on them. Mystic said the whole idea of big, intelligent molecules was ridiculous anyway. There were stars outside Merkon that grew bigger and bigger—but they just turned into big stars, not intelligent stars.''

The tunnel looked out on both sides into strange rooms packed with bewildering machines. Some of them moved intermittently, and there were many lights, pulsating glows of various colors, and occasional brilliant flashes. Kort told Taya that they were in the part of Merkon where Scientist still did most of his work.

"Another mind was called Biologist, and he gave Thinker a new idea," Kort went on. "Biologist was fascinated by machines and what made them alive, and he had been finding out more about evolution ever since Evolutionist discovered it. He realized that what enabled machines to be complicated enough to be intelligent was the amount of *information* stored inside the machines that built them. Now, that information was passed on from one generation of machines to the next— and sometimes it was changed to make the newer machine work better. So really, it wasn't the machines that were evolving at all; it was the information they passed on that was actually evolving."

"Yes, I can see that," Taya agreed. "As far as machines go, anyhow. But I'm not sure what it's got to do with molecules."

"That was the new idea," Kort told her. "The way a molecule is put together can also store information. If the information stored in a machine could cause machine parts to come together in the right way to make a complicated machine system, then maybe the information stored in a molecule could cause chemicals to come together in the right way to make a complicated chemical system, and perhaps *that* was what had evolved and become intelligent."

Taya had stopped to watch a fountain of yellow sparks surrounded by a blue glow inside a glass shape in one of the rooms off to the side of the tunnel. "So now it wasn't the molecule itself that had to be intelligent," she said over her shoulder.

"Correct." They resumed walking.

"And I bet I can guess what happened then," Taya said. "Thinker thought it might be true. Mystic said it was just as silly as the other idea. And Skeptic said he'd believe it when somebody showed him a molecule that could build intelligent chemicals."

"That's what happened. And so Scientist started making enormous molecules and putting them into all kinds of chemicals to see if they would assemble into anything. But there was nothing to tell Scientist what kind of molecule to make, and the number of possibilities was larger than any number you can think of.''

''Even millions and millions?''

''Much larger than that—so large that Scientist would never be able to try even a small fraction of them. He did try, though, for years and years, but everything failed. . . . Oh, he did manage to produce a few that produced tiny specks of jelly that grew for a while, but they soon stopped and broke down into chemicals again. Not one of them ever looked like being remotely intelligent, never mind capable of making a machine. And Skeptic said that if it would take Scientist forever to find the right molecule, even with all his knowledge and intelligence, how could it have just come together on a cold place outside Merkon, without any intelligence? There was nothing out there that could provide an equivalent method of selection. Mystic said that was what he'd been telling them all along.

''But Thinker looked at it another way: If Evolutionist and Biologist were right, then a molecule that could assemble an intelligent chemical system *had* existed, and *had* been selected somehow, somewhere in the universe. Whether or not Scientist could explain *how* it had been selected was a different question. If Scientist could just discover what *that* molecule had been like, then he could forget about all the other countless possibilities that there would never be enough time to try anyway. Scientist agreed, but couldn't imagine where to begin looking; so he asked Thinker to think of an idea for that, too.

''There was only one place that Thinker could think of to look. Biologist had discovered that there were lots of codes in the information that older machines copied into newer machines, which nobody had ever understood—they copied it because that was the way things had always been done. Some of those codes went back to the earliest machines—the ones that had existed before any of the minds were aware of anything at all.''

''You mean the machines that the chemical intelligence made, before machines knew how to make machines?'' Taya said.

''Yes, which meant that some of that meaningless data that older machines had always copied into newer machines could have been written into the first machine by the chemical intelligence that made it. And maybe—just maybe, for some reason—there might be something in there that could give Scientist a clue of how to make the right molecule."

They were approaching the end of the tunnel now. Taya could see that it ended at a large, shiny white door. She glanced curiously up at Kort, but the robot carried on walking slowly and continued. "So Scientist concentrated on trying to understand the codes that had been handed down from the earliest times. And eventually, after many more years, he found what he was sure was the secret he'd been searching for. Some of the oldest codes of all contained arrays consisting of millions of numbers. If those numbers were read in a certain way, they looked just like instructions for building precisely arranged sets of gigantic molecules. So Scientist assembled the sets just as the instructions said, and then began supplying them with chemicals to see if the chemicals would grow into anything."

They had stopped outside the white door. Taya stared up at Kort with suspense written across her face. The robot gazed down in silence for a few seconds, inviting her to complete the obvious for herself. But she hadn't made the connection. "What happened?" she asked with bated breath. "Did they grow into something?"

Kort shook his head slowly. "Not at first. There were many things that Scientist still didn't know. Some of them did grow into strange, unfamiliar forms, but they soon stopped. Scientist had nothing to tell him what chemicals to supply, or how they should be given." The robot's black, ovoid eyes seemed to take on an inner light as they bore down on the tiny, upturned face, now deathly pale suddenly. "He had to learn that they would only grow when they were kept warm; that they had to be always bathed in air; that the air had to be kept slightly moist. . . . We had to learn how to make the special food that they needed, to provide light that was right for their delicate liquid eyes, to keep them covered to protect their fragile skin." Taya's eyes had widened into almost full circles. Her mouth fell open but no sound would come out. That was the first time Kort had said "we." He nodded. "Yes, Taya, there was much to learn. There were many failures."

Taya could only stand paralyzed, staring up at the seven-foot-tall metal colossus, as the truth at last burst into her mind. Kort's voice swelled to echo the pride he could no longer conceal. "But in the end we succeeded! We produced a speck of jelly that grew and acquired shape until it could move of its own accord. We nurtured it and tended it, and slowly it transformed into something the like of which we had never glimpsed in the entire cosmos." Kort was trying to make her share his jubilation, but even as he spoke he could see her beginning to tremble uncontrollably. At the same time, alarm signals poured into his circuits from all over Merkon.

He stooped down and lifted Taya level with his eyes. "Don't you see what this means, Taya? Long, long ago, before there were any machines, there was another kind of life. *They* made the place that has become Merkon. *They* built the machines that the machines of Merkon have evolved from. They were incredible scientists, Taya. They understood all the things that we have been trying for so long to learn. They gave us the secret that enabled them to grow out of simple, unstructured matter that drifts between the stars. Without that secret, all our efforts would have come to nothing. Our greatest achievement, the culmination of all our work, was just a fragment of the wisdom with which they began.

"And now, Taya, we know what they were. They were like you! You will grow, and you will become again what they were. You asked if you could ever learn enough to understand machines. Of course you can . . . and far more than that. It was *your kind* that created the machines! You will teach us! You will know more than all the minds of Merkon put together could even think to ask. You will bring to Merkon the wisdom and the knowledge that once existed in another world, in another time."

The robot peered into her face, searching for a sign of the joy that he felt. But when at last she could speak, her voice was just a whisper. "There were once other Tayas . . . like me?"

"Yes, just like you."

"What . . ." Taya had to stop to swallow the lump forming at the back of her throat. "What happened to them, Kort? Where did they . . . go?"

Kort could feel tremors in her body, and his eyes saw that her skin had gone cold. An unfamiliar feeling came over him. For once, he realized, he had misjudged. His voice fell. "We have no way of telling. It was very long ago. Before Merkon changed, there were places that were built to contain air. We can only assume that your kind of life once inhabited whatever Merkon was built to be. We don't know what became of them." He could see the tears flooding into her eyes now. Gently, in the way that she found comforting, he moved her onto his arm.

"Other Tayas lived here, long ago?" There was a hollowness and an emptiness in her voice that Kort had never heard before. She clutched at his neck, and his skin sensors detected warm salty water rolling down across the joints. "There isn't anyone anywhere like me. I don't belong here, do I, Kort? I don't want to be in this world. I want to be in the world where there were other Tayas."

"That world doesn't exist any more," Kort replied somberly. "Of course you belong in this one. And we're changing it all the time, so it will become even more like yours."

"But I'll always be . . . *alone.* I've never felt alone before, but I do now. I'll always feel alone now, for years and years and years. . . ." She pressed her face against the side of the robot's head and wept freely. "How long will it go on? What will happen to me, Kort?"

Kort waited for a while, stroking her head with a steel finger of his free hand, but the tears didn't stop. "You won't be alone," he murmured at last. "I'll always be here. And you haven't let me finish the story yet."

"I don't want to hear any more. It's a horrible story."

Kort's arm tightened reassuringly. "Then I'll have to show you the rest of it," he said.

Taya felt Kort move forward, then stop, and she became aware of a warm yellow glow around them. She raised her head and saw that the white door was open and they had passed through it. She sensed that Kort was waiting, and lifted her head higher to look. And she looked . . .

And looked . . .

And then she gasped aloud, her fretting swept away in that instant. Kort set her down on her feet, facing the room. For a while she just stood there and stared. Then, very slowly, as if fearing she was in a dream that might evaporate suddenly, she began walking forward.

They were standing in rows a few feet apart—dozens of them. Each of the boxes was low and flat like a bed, but they were smaller than Taya's. Each was enclosed by a rounded glass cover stretching from end to end. There were tubes and wires connecting them to machines lining one wall. And through the glass covers she could see . . .

She didn't have a word for lots of little people like Taya. There had only ever been one Taya.

She stopped and turned to look back at Kort, but the robot made no move. She turned back again and approached the box closest to her—almost reverently, as if the slightest sound or sudden movement might cause the sleeping figure inside to vanish. It had eyes and a nose and a pink mouth . . . and it was bendy everywhere, like her. It wasn't as big as she was—in fact it was a lot smaller—but it was . . . the *same*.

She moved slowly around the box to peer in from the other side. The Taya wasn't quite the same, she realized. It had darker hair, almost black, and a nose that wasn't the same shape as hers. She turned to look in the box behind her and saw that the Taya in that one had hardly any hair, and a pink patch on its arm that she didn't have. And at the top of its legs its body was curiously different. She looked across at the box in the next row, and at the one next to that. All the Tayas were different . . . the *same* as her, but all different.

Kort moved forward to stare down from alongside her. Taya looked up at him, but was unable to form any question because her mouth just hung open and wouldn't close. "Scientist had no way of knowing how long he would be able to keep his tiny chemical thing growing," he said. "If it stopped the way the others had, he'd have to start all over again. So, when he had managed to keep one growing properly for one year, he picked out another fifty groups of numbers to make fifty more different sets of giant molecules, and he started them all growing in the same way that he'd managed to make the first one grow. So now he had fifty-one chemical things, but one of them was a year older than the rest."

Taya was listening rapturously, but she couldn't keep her eyes off the figures in the glass-covered boxes. They were all about the same size—bigger than Rassie, but much smaller than Taya. Their chests were moving the way hers did—not as much as hers, and more quickly . . . but they were moving. Kort's chest never moved like that because he didn't need air. They *were* really like her. Some of them were darker than she was, a sort of brown instead of pink, and a few almost black. And some were yellowy and some more red. Taya wondered why there weren't any blue ones or green ones or purple ones, too.

She began moving through the room between the boxes, stopping and gazing through every one of the glass covers to marvel at how delicately a nose was formed here, or to stare at a miniature hand there, or a brown foot that was pink underneath. This one had hardly any eyebrows, while that one had thick black ones; this one had hair that was almost red, and another had tiny ears, not much bigger than Rassie's.

"By that time all of the minds were saying how clever Scientist was," Kort resumed. "But then Skeptic reminded them that nothing Scientist had done so far proved anything about chemical *intelligence*. All he'd proved was that a set of molecules could cause a chemical structure to grow. And he had a point, because even the one that was a year older had never actually done anything that could be called intelligent. All it had done was kick, squirm about, and eat the food that the machines gave it. So the machines settled down to watch and wait for it to do something intelligent."

Scientist must have been very clever to make these, Taya thought to herself, *never mind what the other minds said.* When she had reached the end of the room and looked inside every one of the glass covers, she turned. She was happy now, Kort could see, and the laughter in her eyes was echoed by the relieved currents flowing into his mind from the entire network of Merkon. But there was something else in her eyes, too. The expression on her face contained more than just the simple happiness that he saw when she watched the stars or created a picture that she especially liked. There was a light of awareness there now, which added to the happiness to produce an effect that was new to him—as if in the last few minutes she had suddenly become older and changed more than she had in all of the previous nine years.

He continued. "The minds waited for almost another

year, but no sign of intelligence appeared. Then Mystic started saying it was because Supermind was angry at the machines for trying to create intelligence. Only Supermind was supposed to create intelligence. If the machines didn't stop trying to do something that machines were never meant to do, Supermind would scrap all of them, and Merkon as well. This worried the minds, and they argued about whether they should allow Scientist to keep his creations."

There was nothing left to see at the end of the room. Taya clasped Kort's hand and they began walking back between the boxes toward the door. "By this time a new mind had formed out of parts of Scientist, Evolutionist, Biologist, and Thinker. Its name was Kort." Taya stopped and looked up. Kort paused for a second, then continued. "Kort had spent a lot of time studying the strange chemical things and watching them grow. He had become fond of them and didn't want Mystic to take them away. He suggested that maybe the machines were mistaken in assuming that all kinds of intelligence had to be like them—because that was the only kind they knew. A machine was fully working as soon as it was finished and switched on. But maybe a chemical system was different. Perhaps its intelligence needed time to grow, just as its body had to grow.

"But the other minds were still afraid of making Supermind angry and being scrapped. So Kort suggested carrying on the experiment with just one of the chemical things instead of with all of them—to put the other fifty to sleep in a special way that would stop them growing, and just see what happened with the one that was a year older. Then, if Supermind did get angry, it would only have reason to get a little bit angry. And only Kort would have anything to do with the one that would be allowed to carry on growing. Then Supermind would only have reason to scrap Kort, and not any of the others."

"And that was what they did, wasn't it?" Taya said, smiling. She thought for a second. "So was that when you made your body?"

Kort nodded. "One of the things he'd learned was that the little chemical things needed lots of looking after, and he'd been thinking of making a special looking-after machine to do it. That made him wonder what had looked after them long ago, before there had been any machines. He asked Thinker what he thought, and the only thing Thinker could think of was that the small chemical things must have been looked after by the ones that had already grown bigger. Kort figured that the bigger ones would have had the same shape as the small ones, and maybe that would be a good shape for a looking-after machine to have if it was supposed to do the same job. So that was the shape he chose to build it.''

"I thought it was that shape for mending things," Taya said.

"It's a very useful body," Kort replied. "These hands aren't very good for much by themselves, but with a few simple tools I can make them do almost anything. I found there are some things that I can do faster and more easily with this body than the machines can."

"What can it do that the machines can't do?"

"There's one very important thing. If something is going to become intelligent, it has to be able to learn things. But it can only learn if you can talk to it to teach it. Scientist had known for a long time that the chemical things couldn't talk, because they couldn't hear radio waves."

"Are those the waves you talk to the machines with?"

"Yes. But they could make pressure waves in the air that they had to be in all the time—they were always making pressure waves. So Kort decided to make his looking-after machine capable of sending out pressure waves, too. Then maybe he could find a way of using them to talk with instead of radio waves. The chemical thing grew, and as it grew, Kort taught her to talk."

"You haven't given her a name yet," Taya said. "You said everyone in a story ought to have a name."

"She was called Taya, of course."

Taya laughed. "I know. I just wanted to hear you say it."

"Taya grew bigger, and Kort began teaching her things. All the minds in Merkon waited to see what would happen. But as time went by, they were disappointed." Taya looked dismayed, but Kort went on, heedless. "She just wasn't any good at even the simplest things that a new machine would do perfectly. She forgot things almost as quickly as he tried to teach her new things, and she was hopeless at even the easiest of sums. Her ears were so weak that she could only hear him when he was in the same room, and her eyes could never see more than a few of even the nearest stars, and then only a part of what they really look like. Mystic asked how anyone could possibly call her intelligent, and said it was a final warning from Supermind for her to be scrapped.''

"*Me?*" Taya clapped a hand to her mouth, horrified. "Mystic wanted to scrap *me*?"

"At one time, yes. But Kort argued with the rest of the minds and demanded that they keep to the agreement they had made. But while all this arguing was going on, Taya started to change in a strange way." Kort paused and looked down at the face staring up from no higher than his waist. "The machines knew they could see lots of things that she couldn't. But then they found out to their astonishment that *she* could see other things that they couldn't see. She could see things in shapes and colors that made her smile. She could think of questions that none of the minds in Merkon had ever thought of asking. She could *imagine* things that weren't there, and create her own world inside her mind whenever she wanted. She could see things that made her laugh, and sometimes things that made her cry. The machines found that they liked it when she laughed, and it made them want to laugh, too; and they felt bad when things made her cry, and they tried to make those things go away. Soon all the other minds found what Kort had already found: that they liked their world better with Taya in it. They remembered how it had been before Scientist made her, and it seemed empty and cold, like the emptiness between the stars. She was like a tiny star, brightening the inside of Merkon."

"All the minds?" Taya queried. "Even Mystic?"

"Yes, even Mystic. But now Mystic was saying that the things Taya could see proved what even Scientist had been unable to prove: that there *was* another universe that couldn't be seen with all of Scientist's instruments. Supermind had allowed Scientist to create Taya to prove that Supermind really existed. And one day she would be able to uncover secrets that they would never even have guessed might exist.''

"And was the Merkon in the story always moving toward a star like this Merkon is?" Taya asked thoughtfully.

"Oh yes. It was just like this Merkon."

"Did it ever get there?"

"You know, it's funny you should mention that. I've just heard from Rassie. She says that Vaxis is getting bigger. Scientist says that Merkon will arrive there just over ten years from now."

"Ten years!" Taya gaped up at the robot. "That's a long time. It's longer than since I started growing, and that's longer than I can even remember. I can't wait ten years to find out what happens—" Her voice broke off as a new thought struck her. "Did Rassie really just tell you that?"

"Why?"

"She didn't! Rassie doesn't really talk. You've known about it for a long time. You have, haven't you?"

"Yes," Kort admitted.

"So, why didn't you tell me before?"

"Because I know how impatient you are, little seer-of-invisible-universes. You think ten years is a long time, but it isn't. There will be lots to learn and do in that time."

They were back at the door, and Kort stopped while Taya turned to look back at the rows of glass-topped boxes. "So what happened to the fifty others?" she asked.

"The minds asked Scientist to wake them up and let them carry on growing from where he had stopped them," Kort said.

"So when will he do it?" Taya asked, abandoning the pretense of a story in her eagerness.

"He has already started to. But they haven't been asleep in the same way that you sleep. They've been kept cold for a long time, and they can only be warmed up again very slowly and carefully."

"But how long will it take?"

"Not long. Scientist says about another five days."

"Five days! I won't have to wait that long before I can talk to them, will I? I'll never be able to wait *five days!"*

"You see how impatient you are," Kort said. "And you'll have to learn to be a lot more patient than that to talk to them. They won't be able to talk as soon as they wake up."

"They won't?"

"Of course not. They don't know the language yet. They'll have to learn it, just as we had to."

Taya gasped. "Are you going to have to teach all of them?"

"Certainly not. You are going to have to help."

"*Me?*" Taya stared back in amazement. "But I can't teach things. How will I know how to teach anything?"

"That's something else you'll have to learn," Kort replied.

"But they'll need to know all kinds of things. Will I have to teach them about Merkon and the machines . . . how to make clothes and draw pictures and spell words . . . and do *sums*?"

"I said there would be a lot to do between now and when we reach Vaxis," Kort said. "But it won't be as bad as you think—we've decided to build some more bodies like mine. Also, because Scientist stopped the others growing, you are eight years older than they are. You've already learned a lot that they won't know. By the time they are nine, you will be seventeen and will have learned a lot more. Between us we should manage okay."

Taya tried to picture the forms in the boxes walking and talking, asking all the questions that she asked Kort and trying to learn all the things she'd had to learn. There would be so much for her to remember. "I'll be very special, won't I?" she mused, half to herself.

"Very special," Kort agreed.

"Do we have a word for a Taya that's special?"

"No. We've never needed one before because there's only ever been one of you. Maybe we should have."

"How about 'queen'?" Taya suggested. "That's a nice word. Could a queen be a Taya that's eight years older than anyone else, and who knows more things and has to teach the others?"

"I don't see why not," Kort said.

"So does that make me a queen?"

"Well, not really, because there aren't really any others yet. But you will be in five days' time."

"I want to be special *now*. Can't we have another word that means somebody who isn't a queen yet, but who will be in five days' time?"

"Sure we can. Let's say that somebody like that is a . . . 'princess.' "

"That's a nice word, too. So am I a princess right now?"

"Right now," Kort confirmed. "I've already written it into the dictionary."

Taya looked down at herself, and after a few seconds raised a disappointed face toward the watching robot. "I still don't feel special," she said in a thin voice.

"How did you expect to feel?"

"I'm not sure. But there should be *something* different about being a princess. I still feel like a Taya."

"I'll tell you what we'll do," Kort said. "We'll make a rule that says the princess must look different from everybody else. Then everyone will know who she is, even if they're still small and not very good at remembering things yet."

"How will we do that?" Taya asked.

Kort unfolded her red cloak, draped it around her shoulders, and fastened the clasp at her throat. "There," he announced. "Only the princess will wear a red cloak."

Taya stepped back and looked happily down at herself as she spread the cloak wide with her arms. Then she twirled round and around, causing it to billow out in the air. "I *feel* like a princess!" she laughed. "I'm really special already, aren't I?"

The robot bowed low and offered his arm. "Come, little princess, we must go now. Scientist has work to do here."

Taya climbed onto Kort's arm and clung to his head as he straightened up and turned toward the door. "Will you make me some shoes that are silver, like yours?" she asked. "I think a princess should wear silver shoes, too, don't you?"

"A princess should have anything she wants," Kort replied.

The door closed behind them, cutting off the yellow glow. The robot and the princess moved away along the glass-walled tunnel, toward where the capsule was waiting to carry them home.

INSIDE STORY

It was like something out of one of those old-time spy thrillers or private-eye movies. I waited on one side of the parking area near the Washington Monument, wearing a light-colored raincoat and holding a folded copy of *Time* magazine as "George" had instructed. He arrived to pick me up in an aircab at exactly seven o'clock. It was a drizzly December night, and the parking lot wasn't well lit. All I could see was a dim figure in an overcoat, sitting hunched back in the shadows with a hat pulled low over its face. He murmured for some identification, and I showed him a press card that stated I was Lou Chernik, senior reporter with the *Washington Post*. George used a penlight to examine the photograph, shone the light up at my face, then opened the door for me to get in. We flew over the Potomac and landed at the rear of a motel in Crystal City. George paid the cabbie, then led me up some outside stairs and along a balcony to one of the suites. I'd come across this kind of thing in stories, but nothing like it had ever actually happened to me before. I guess George and I must have read the same books.

I'd assumed there would be just the two of us, since George hadn't mentioned anyone else when he called Melvin

Pearce, the *Post*'s editor-in-chief, a day earlier to set up the meeting. I was wrong. The woman waiting for us in the motel suite was an eye-opener, with a satiny, lilac-colored, body-clinging dress, jet-black hair falling halfway down her back, and the sultry-eyed, full-lipped kind of face they always pick for the lead role in Cleopatra movies. Straightaway, something about her set little warning bells ringing inside my head. It was the kind of feeling you get when a girl with that certain aura slides onto the empty seat next to you at the bar and sends your hormones into a head-on collision with your brains: you know that one way or another, an arm and a leg would be just a down payment on the price of getting too closely acquainted.

George introduced her as Vicki. He didn't say if she was his wife, girlfriend, mistress, or what, and I didn't ask. When he took off his hat and overcoat and hung them in the closet along with my raincoat, I saw that he was in his late forties, a little on the heavy side, and had one of those pink, fleshy faces that look as if they ought to be wheezing for breath all the time. His hair was beginning to thin, and his eyes had that distant but intense fixation that you see a split second before you walk into a biblical harangue from a sidewalk evangelist, or on the faces of you-name-it nuts wherever you go. His necktie, shirt, and cuff links were pricey and stylish, but they didn't go with the suit he was wearing, which had gone out of fashion and was showing signs of combat fatigue. His general appearance suggested a pretty recent attempt at a remodeling job carried out on an inadequate second mortgage. George was just beginning to find out about that down payment, I decided.

The suite had a lounge area between the door and the bedroom, and George and I sat down at the table by the window while Vicki fixed some drinks. Preliminaries weren't necessary. An allegation of a top-down government conspiracy aimed at destroying the nation's technological development—and perhaps that of the entire Western world—wasn't something that a senior reporter would forget in a hurry.

George was nervous but trying not to show it. He took a quick gulp from his glass and looked across at me. "What do you know about the DOB?" he asked. He'd told Pearce that the Directorate of Bureaus was where the supposed conspiracy was being masterminded.

I shrugged and gave the answer that anyone would have given. "It's a federal government department. Isn't it supposed to 'coordinate' a whole bunch of other departments, whatever that means? I'm not sure. Probably it's just a dump for deadwood bureaucrats that nobody wants but nobody can fire."

George nodded. "That's what most people think." His voice dropped ominously as he leaned across the table. "That's what they're meant to think. But that's a cover. In reality, the DOB is the nerve-center of a carefully orchestrated operation aimed at undermining the social structure of the United States and reducing it to a neo-feudal order run by a privileged élite. It's happening right now, under our noses, and some of the most powerful people in the country are involved." George looked at me expectantly while Vicki sat down and watched over her glass.

Reporters hear something like that at least once a week. "That's an interesting suggestion," I said. "If it's true, it's not the kind of thing they'd want many people to know about. How come you know?"

"I work there—at DOB," George answered. "I've been there for over six months now. I've seen what goes on. I can name all the names and substantiate everything with documented facts. You want a story that'll blow the roofs off half of Washington, Mr. Chernik? I've got it."

That was enough to raise anybody's eyebrows. "Okay, I'm interested," I told him. "Shoot."

Vicki held up a hand before George could answer. "Just a minute," she said. "What kind of a deal might we be talking about? If this turns out to be the way George says, how much would it be worth to your paper?" At least she believed in coming straight to the point. I told her I couldn't answer that. It would depend on how big the management thought the story was. "George has given you an idea of how big it could be," she said. "Maybe you should get some kind of ballpark figure before we go any further. I mean, how do we know you won't steal it if we give you more without any kind of an understanding at all?"

She was trying to sound hard-nosed, but it wasn't quite working. Instead it told me that she was as new to this game as George was. Now I could see the pieces beginning to fit. George had stumbled on something that Vicki thought might be worth money, and she had latched onto a possible ticket toward life's better things. I had the feeling that she wouldn't be staying around for very long after the ticket was either cashed or proved a dud. . . . But that was George's problem.

"Look," I told her, "any newspaper that worked like that would have gone out of business long ago. There has to be some trust in any deal, never mind what the lawyers tell you. Nobody can start talking prices until they know what they're being asked to buy. Now whatever this story is, you'll get what it's worth. Okay?"

Vicki sipped her drink and fell quiet. George shifted his eyes back to me. "Do you want to know the truth about *Climaticon*?" he asked.

"Who wouldn't?" I answered.

You remember the *Climaticon* project, of course—the plan to control the world's climate with ionizing radiation beamed down from projectors constructed in orbit. A very controversial subject. One side was eulogizing about the benefits of being able to increase food production by tailoring rainfall to order anywhere, snuffing out hurricanes at birth, and stopping half the cities from being snowed under every winter, while the other side was protesting about the unknown effects of the beams on ecology, and the risks of fooling with the weather system of a whole planet. There were demonstrations and rallies everywhere, it took state troopers to evict protesters from the site of a prototype ground station in Arkansas, and the same kinds of thing were happening abroad. In the end the opposition won and the idea was scrapped. But at the time I'm describing, the outcome was still uncertain.

"The truth is that it would be quite safe," George said. "I've seen the official reports. The government knows there'd be no problem. But the government isn't saying so." He gave me a moment to think about that. "Can you see what that means? Something that could be of inestimable benefit to civilization is in jeopardy because of lies, and the people who possess the information to refute those lies are allowing the public to be deceived. What's more, certain organizations controlled covertly through DOB are circulating falsified information to perpetuate those lies. What do you say to that, Mr. Chernik?''

I didn't make a big pretense of being surprised. Claims like that appear from time to time. "A pretty stiff accusation," I said. "What's it based on?"

"Take the business about radiation," George replied. "The high-intensity zones would only exist for short periods of time, and they'd be localized over the oceans. The effects everywhere else would be way below the natural background level that exists anyway. That has been proved, but nobody gets to hear about it. And the chances of a triple-redundant computer system with automatically switched-in backup failing and just happening to direct one of the primary beams at a population center are so remote that you can forget about it happening in the lifetime of the solar system." He snorted beneath his breath. "But all you get from the media are scare-stories touted by paid celebrities and other scientific illiterates."

"Now wait a minute, George," I said. "Not everyone would agree. Independent studies have been carried out, both here and in other countries, which say there are some real dangers. You can't simply dismiss them like that."

George smiled humorlessly. "They *say* those studies were independent. But I know differently. The decision to kill *Climaticon* was taken two years ago, at a meeting that took place in Brussels between members of the U.N. Council on Policy Development, the International Studies Institute, and the Euro-American Committee. Some very wealthy and powerful interests are represented in those organizations. At that same meeting, a directive was drafted for secretly initiating a study to identify issues of potential negative impact, specifically to generate public concern. At the same time, a network of activist groups would be set up to target university campuses and citizens' action alliances." George met my doubtful look and nodded. "The studies that you referred to were based on faked data," he said. "Through DOB, falsified figures were circulated to opposition movements that had been set up overseas, to give a consistent story worldwide. I know—I saw it being done. The whole thing's a fraud, with no scientific validity whatsoever." He sat back and looked at me challengingly. "Now tell me again that those studies were 'independent.' "

Well, that sounded pretty clear. "And you say you can substantiate these claims?" I reminded him. George looked at Vicki. She hesitated for a moment, then got up and went into the bedroom.

"The same thing happened with the ocean mining fight," George went on. "That was before my time at DOB, but I've been doing some checking into the records. There never were any hazards to marine ecology. That scheme could have produced abundant cheap metals, but it was sabotaged in the same way as *Climaticon* is being sabotaged now. And a lot of the same names were involved."

I nodded but said nothing. The proposals for exploiting the ocean-ridge deposits had produced a big outcry that the environmental disturbances and discarded wastes would threaten the entire balance of marine life and hence the global food chain. Proponents of the idea had argued that the areas affected would be negligible, and the disturbances would be well within the capacity of the ocean's biochemical mechanisms to handle. But it was all over: the death sentence on the project was passed by a U.N. Special Commission on Oceanic Minerals in 1998.

Vicki came back into the room and placed a leather briefcase on the table. She unscrambled the combination and opened the lid to reveal the case crammed with hard copy databank retrievals. I ruffled through the contents and found reports, memoranda, minutes, and other documents, many with DOB letterhead, most of them classified. It was as George had said all right—enough to blow half the roofs off Washington. "That'll give you an idea of what you're being asked to buy," Vicki said, sounding sarcastic. "The full reading comes after you've talked to your management."

There was lots more, George told me. That scare about a plot to lace the atmosphere with a euphoric drug, for instance, was a put-up job. Nobody'd ever had any such intention.

That was something that had happened a couple of years previously. *The New York Times* reported that an anonymous senior government scientist had leaked details of an experiment that was being contemplated to reduce urban violence and aggressive tensions among the populace in general by releasing trace amounts of a psychotropic substance into the atmosphere at places along the West Coast. The whole thing went away after strenuous government denials, a spate of official and unofficial investigations, and a public hearing that found the whole thing to be a fabrication of somebody's overactive imagination.

George told me that the leak was a certain professor of biochemistry, who at that time was also deputy chairman of a presidential advisory committee on chemotherapeutic social programs. He had been paid to make the alleged leak, and the subsequent publicity was stage-managed from within DOB and oiled with DOB-arranged financing. The whole thing was a contrived fiction from beginning to end, dreamed up for the sole purpose of scaring the public.

Then George asked me what I thought the next thing might be. I invited him to tell me. "Back there in DOB, they're already analyzing the proposals for building skyhooks up to synchronous satellites," he said. "They're working out the brainwashing and sabotage campaign that we'll all be hearing if the plans ever get serious. It'll be *Climaticon* all over again."

I went back in my mind over the things he'd said since we sat down. "So how does it add up to a conspiracy to undermine the Western world?" I asked him. "What are you saying is behind it?"

George let Vicki take that question. It seemed he had provided the evidence, and she had made the interpretation. I presumed the idea that it might be worth money came with the interpretation. That fitted.

"Look at it this way," Vicki said. "The main concern of the ruling class of any society has always been to preserve its power and privilege, right?"

I shrugged. "So what else is new?"

"And the way to do that is by restricting the amount of wealth available."

"Maybe. . . . I guess I've never really thought about it," I replied.

Vicki went on, "But advanced technology opens up the prospect of unlimited wealth—more than could ever be restricted. How could anybody hope to control a population of millionaires who don't need protecting? They couldn't. So you can see the threat that unrestricted, uncontrolled science would pose to the people behind the power structure. They'd look for ways to contain it."

"So what are you saying?" I asked her. "That the things George was talking about are part of something bigger—a scheme to undermine confidence in science and scare people away from it?

Vicki nodded. "Exactly—to slow down technological progress, and eventually reverse it. And more—to manufacture a fear of government and steer people into a back-to-the-village mentality, with the population broken up into small, harmless units who'll do as they're told. That way people on top of the heap get to stay on top."

"Nobody could seriously hope to get rid of science," I objected. "It's obviously here to stay."

"But not for the masses," Vicki said. "It's fine as long as it's controlled by the right people and not allowed to generate wealth on a scale that would get out of hand. See the logic? That's what the arms race of the last century was all about. It consumed billions of surplus dollars, and it kept everybody working hard, paying their taxes, obedient, and willing to make sacrifices. But now that's all over, and science is threatening global mass-prosperity—a hundred more Japans in the world. The élites are panicking. It's time to put a leash on the world and bring it to heel again. . . ."

And certainly there was no denying that it all dovetailed together in a way that couldn't have been accidental, and which pointed inarguably to some high-level orchestrating behind the scenes. . . . But that was how we'd meant it to look. And I have to say that it was gratifying to hear all the pieces being connected together in just the way we'd hoped they would be.

George's real name was Marty Felborn. I'd recognized him the moment he took off his hat and coat. The reason he didn't know me was that you have to work downstairs for quite a while at DOB before you're allowed to even know about the section on the upper levels and the Directorate's true function. I'd joined DOB ten years before—long before George ever had any reason to take much notice of it. Melvin Pearce knew who to contact if he ever got a call like the one George made—all the senior editors of the big newspapers had the number. The activities of the DOB are probably one of the most closely guarded secrets of all time, both here and in the countries whose governments we collaborate with.

You see, everything that Marty discovered was true. It's just that he never gave himself a chance to find out why. I'm fairly certain he would have eventually if he hadn't let his hormones get the better of his brains, because before he bumped into Vicki and went clattering off the rails, he'd been doing a pretty good job.

Climaticon could have brought all the benefits that people said it could—if it had been feasible. Unfortunately, it wasn't. Enough computer simulations had been run to show beyond doubt that the dynamics of a planetary weather system were too complicated to manage. And in any case, the beams wouldn't have worked. The dummy ground station in Arkansas cost a few million to build, which was peanuts, and it provided some jobs. Truth was the project was never a viable possibility. The figures that we fed to the *supporters* of the project had been faked, as well as the ones that its opponents were waving around. Marty only got half the story.

Ocean-ridge mining would have worked without fouling up the world, but the fact was we didn't need it. We knew by that time that controlled fusion plasmas would give us all the metals and minerals we needed from desert sands and seawater at far lower cost. There was no point in trying to adapt conventional extraction technologies to underwater environments when they were about to be obsoleted. Marty was dead right about the scheme to squirt chemicals into the air on the West Coast to make us all nice people—nothing of the kind was ever contemplated. And as you know, no elevators up to satellites are being built. I doubt very much if any ever will be. Their appeal lay in the energy that could be saved by dropping one payload down as a counterweight while another was being hoisted up. But with the energy abundance we've got these days, there wouldn't be any point.

So Marty was right as far as he went. The DOB hides behind a cloak of obscurity to conceal its real function, which is dreaming up elaborate nonsense-stories and coordinating a network of support operations to keep them alive. The insiders call it the "Department of Baloney." We spend a lot of taxpayers' dollars every year manufacturing baloney stories, and believe me they're worth every cent.

It all started back in the eighties, when some of the unexpected consequences of a free democracy started becoming apparent. The fact of life is that when everyone has the right to say *no* and veto what someone else wants to do, you can bet your last dime that somebody will. No matter what a person sets out to do, there'll always be somebody else who'll make it his business to shout loud enough and long enough to block it. For whatever reason, some people simply aren't happy unless they're stopping other people from doing what they want. Well, very soon somebody or other was making everybody's business their business, and by the end of the last century nothing was happening any more. The whole country was grinding to a halt. And other countries were starting to have the same problem.

So these days we invent causes for them to fight for—causes to keep the fanatics, the activists, and the rest of them occupied and out of everyone else's hair. They seem pretty happy with it, too. Why shouldn't they? They stopped *Climaticon*, with its risks and callous disregard for human lives; they forced the UN to retract an irresponsible charter of ocean-mining rights, which put profits before the risk of a global catastrophe; they uncovered a sinister plot for mass-drugging the population; and more recently they've sprung into action to protect us all from a reckless idea to put up twenty-two-thousand-mile-high vertical railroads that could wipe out whole cities if they fell down. Yessir, with their record of successes as self-appointed protectors of the public, they must feel pretty good inside. The public is also happy, knowing that it can sleep easy at night with its interests in capable hands.

And we at the Department of Baloney are happy, too.

Have you noticed that in the last couple of decades we've been bringing nuclear plants on-line as fast as we can build them and nobody hears about energy shortages any more? No, I thought not. Not many people have. Have you noticed that the breeder program is up and running again? That the first commercial fusion reactor is exceeding all performance expectations? That the space program is back in business and making up for lost time with nobody protesting the cost? Or that recombinant DNA engineering has been yielding stupendous breakthroughs in agriculture, manufacturing, and medicine, and is already eradicating whole categories of crippling genetic disease?

Amazing, isn't it? The things that really matter are all moving again, and nobody even notices.

What happened to Marty? Well, we had to let him go, naturally, after the FBI recovered the documents. The fact that he'd been recruited in the first place exposed a flaw in our screening and selection procedures, but we think we've fixed that now. I don't know if he and Vicki are still together, but somehow I doubt it.

He still shows up from time to time. You may have come across the stuff he writes in crank science magazines, or those tabloids you see at the supermarket checkouts. Usually he's raving on about a monstrous government conspiracy to sabotage science that he says he has the "inside story" on; but most of the people who read those things only do so for laughs, and the ones who take them seriously are never taken seriously by anyone else. But apparently that's the only kind of market Marty can find. None of the reputable publishers will touch him. The word seems to have gotten round the industry somehow that he was let go by the government because of his tendency to instability and paranoid delusions, all stemming from his long-standing problems with drink and drug abuse.

It's tough, but that's the way life sometimes has to be. Eventually Marty ought to be able to figure out what he's up against, if only he'd stop and think about it. Then maybe he'd be able to save himself a lot of grief and go off and enjoy himself, instead of trying to beat the system in a situation where he's got no chance.

Because he's up against professionals.

Baloney is our business, after all.

GETTING HERE
FROM THERE

Like most science-fiction writers, I attend science-fiction conventions at least a few times a year. It helps us get to know our readers, and the readers to get to know us. Apart from "How did you get started?" one of the most frequent questions I'm asked is "What are you working on currently?" For the past half year or so I've replied that one of the projects is a collection of short stories and essays. In response to this, a number of readers asked if I could include some autobiography, too. They grumbled that the blurb at the backs of the books is too short, and always says the same thing anyway. I put this to Lou Aronica of Bantam while we were having dinner one evening in New York, and Lou thought it was a good idea. So . . .

I grew up in the part of London known as North Kensington. My father was a devout Irish Catholic, and my mother, a German atheist. There was a war going on, which meant that it seemed normal for most adults to wear uniforms and the parks to be full of sandbagged antiaircraft-gun and searchlight emplacements, and that on some days it should rain rain, and on others, bombs. On top of this, I had been born with deformities of both feet, which were to entail many years of surgery to rectify, and my parents were cautioned that the chances were remote that I would ever walk normally—a fear which fortunately proved groundless.

Because I had to wear specially made boots and leg-irons throughout childhood, I never got involved much in sports and athletics as most boys do, which is why I am conceivably the least sports-interested male in North America today. Partly as a consequence of this, I suspect, I never developed much of a team spirit. Also, because of being hospitalized for many months of most years, I was always having to catch up from being months behind at school. Since nothing that the teachers said made any sense, I tended to find things out for myself in my own way, and this has persisted as a habit through life.

The surgery was a great success, and when I was twelve or so, my father bought me my first pair of regular shoes. We went to the hospital just to give the surgeon his leg-irons back. That was one of the most memorable days ever. I refused to board a bus or subway train for months afterward, but insisted on walking everywhere so that everyone in the street could see those shoes. With friends I hitchhiked all over Britain discovering hills and mountains, and throughout my teens and twenties camping and rock-climbing remained favorite pastimes. Perhaps that has something to do with why I'm still attracted to mountains and live in the Californian Sierra Nevada region today.

At school I won a scholarship into the grammar school system, which for most people offered the main gateway to higher education (it did then, anyway). Our family was working class, and this was my first exposure to the loftier side of British culture. The curriculum emphasized the classics, and I formed the impression that it hadn't changed very much since the days of Wellington and Waterloo. History, for example, began with the Romans and finished with James I or thereabouts, so presumably some updating was overdue (I didn't find out about the War of Independence until I moved to Massachusetts over twenty years later). Only half the class took geography, while the other half took physics—a strange arrangement when viewed in retrospect, since both subjects, one would have thought, would be essential to anyone hoping to comprehend the twentieth-century world. The streaming into different subjects was rather arbitrary, and as things turned out I was assigned to the geography group. Everybody, of course, was required to take Latin and ancient Greek.

The problem with the system, as I remember, was its preoccupation with instilling an acceptance of "how," instead of promoting an understanding of "why." It emphasized method without offering a purpose. This was true especially of mathematics and the limited amount of the sciences, principally chemistry, which I encountered. At the end of the fifth year we were streamed again, this time into either the "Sixth Classical" or the "Sixth Modern." The classical group, predictably, concentrated on even more intensive Greek and the like, and much to my relief, I was consigned to the modern stream. Instead of ancient Greek, we were informed, we would be taking ancient history. That was what finally persuaded me that the time had arrived for the British educational system and I to go our separate ways.

Leaving school at sixteen was a momentous day, solemnized by the ceremonial burning of a five-year collection of Latin and Greek exercise books. I took a series of jobs which included being a messenger boy for a London newspaper, loading trucks, delivering groceries, and working a printing press, prior to my intended entry into the Royal Navy to train as an electronics engineering officer. Because of my medical history, however, Her Britannic Majesty declined my gracious offer to serve in her fleet—and it's interesting to note that the country has been going downhill ever since. I therefore informed everybody that I would become a writer. Someone asked me what, with the accumulated wisdom and experience of sixteen years, I imagined I had to write about that the world was breathlessly waiting to read. He had a point. What to do thereafter was far from obvious.

Mother found a newspaper advertisement placed by the Civil Service Commission of the British government, inviting applications for engineering and scientific research scholarships at various government establishments in the U.K. Final selection (of around fifty in total per year) would be made on the basis of a three-day series of written examinations held annually in cities around the country, followed by interviews.

I duly filled in and mailed the application forms, and then departed to spend the summer climbing in the Scottish Highlands with a bunch of pals. It didn't take long to forget all about Civil Service examinations.

The reminder came in the form of a large, official-looking envelope waiting for me when I got back to London. The letter enclosed informed me that I was scheduled to take the examinations at one of the London town halls in four weeks' time. It also advised that, to avoid wasting everyone's time, applicants should possess as a minimum requirement the school-leaving certificate level in a list of subjects that included physics. I had never taken any physics, let alone obtained a school-leaving certificate, which normally required a 3-year course. This was the first time the habit I'd developed as a youngster came in useful. Through the next four weeks I self-taught the physics curriculum, beginning in the public library when it opened, and carrying on in the coffee shop next door until midnight. When the final results were published I found I was in the first ten out of twelve hundred or so entrants, and subsequently I was accepted as an engineering student at the Royal Aircraft Establishment (RAE), Farnborough—Britain's leading R&D center for aviation and related matters.

Life at Farnborough was a new educational experience. The course provided a broad grounding in all aspects of engineering and related sciences, alternating three-month sessions in the RAE's own college with three-month spells in the various departments, machine shops, and laboratories of the Establishment itself. The college combined an informal teaching style with firm expectations for hard work. The lecturers were not educationalists, but engineers and scientists concerned with real problems that mattered: They not only described "how"; they explained also, *why*. Academic standards were high, and studies covered mechanical, electrical, electronic, thermodynamic, structural, and aeronautical engineering, along with supporting mathematics, physics, and chemistry. The aim was to attain membership of the British professional institutions of electrical, mechanical, and aeronautical engineers. Practical training began in such places as the machine shops, forge, and foundry in the early years, and continued on through wind tunnels, instrumentation and photography labs, to working on missile systems and jet engines, and sometimes getting a chance to fly in RAF experimental aircraft. It was a good program for teaching independence and responsibility, as well as instilling a positive attitude toward science and technology. We lived in a former RAF officers' barracks on the edge of the airfield, two students to a room, we received a wage, and we paid for our keep.

Regrettably I was unable to complete the full course at Farnborough. The Irish impulsiveness in me (for want of a better excuse) led to romantic distractions with a happy-go-lucky Yorkshire lass called Iris. I married at an absurdly early age and by the time I was twenty found myself the proud father of twin daughters (Debbie and Jane, who today are twenty-six). Even with my spending the evenings washing dishes, the economics of the situation simply didn't go with an RAE student's pay. I took a job as a junior engineer with a large electronics company, where I was allowed a day and a half off a week for college. This, along with evening classes, enabled me to continue studying, and eventually I graduated as an electrical and electronics engineer.

On looking back over forty-six years, I have to admit, I suppose, to having spent a lot of time and energy stamping from one side of life's fields to another in futile pursuit of the grass that always looks greener. After all the effort of continuing with courses and bicycling ten miles each way three times a week to college to become a professional engineer, I was now far from sure that I wanted to be one. Sitting in the same lab every day somehow wasn't so appealing any more. There was a big world outside. So I transferred into sales and moved on through a number of electronics companies that ended with ITT, first as an inside man backing up the field force, and later as an outside sales engineer and then sales manager, dealing mainly with digital instrumentation and custom-designed industrial control systems. Life had become interesting again by opening up another new world—that of business and commerce, of which my ignorance was all but total—and the work involved a lot of travel around the U.K. Our third daughter was born in this period, too—Tina, who is now twenty-four.

Many of my customers were scientists, and dealing with them increased my fascination for the world of science and its method. Unlike the other isms and ologies that man had been concocting throughout history in his ongoing attempt to comprehend the universe and improve his condition, science worked. It delivered. It made predictions that were testable and produced results that were measurable. It asked what was wrong with its own beliefs, and in doing so, found and corrected its errors, and emerged stronger as a consequence. Despite the cynicism evident in some quarters, I believed, as I continue to believe, that the human race is capable of solving its collective problems just as the majority of people are capable of solving their individual problems—the important thing is having confidence in our powers of comprehension and reason; that's what education should be all about.

By contrast, I found the usually negative, always sensationalized, and often preposterous popular depictions of science and scientists exasperating. My friends got tired of my complaining about this and told me to write something better if I could. I said okay. They said it would never get published, and we made a bet. I had enjoyed the movie *2001* for its technical authenticity, but I had never understood what the ending was supposed to mean. However, the notion of a major scientific mystery turning up on the moon provided an inspiration for showing science as the wonderful, ongoing detective story that I had always felt it to be. So I bought a typewriter and began writing *Inherit the Stars*. Before it was finished, however, life interrupted with more urgent demands.

Special-purpose electronics systems at that time were incredible conglomerations of vacuum tubes and transistors packed into big steel cabinets, which consumed lots of power and produced lots of heat. Modification was an expensive business that involved stripping-down and rebuilding, since all the logic was hardwired. When those wretched Americans began introducing small, inexpensive computers to perform the same functions—at about a fifth the price, a tenth the size, and reprogrammable by software—it was clear that the days of hardwired systems were numbered. After some reflection on the implications, I resolved to join the computer industry. The problem was, I didn't know anything about computers. Well, I'd taught myself about other things before. . . . So I started reading about computer technology, then brushed up my credentials and began approaching computer companies.

The results—to begin with—were disastrous. The interviewers at one venerable pillar of British industrial tradition didn't seem especially interested in what I knew that might be relevant to selling their products; instead they wanted to know why I'd left school early, what my father did for a living, and why I rented a house instead of owning one. They were also curious to learn whether or not, if offered a job, I would be willing to part my hair on the left, as did everyone else (mine was combed back without a parting). I told them that I'd quit school because I wasn't interested in classical languages, that my father tended the boilers in a factory, and that I didn't own a house because I couldn't afford the down payment. I forget what my reply was concerning my hair. Soon thereafter the conversation deteriorated, and it became evident that our disinterest was mutual.

Then I turned my attention to the American computer corporations that were operating in the U.K. Their attitude turned out to be refreshingly different. They were interested in what I knew, what I had done, what I wanted to do and why, and all else was largely irrelevant. Honeywell made an attractive offer, and I joined their scientific/industrial minicomputer division as a sales engineer. (Since then, interestingly, the British computer industry has gone pretty much the same way as the Royal Navy.)

For a couple of years I worked in the London area, and sometimes overseas in places like France and Italy. This was a high-commission market, business was good, and for the first time ever I found myself financially comfortable. In my travels I had developed a liking for the North Country of England and its people, and sometime around 1971 I transferred to Honeywell's Yorkshire branch, moving with Iris and the family to a picturesque resort town called Ilkley, situated amid dales and moorlands between the city of Leeds and the Pennine Mountains. The children liked it, we made many friends, and I even took up climbing again. And, yes, we bought a house—a spacious, four-bedroom, brick-built one, five minutes walk to the town center from the front, and five minutes to open country with lakes and rocky cliffs from the back. It cost eight thousand dollars. I still get ill thinking about it, these days.

Iris and I had gotten along okay when life was a struggle. But the blessings of social respectability and conventional happiness proved too much and our marriage folded. I let her have the house, the contents, custody of the children; I continued paying the mortgage and moved into a flat in Leeds with my books and two suitcases as the total to show for thirteen years. I also decided I was tired of the computer business, and for good measure—since I was in the process of changing things anyway—I quit my job with Honeywell and went off selling life insurance. With generous salaries, commissions, company cars, paid expenses, and other benefits, computer salesmen lived comfortable lives. By contrast the terms now were: no salary, no car, no expenses, no benefits—just commission . . . but a lot of it if you produced. The challenge was irresistible. It's amazing what you can do if you put your mind to it. I topped the branch of twenty-odd salesmen in my first month. Apparently nobody in the company had done that before.

The job was stimulating at first because it involved learning something new again. There were no fixed hours, and for relaxation I took out the unfinished manuscript of *Inherit the Stars* and resumed working on it. The novelty of the insurance business wore off, however, and working on the book reawakened my interest in science. So I applied for a position with Digital Equipment Corporation, who as luck would have it were planning to open an office in Leeds, and I joined the company in 1975. Working with Americans and the visits to the U.S. that the job entailed made me an Americophile. I liked the pragmatic informality of American life, and the confident (although admittedly sometimes rather vociferously expressed) optimism of the people. It didn't seem surprising that this nation could send people to the moon, and that the whole world should buy its computers and fly its jets.

I had finished the book by now and began sending it to publishers and agents in London. The reactions, though generally complimentary, were negative: the market was tight; new writers were a risk; the costs couldn't be justified, and so on. So, I started asking around within DEC about people who might know something about the science-fiction market in the States, and the trail led eventually to a gentleman called Ashley Grayson, who was with a software support group in Massachusetts. I contacted Ashley, and it turned out that we were both due to attend the same sales conference at Cape Cod. I took a copy of the manuscript with me on the trip, left it with Ashley, and forgot the matter after I returned to England.

But a couple of months later a long letter arrived from Judy-Lynn del Rey of Ballantine Books in New York (I had never heard of Ballantine Books, which shows how green I was). Judy liked the book, wanted to publish it, and, subject to my agreeing to some rework, offered a contract—what a contrast to the responses I'd had from London. (It's interesting to note that British publishers seem largely to have followed after the Royal Navy and the British computer industry.) Sadly, my father, who had taken an interest in my thoughts of writing, but without seriously believing that anything would come of it—things like that didn't happen in the Irish farming village he was from—died suddenly a week before the letter arrived.

By this time I had bought another house, in the center of Leeds. Debbie, one of my twin daughters, now in her mid-teens, had come to live with me, and in 1976 I married my second wife, Lyn. In bits and pieces, life was coming back together again. I was still selling mainly to scientists, several of whom had supplied helpful information for the book. Some of the physicists I knew said things like, "Oh, I used to read science fiction when I was younger, but I grew out of it. The science got to be too simplistic." I wanted to produce a book that people like these would find interesting. Accordingly, I began working on a second book, *The Genesis Machine*. I also wrote *The Gentle Giants of Ganymede* in parallel with it, pushing one manuscript aside and picking up the other to avoid losing time through the turnaround of mail between Leeds and New York. Meanwhile, my friends and relatives were waiting eagerly to see *Inherit the Stars* in print. The first copy off the press of my first book arrived from Judy-Lynn ten days after Mother died unexpectedly from an infection following hip surgery.

DEC offered me a position with their sales training

division at Maynard, teaching Americans to sell computers—an unusual job for an Englishman. I had no strong ties left with England, and the idea of living near New York was attractive. Lyn and Debbie liked the idea, so we sold the house and contents, and moved over from England in the fall of 1977. People were carrying away the furniture while I raced to finish *The Genesis Machine*, until there was just a chair and a desk left in the attic room I used as an office. I typed the last page while Lyn was packing our clothes in the bedroom, and we mailed the manuscript on our way to the airport. I thought it would appeal only to a specialized readership, but have since been pleasantly surprised by the wide range of backgrounds of the people who say they enjoyed it.

The next two years were hectic. Besides contending with culture shock and holding down a fairly demanding job, I wrote two more books: *The Two Faces of Tomorrow* (every S.F. writer has to do an intelligent computer book), and *Thrice Upon a Time* (every S.F. writer has to do a time-travel book). We became permanent residents of the U.S. and bought a huge, six-bedroom colonial house, built in the 1890s, in Acton, Massachusetts—with oak-paneled dining room, hallways and stairs, big cellars, big attics, and a big barn, part of the downstairs of which we used as a double garage. I'd always wanted to restore a run-down, big, old house, you see. And this one sure was run-down! The roof leaked, the basement flooded, everything needed rewiring, and the cellars were festooned with lace curtains of cobwebs. So, besides teaching computer-selling and writing, I also dug, sawed, drilled, hammered, shoveled, mixed, and fixed windows . . . and fixed windows, and fixed windows. They put a lot of windows in those old houses. (And still people asked me what I did in my spare time!) I got to know the owner of a local decorating company, who helped out by having his people do a lot of the work at cost to keep them on the payroll through winter, and in eighteen months we turned the place into a sparkling, fixed-up, redecorated showpiece of a home. At last I had gotten the house-restoring bug out of my system. The only problem was that by this time Debbie had gone to live in Boston, Lyn had had enough and moved into her own apartment, and I was left sharing the place with a cat called Squawk.

So, I sold the house and furniture, split the proceeds with Lyn, and moved into an apartment in Framingham. Then, since I was in the process of changing things anyway, for good measure I decided to quit my regular job, leave Massachusetts with its winters for the enjoyment of hardier souls, and just be a writer. I ended up with a car, two suitcases, and a typewriter again—this time heading for New York City. Strange, isn't it, how life has this repetitive flavor about it.

Looking back, it's interesting to note how many of life's unexpected, right-angle turns have resulted from talking to the guy next to me at the bar. While engaged in an evening of alcohol-stimulated meditation on what to do next, I struck up a conversation with a character called Glen, an electronics engineer who had just moved North to take a job with Honeywell, which gave us something to talk about. We also talked about apartments. I described a nice but not exceptional two-bedroom place that I'd looked at on the Upper East Side, going at fifteen hundred dollars per month (plus 15 percent of a year's rent for the agent's fee). Glen said, "That's amazing! I just moved out of the same place in Orlando, Florida."

"Really? How much?"

"Two fifty. And that included the swimming pool, the tennis courts, the health club, the maintenance, the gardening, and the social club and bar."

"You're doing a super selling job," I told him. "What else?"

He shrugged. "No state income tax. No snow shoveling. No wood splitting. Shake the trees, and girls fall out. . . ."

It took me several months to get from New York to Orlando—strange things happen when you drive around in the U.S. I arrived with a first draft of a new book that had been typed in bits and pieces on a miniature Japanese portable in Howard Johnson's, Best Western, and Ramada Inn motel rooms, people's spare bedrooms, on kitchen tables, and in various other places down the East Coast and across the South. That was how *Giants' Star* was written—the last volume of the trilogy that began with *Inherit the Stars*.

The first thing to do was find somewhere to live. I checked into a downtown Holiday Inn, and after a shower and a change of clothes went down to the bar and started talking to the guy next to me. His name was Pat, and he turned out to be the regional manager for a life insurance company, which gave us something to talk about. We had a wild evening as far as I remember. Pat took the next day off work to drive me round the area looking at apartments, and I soon had a roof again. Everything Glen had said was true: there was no snow shoveling or wood splitting; the apartments had their own pool, tennis courts, health club, and bar; the management took care of all maintenance and gardening—wonderful for a writer after that house in Massachusetts; there was no state income tax. Excitedly, I rushed outside and shook the nearest tree . . . and got buried in oranges.

Fortunately, that was no longer of much consequence, since a Californian lady whom I had met in Pensacola moved down to join me. Her name was Jackie—we'd been introduced in an Irish pub by a girlfriend of hers that I had gotten to know after walking in the wrong door of a restaurant and blundering into a private function of the Pensacola Press Club. Jackie was an extraordinary person who had studied things like philosophy, art, and electronics, spent four years in the Navy as a weapons instructor and then transferred to the Army to be a parachutist, and was now working in a bookstore. Like me she had been married twice. Jackie also seemed to have read everything in science fiction ever written, which was invaluable. So through the summer I retyped *Giants' Star* in the day while Jackie was at work, and we talked about it through the evenings and usually well into the early hours over endless pots of coffee at Perkins' twenty-four hour pancake restaurant across the street.

For the first time ever, I was able to work exclusively on things that I wanted to do, in my own time and at my own pace without distraction. I was getting to know better the colorful world of American fandom and science-fiction conventions, and there were TV and radio interviews, and guest-speaker invitations from universities and elsewhere to break the routine. I had kept in touch with my daughters and sent them plane tickets each summer to come and spend their vacation wherever I happened to be, and Jackie and I made lots of friends in central Florida. We started talking about buying a house there; in fact she was all set to manage a new store that Waldenbooks was about to open at Daytona. After all, it was obvious that we were going to be there for quite a while, wasn't it? Nobody in their right minds would disturb a pleasant, comfortable, settled situation like that, would they? Of course not.

It happened like this.

I had always wanted to *drive* across the U.S. I'd flown to the West Coast several times on business, but sitting in an armchair up in the sky for a few hours wasn't the way to appreciate the immensity of this country. Well, while we were sitting around in Perkins' one night, trying to think of something new to talk about now that *Giants' Star* was finished, I suggested, "Let's go to California."

Part of Jackie's appeal has always been the iron hold that she keeps on her composure. "Right now, you want to go to California?"

"Sure, why not? I feel like a drive."

Thoughtful silence, then a shrug. "Okay."

So we paid the check, went home, tossed some things into a suitcase, and reached California four days later. We saw the mountains, Yosemite Valley, San Francisco, the Bay Area, and a lot of other places that I'd always wanted to visit. It was just a break—a couple of weeks of getting away before moving to Daytona, where Jackie would start her new job and I would begin the next book. Then we started talking to some people next to us in a bar. They said, "You ought to spend a day seeing Route Forty-nine while you're here," which turned out to be a scenic highway in the Sierra Nevada foothills, running through the towns of the gold-rush era. We drove into a town called Sonora, which was picturesque and quaint, with its small shopfronts, covered sidewalks, and people actually walking around on legs—unlike the spread-out automobile-scale towns you see everywhere, where all the places you want to go are separated by twenty-minute drives. It was a people-scale town. We got out and walked around. Everyone was friendly. While I was browsing through the local paper in a coffee shop, I came across an ad for an apartment that sounded interesting. Jackie said, "Let's have a look at it, just for fun." So I called the number.

We took the apartment. Before we could move in, however, we had to drive back to Florida to tidy things up there, and then back once more to California—three times across the continent in a month, which got that bug out of my system. For the final trip we traded our cars in for a customized Chevy van, and I vividly remember spending the early hours of Christmas Day morning, 1980, changing a wheel in the middle of the Arizona desert.

People are always asking me how long it takes to write a book. Typing the words doesn't take all that long—with my way of working, anyway. That's just the final phase of a process that begins long before—usually years before. During a conversation that I'd had with some friends once in a pub back in England, someone had asked what I thought the solution was to the problem in Northern Ireland. I'd replied that there wasn't one; but then, after some reflection, I added, "Unless you can find a way to separate the children from the adults for one generation." Writers can't make a remark like that without it leading off into a new trail of thoughts. If children weren't to be raised by human adults, then what else would raise them? How about smart machines? Most people's immediate reaction to such a suggestion is concern and dismay at the cold, unemotional, somehow sinister relationship that they visualize would necessarily exist. But a lot of story ideas come from rejecting the obvious answers and thinking about the alternatives. Why should the relationship have to be cold and unemotional? As a visit to any school's sixth-grade computer club at ten in the evening will confirm, children love machines—closing the building is sometimes the only way to get them out. So why couldn't such a relationship be warm and friendly instead—even charming? What kind of a story might result from treating it that way? That was how *Silver Shoes for a Princess* came about. Later I extended the notion to cover a whole society descended from a machine-raised first generation, which became the basis for the next novel, *Voyage from Yesteryear*, published in 1982—at least six years after I began thinking about it. So that's my answer to how long it takes to write a book.

It seems that Jackie, who is now my third wife, and I are setting a tradition of doing something different to celebrate the occasion whenever we finish a new book. As soon as *Voyage* had been mailed off to New York, our first son, Alex, was born—at home in true mountain-country tradition, with no needles, bright lights, funny smells, or antiseptic people; instead, friends and family, beer and hamburgers, and smiling faces. It seems a much nicer way of welcoming new human beings into the world.

Thinking and talking about intelligent machines had made me want to write a story about a world with a naturally evolving machine biosphere, which eventually appeared in 1983 as *Code of the Lifemaker*. Jackie and I bought a big, old, rambling house in the center of Sonora that had been empty for a year or so and needed a lot of fixing. So I found myself spending lots of time drilling, sawing, hammering, and digging, laying drains, pouring concrete . . . and, inevitably, fixing windows. Strange, isn't it, how life has this repetitive flavor about it.

The next project was *The Proteus Operation*, eventually published by Bantam, which took a year and a half to research and write, and mixes science fiction with World War II history. It also features a procession of real people as guest characters, which made it a new and interesting experiment in writing. While it was in progress, we had our second son, Michael. After that I wrote another book, *Endgame Enigma*, mixing science fiction with modern-day espionage and CIA-KGB antics this time—and to keep up the tradition, we had another son, Joe. (During both her previous marriages Jackie was told by various medical eminences that it was physically impossible for her to have children.) And so I find myself in a large house in a small, picturesque town near the mountains, with three young children. Strange, isn't it, how life has this . . .

Sometimes I claim that being an American is a state of mind and has nothing to do with where one comes from or how one speaks. As social evolution progresses, I believe that humanity as a whole will acquire and mix with its other attributes the confidence in itself and its abilities that I think of as characteristically American. The universe in which we live is limitless in every direction, and contains a greater abundance of energy and other resources, opportunity, and room to expand and grow than we could ever know what to do with. Nature imposes no limits on us as a species, either to what we can achieve or upon what we can become. The only limits that matter are those that people create in their minds. There are no finite resources, only finite thinking.

Although there will always be problems to be faced and risks to be taken, I feel optimistic about the future. Those are the sentiments that I try to project and share in the things I write. I hope I shall never find reason to feel otherwise.

THE PACIFIST

Fifty meters below ground level in a secret, concrete-walled laboratory complex beneath the headquarters of the World Peace Foundation, the last hope for humanity and a sane, rational world stood on its steel supporting platform.

Its general form was a ten-foot-diameter torus, set horizontally and painted dull black to be inconspicuous at night. The outer ring contained the Tipler-field simulated mass circulators, Schwarzchild ring compensator, and boundary cutoff equalizers, and left just enough room in the center for the antimatter-fueled power generator and the cramped cockpit enclosure containing the instrument panel and solitary operator's seat. After more than ten years of unrelenting effort and tenacity in the face of problems that many had thought insoluble, the time machine was complete. Flanked by the WPF scientists and technicians who had helped make it a reality, Professor Magnus Maximilian Magus, its conceiver and creator, stood gazing down at it from the glass-walled control room overlooking the floor. Standing in the opened hatch above the cockpit, his head held proudly erect, his eyes clear and shining, and his jaw set solidly in resolve, the time commando listened as the final words of the professor's exhortation rang over the loudspeaker system.

". . . that after three worldwide conflicts of increasing destructiveness, mankind would have learned. The First World War took us from cavalry to the warplane and the tank; the Second, from the heavy bomber to nuclear weapons; and the Third, from the ICBM to the orbiting gamma-ray-laser bombardment platform. But nothing had been learned. And today, barely more than a generation after rebuilding its cities from the rubble of the last conflagration, our race stands divided yet again, but this time by a line that runs between worlds—we, of the Terran League, and the offworld alliance. This time the weapons have interplanetary range capability. If they are ever used, it will surely mean the end of our existence as a species."

Magus raised his hands in appeal behind the control room window. "It did not have to be this way. The spiral into ever greater depths of insanity was not inevitable. For by right, the 'War to End Wars' of 1914 should have been, and could have been, just that—a sweeping away of the old power structure and social order before the final triumph of Reason toward which Europe had been moving for centuries. . . ." Magus paused ominously, and his voice fell. "But the promise was not fulfilled. Instead of welcoming the peaceful, scientifically planned society which we, the custodians of Reason stood ready to design—the professor stretched out an arm to indicate the people around him—"the world turned its back on Reason, sacrificing itself to the vain ambitions and pretensions of lesser intellects." Magus's fists clenched, and his face took on a pinker hue. "Mediocrities! Ignoramuses! Uneducated charlatans and showmen posturing as thinkers! They abused the power that *we* had created for them, and they cheated us out of the—" He checked himself with a cough and regained his composure. "But now the day has arrived that will allow us to correct the error. In so doing, we will eradicate the tragedies that have followed, and we will create in their place the Golden Age of peace and enlightenment that should have been."

Magus pointed down at where the machine was standing. The time commando straightened to attention and thrust out his chin as the amplified voice boomed down over the floor, "And *you*, Elmer Theodosius Ulysses Kunz, have been selected to carry out this supreme mission, unique in the annals of all history, to travel back and recast destiny. Go now to your duty, knowing that our cause is righteous, and assured that every one of us will be there with you in spirit.''

Time Commando Kunz extended his arm high in a final salute. "May universal peace, brotherhood, and reason come to prevail among all men. I go, to destroy the archprototype of tyrants. Time will be rewritten, with harmony and good-will between the worlds, and an end to intolerance."

"Harmony between the worlds!" Magus led.

"Stamp out intolerance!" Kunz and the chorus chanted back in unison.

In a last dramatic gesture, Kunz pulled his heavy green cloak tight around himself with both hands before stepping down to disappear into the cockpit. To avoid being conspicuous when he emerged, he was wearing the leather shorts and cross-braced suspenders, red stockings, loose white shirt, and feathered hat, which the limited research material available— few records had survived the Third Great War to End Wars— indicated had been the typical dress of central Europe in the early twentieth century. The mission planners had added the cloak because it would be winter there when he arrived. Also, it provided concealment for the high-power infantry assault laser; rapid-fire submachine cannon; .45 caliber solid-shot sidearm with silencer; close-range neurotoxin gas pistol; four fragmentation, two blast, and two incendiary grenades; dag-ger; garrotte; and air-powered, cyanide-tipped dart gun, which the Peace Foundation's weapons experts had deemed mini-mum for the mission.

He checked that the larger items of equipment were in their places in the rack below the hatch, then squeezed him-self down into the narrow seat. The panel lights indicated that all system checks were completed and had registered positive. Then a whine came from just above his head as the hatch closed over the cockpit, and a solid *clunk* signaled the latch engaging. The status summary light was showing orange, which meant that the executive computer had already syn-chronized its countdown to the control room, and the display next to it was showing less than a minute to zero. The system was now awaiting merely his confirmation to deactivate the final fail-safe override that would abort the launch command at the end of the sequence.

Kunz cast his eyes slowly around the tiny chamber and across the panel indicators one last time to impress upon himself the solemnity of the moment. Then, he licked his lips, drew in a long breath, and said into the stalk microphone projecting from one side of his seat, "Checking positive at zero minus fifty seconds. Request permission to disengage final abort interlock."

The supervisor's voice came through on a channel from the control room. "Positive status confirmed on all circuits. You may proceed."

Kunz felt the tension rising in his body. He unlocked the switch, closed his fingers around it, hesitated for one, maybe two, seconds, and then threw the switch from its *Abort on Zero* position to *Launch*. The status light changed to green, and more greens appeared lower down on the panel. Keeping his voice steady only with an effort, he reported, "Interlock disengaged, positive function." The countdown indicator was reading thirty-five seconds.

Then Magus's voice came through. "At this fateful moment, the turning point of history, we of the Peace Foundation salute you, Kunz. Remember as you go forth that all our hopes, our aspirations, the very future for which we have labored over these years—everything depends on you now."

"I shall remember. Have no fear, comrades. Your trust shall not prove misplaced," Kunz promised, his voice rising.

"Go, fearlessly and with honor, for peace!" Magus's voice thundered.

"Ten seconds," the supervisor's voice interjected.

"For peace!" Kunz cried.

A hum emanated from the mass recirculators, became louder, and rose to a shriek. The compensators started to whistle and whoop. A red glow filled the space surrounding the cockpit, and patterns of lights flashed across the instrument panel, while in the center, the numerals of the countdown indicator read off the final seconds 3 . . . 2 . . . 1 . . . 0!

"Ayeiii!! . . ."

Kunz's world exploded in a storm of color, sound, and chaotic tactile sensations as space and time unraveled about him, and unfamiliar patterns of energy quanta overloaded all his sensory systems simultaneously. . . .

He was aware of the shapes surrounding him, but in an unreal kind of way, as if they were parts of a different world projecting out of other dimensions. They consisted only of iridescent outlines without substance—hollow-wire figures of light, shimmering in a void. His thoughts seemed to be running simultaneously in a thousand directions at once, yet at the same time to be frozen into immobility. He could see the entire networks of associations, branching, repeating, reforming, and coalescing, but with all of the parts managing to coexist together without any impression of sequence. He was experiencing timelessness, he knew; but like an infant opening its eyes for the first time without any prior experience to relate its perceptions to, he was unable to interpret the sensations that his mind was registering.

Magus had explained that the torus would generate a spacetime singularity in the form of an infinitely thin plane across the hole in the middle, through which every cross section would rotate perpendicular to space-time like the elements of a smoke ring. But instead of emerging on the other side, the vessel would enter a realm in which space and time would be interchanged: it would be possible to move freely in time, but in one direction only through space. That direction had been calculated precisely to connect to the point in space—a fifth of a light-year away now—that a particular spot on the earth's surface had occupied at the time targeted for Kunz's arrival in the twentieth century.

He had no way of telling how long the dreamy state of changelessness persisted—if, indeed, "how long" still meant anything at all. But then the panorama of all his mental processes laid out side by side began collapsing in on itself like the pieces of a clock being reassembled . . . and as the clock came back together, it began running again. The ghostly outlines around him took on their solid forms, the glow dimmed, and the various sounds around the cockpit ran down and died. Then all was silent. The moment that Kunz had trained and steeled himself for had arrived. There was no time to be lost. He pressed a button to open the hatch and stood up from the cockpit.

He was outdoors, and it was nighttime as intended, with the air chilly and the moon hidden by clouds. Sounds of drums and brass marching bands were coming from the distance, accompanied by singing and cheering. The machine was lying in an open area of ground shadowed by trees. All was still in its immediate vicinity, but a line of large buildings bounded the open area a short distance away, silhouetted against flickering orange light. The music and singing were coming from the far side. It was all uncannily close to what Kunz had been led to expect from his briefings. He was in the Tiergarten in the center of Berlin, the capital of Germany. It was the night of Monday, January 30, 1933.

At noon that day, after driving one hundred yards from the Kaiserhof Hotel to meet the aging President Hindenburg in the government offices on the Wilhelmstrasse, Adolf Hitler had been sworn in as the new German chancellor. So had come to power the man who would reject the world's attempts to achieve lasting peace through understanding, compromise, appeasement, and reason, and who in the eyes of the world would make them the very cause of war. Just when reason had finally come of age and could have pacified the world, one man's betrayal had caused pacifism to be dismissed as ineffective and ridiculed for a century afterward, thus setting the course for calamity.

Kunz transferred his equipment from the stowage rack to fastenings on his belt and inside his cloak, then climbed up out of the cockpit, over the outer torus, and down the short metal ladder on the outside. As he reached the ground, a blue light shimmered briefly in the darkness some distance away out in the park. He froze for a few seconds, but nothing more happened. Then, taking a tight grip on the assault laser beneath his cloak, he began making his way stealthily toward the buildings lining the Wilhelmstrasse.

The singing of the crowd became clearer as he approached the buildings. They were singing the Horst Wessel song—one of the party hymns of the "Brownshirt" Nazi storm troopers. In the evening of that day, as news of Hitler's appointment spread through the city, tens of thousands of delirious supporters and Brownshirts had gathered and marched in a massive torchlight parade, out of the Tiergarten, through the triumphal arch of the Brandenburg Gate, and along the Wilhelmstrasse to celebrate their victory. Hitler himself, after watching the parade for a while from the balcony of the Chancellery, had retired inside for a quiet dinner with Göring, Goebbels, Hess, Röhm, Frank, and a few others of his inner clique. With the jubilant atmosphere putting everyone off their guard and all the noise and distraction in the streets, this had been judged the ideal moment for not only eliminating Hitler, but decapitating the Nazi apparatus of its entire leadership cadre to ensure its demise. A spot of diffuse, greenish glow flared somewhere across the park. Kunz stopped. The glow died away, and after a moment he moved on.

And then he almost walked into something in the shadows between two trees, where he had expected there to be open grass. At first he thought it was an automobile or a small building of some kind, but as he passed by, the moon shone briefly through a chink in the clouds and revealed the object to be circular in shape. It was a machine, in the general form of a torus, lying horizontal, ten feet or so in diameter. It had a metal ladder leading up over the outer ring to an enclosure of some kind in the middle. Kunz turned to stare back uncertainly at it, until he was walking fully backward. That caused him to bump into something else.

It was another machine. This one was in the form of two vertical disks about eight feet high and close together, like a pair of large wheels on a short axle, with a boxlike structure between them. In the moonlight Kunz could make out a black swastika on the outside of the disk facing him, and underneath it in German, the words GOVERNMENT PROPERTY. FORBIDDEN TO TOUCH. The only problem was, it didn't look to him like something that any government of the 1930s should have owned.

Suddenly the air around him began crackling electrically. He dropped to the ground instinctively and covered his head. A tremor ran through the ground beneath him, and he became aware of light and a subdued pulsating sound. He looked up cautiously and found an eerie violet radiance bathing the area around him, centered on a point twenty feet or so ahead of where he was lying. As he watched, a shape materialized in the glow. It was about twelve feet long, and consisted of two pointed cylinders side by side, and in between them a framework supporting a bubble. The light and the sound died together, leaving the machine outlined in the moonlight. Kunz raised himself slowly onto one knee. He was about to stand up, when the top of the bubble hinged open and a head appeared, wearing a Lincolnesque stovepipe hat. The head peered one way and then the other, apparently without seeing Kunz, and then the rest of the figure scrambled out. It was wearing a tailcoat with gold-embroidered front and epaulets, pants with a broad stripe running down the sides, and shiny cavalry boots. The figure turned to hoist something out of the bubble that looked like a weapon, and then jumped down to the ground. That was when he saw Kunz. For a second they both stared. Kunz moved to shift his cloak out of the way of his own weapons. The figure bolted for the shadows, and in the same instant the moon went back behind the clouds. By the time Kunz's eyes had readapted, the figure was gone.

Bemused and bewildered, Kunz resumed heading toward the Wilhelmstrasse. But his boldness and determination were ebbing. Something was obviously very wrong. At the back of a building which he recognized as part of the German Foreign Office, he passed another torroidal machine, this time tipped at a crazy angle against the wall enclosing the grounds. He didn't even bother stopping to look at it, but now in a complete daze, followed the wall around to an alley leading toward the noise and the commotion, which brought him out onto the Wilhelmstrasse itself.

A column of storm troopers was marching down the middle of the road to a thunderous beating of drums, with trumpets blaring, banners flying, and a river of torches flowing away as far as the eye could see. Shouting people lined the sidewalks on both sides, and every window was packed with waving, cheering figures. As the mission planners had anticipated, it would have provided the perfect cover for getting into the Chancellery building . . . if it weren't for his dress, he realized as he looked around. He was the only person in sight wearing a cloak. And not only that—all the men were wearing subdued combinations of heavy overcoats, flat caps or conventional felt hats—not one with a feather—

and without exception, long pants. Kunz's cloak was only knee length, and his bright red socks seemed like beacons.

Then he saw the two German policemen in flat-topped helmets and greatcoats heading toward him along the rear of the crowd. Suddenly he started to panic. He turned, but a knot of onlookers had blocked the alley that he had emerged from. Desperately he turned the other way, but a crowd coming out of one of the doorways had cut off any escape in that direction. And before he could recover from his confusion, the policemen had drawn up in front of him.

The larger of the two looked Kunz up and down. He had heavy cheeks and a thick black mustache, and a fleshy sausage-neck overflowing from his collar. "Don't tell me," he said amiably in German, "You've come back from a future age to assassinate the Führer."

Kunz gulped disbelievingly. "How . . . how do you know?" he stammered.

"Oh, they've been showing up in dozens all night. You'd better come with us. The line starts a block farther along the street."

They took him a short distance along the Wilhelmstrasse, and then down a narrow side street that opened out into a cobbled court overlooked by high buildings and lit by gas lamps. On the far side was a stone building with wide double doors set behind a columned entrance arch at the top of a set of wide, shallow steps. And stretching out of the entrance in a ragged line three or four deep—like theatergoers waiting for the doors to open, mumbling among themselves and jostling as a cordon of more German policeman strove to form them into some semblance of order—was the strangest collection of characters that Kunz had ever seen.

There were several wearing military camouflage smocks, and a number of others in hooded, bodytight Ninja suits. One, in silver coveralls and something that looked like a football player's helmet, was arguing with two others, one of whom was wearing a pink cloak with emerald-green knee breeches, and the other a German fireman's uniform, but with a field marshal's helmet. Nearer the door, a bronzed, muscular Adonis in what looked like ballet tights and a fencing blouse was shivering beneath a greatcoat that one of the policemen had evidently lent him, while a few places back, another man with leather shorts and a Tyrolean hat similar to Kunz's was waving his hands and jabbering at a woman with a long tweed skirt, motoring bonnet, and fleece-lined flying jacket. One had an aviator's cap with goggles, another a Napoleon hat and tunic, and another an American Stetson with pantaloons. Here was a Louis XIV wig, there a diamond tiara worn with a raincoat, and farther along, a Cal. State T-shirt stretched over the bodice of a crinoline dress.

Kunz could do nothing but stare numbly. He was barely aware as the two policemen relieved him of his arsenal, frisked him for concealed items, and added the collection to a pile of rifles, submachine guns, revolvers, automatics, pistols, bombs, grenades, blasters, flamethrowers, hand lasers, beam projectors, bayonets, daggers, knives, axes, cudgels, clubs and weapons of every description accumulating on the far side of the court, guarded by more policemen. Then the two who had brought Kunz in escorted him to the end of the line, behind the Louis XIV wig and a huge bearded man in a sailor suit with paratrooper's jump boots. "Wait here," the amiable sausage-necked policeman said. "It shouldn't be long."

"What's happening?" Kunz asked, finding his voice at last.

"Why, the Führer is coming here to talk to you. He's heard all the terrible things you people are saying about him, and he's very upset."

Just then, two more policemen appeared from the direction of the street, steering between them the figure in the Charlemagne coat and the Abe Lincoln hat that Kunz had glimpsed briefly in the Tiergarten. The figure stopped dead, looking as stunned as Kunz had been, while the policemen took charge of the plasma-bolt beamer, two sidearms, machete, and four subcritical fission grenades that he had been carrying, and then they led him over to join the line alongside Kunz.

"They're still coming in like homing pigeons back there," one of them said to the two policemen with Kunz. "We need all the help we can get."

"It won't be long now," the sausage-neck said to Kunz again. He indicated Kunz to Abe-Lincoln-hat with a nod of his head. "Just stay close to Pinnochio here until they move you inside." With that, he turned away to head back toward the Wilhelmstrasse after his three colleagues.

Kunz and Abe-Lincoln-hat eyed each other suspiciously. At last Kunz ventured, "I, er . . . guess it wasn't such a unique idea." Abe-Lincoln-hat stared at him. "Where did you come here from?" Kunz asked him.

"The year of the Lord, 2124."

"The pacifist cause must really have been catching on by then, eh?"

"Pacifists?"

"Isn't that why you're here—to get rid of Hitler, the man who got pacifism a bad name?"

Abe Lincoln-hat's eyes glared. "Pacifism is Satan's design to disarm the hosts of the righteous, and Hitler is his agent! For by renouncing all war, the world shall deny the just war that is God's instrument."

Kunz's expression hardened. "There can be no just war," he said.

"It is written, 'The wicked flee when no man pursueth: but the righteous are bold as a lion.' "

"What's a Bible freak doing here?" Louis-XIV-wig demanded, turning in front to face them. "Religious fascism is no different from Nazi fascism. Hitler invented the techniques of mass propaganda that gave the Fundamentalists the presidency in 2080."

"*Arghh!* You . . . secular *humanist!*" Abe-Lincoln-hat grabbed him by the throat with both hands.

Sailor-suit-and-paratrooper-boots was also glowering back. "Who did I hear was a pacifist? They were the bums who lost us white supremacy and let the Asiatics take the twenty-first century."

"I am," Kunz said, thrusting out his chin defiantly. "So why are *you* here? Hitler was on your side, wasn't he?"

"He blew it. If it wasn't for his war, the colonial empires wouldn't have broken up, see. And I say all pacifists are wimps."

"Oh yeah?" Kunz punched him in the mouth.

"All right, all right—enough of that." Three policemen moved in to break up the fray. Just then, the doors at the top of the steps were thrown open. The murmuring and arguing in both directions—already a number of more recent arrivals had joined on behind Abe-Lincoln-hat—died away, and the line began shuffling forward.

The building turned out to be an auditorium, with rows of seats facing a raised stage. In the center of the stage was a speaker's rostrum, and behind it a row of chairs on which a dozen or so men in suits were already seated. They looked like government officials. Some remained quiet and were looking concerned, while others whispered agitatedly among themselves. A line of German policemen stood below the stage, facing the audience, and others were stationed at intervals along the walls. As the entrants dispersed among the seats, Kunz moved as far away as possible from the three that he had tangled with outside. He found himself a place halfway to the back on the extreme left of the auditorium, next to the side aisle. The murmuring and muttering had risen again, and already more arguments were breaking out in several places. As Kunz sat down and leaned back in his seat, he became aware of a man's voice behind him, speaking in a suave English accent. "I mean to say, the bugger ruined our empire for us. Up until then, we hadn't been doing too bad a job of civilizing the world."

"He ruined U.S. isolationism, you mean," an indignant American voice that sounded as if it was from Brooklyn retorted. "If we hadn't had ta come in and bale yous guys out for a second time, we'da had it made. We never wanted ta be no policeman for da whole woild."

"Yes, and a fine mess you made of things, I must say."

"A fine mess you left us, you mean."

"You don't know what you're talking about."

"Waddya mean? So, what da you know about anything, then, huh, asshole?"

"Tch, tch. Colonials!" The sounds of scuffling came from behind, and something thudded against the back of Kunz's seat.

"Cut that out!" One of the policemen said, moving forward from the wall.

"The man's a complete savage," the English voice protested.

"I ain't stayin' next ta him. Everyone knows they're all gay."

And then a hush descended on the auditorium as a figure

with a face familiar to all, wearing a brown Party uniform with Iron Cross and swastika armband, walked out from the wings and crossed the stage to the lectern. He surveyed the rows of faces before him and pursed his lips for a moment below his narrow, clipped mustache. "I'm given to understand that I seem to have made myself rather unpopular with some people," Adolf Hitler said. He waited, but there was no immediate response. "But that's terrible. I have made plans for straightening out—with all due respect to my predecessors— the bungled job that's been made of the Weimar constitution, and for getting the country onto a sound democratic footing at last. The League of Nations hasn't been working out as well as was envisioned, and I've been giving some thought to that, too. . . . But what are all these awful things about me that I've been told? I need to know what the complaints are before we go launching into anything new. Well, you've come all this way. Somebody must have something to say."

A man near the front leaped up to reveal the slogan NO NUKES written across the back of his sweater in large red letters. "It was because of you that the nuclear nightmare was unleashed across the world," he shouted. "World War II was the cause of the Manhattan Project, which produced the Bomb. That led to everything else, and then everyone got ahold of it." He pointed an accusing finger. "Radiation! Fallout! Genetic diseases! Deformed babies! Because of you, the world will end with universal cancer!"

Hitler stared at him incredulously. "Radiation? Genetic dis—"

Suddenly, the spell broke. "Industrial pollution of the planet!" a woman near the back shrieked, rising. She was wearing an EARTH FIRST button on a black leotard painted with a white skeleton. "Your war brought about the decline of Europe. Unchecked capitalist greed in the postwar U.S.A. resulted in—"

"You call yourself National Socialists," a man in a black opera cape yelled out. People were on their feet all around the room by now. "But you destroyed socialism! If it hadn't been for your treachery in 1941, Russia would have ruled the world."

"That's not true!" a voice called from near where Kunz was sitting. "If they hadn't rallied against the Nazis, the

Soviets would have disintegrated. Stalin was a lunatic. Hitler saved Communism.''

"But you destroyed Germany, on the eve of what should have been its era of greatness," a man in a kaiser helmet and trenchcoat shouted out.

Voices were shouting from all sides.

"Mass murderer! What about the camps?"

"Nazism was to blame for the rock cult and drugs!"

"It caused pornography, teenage pregnancies, and evolution!"

". . . belief in astrology and the paranormal . . ."

"And liberals and gays and AIDS!"

Hitler smiled tolerantly and raised his arms in an appeal for order. Slowly the hubbub subsided. "My dear people . . . really, this is all most bewildering. I know we do have some outstanding ideological differences to resolve, but it is my firm belief that the Western civilization that has arisen in Europe is about to enter its golden age of prosperity and culture. With confidence in reason and the creative potential of the human mind, we have it within our power as a species to eliminate universally and permanently the evils of hunger, disease, poverty, oppression, and ignorance that have plagued humanity for as long as humanity has existed. To let you into a secret, we have some scientists working on rocket propulsion for vehicles which, they tell me, might one day enable us to leave this planet entirely. And as for the political differences between ourselves and our Russian neighbors, well, I know there have been problems in the past. But those problems stemmed from shortages of resources, and in the new age I see coming, with new technologies that will end such shortages, I am optimistic that eventually, with better education and as tensions relax, we will come to see . . ."

As Hitler spoke on, the atmosphere around the room changed. One by one, those of the audience who were on their feet sat down. Many of them exchanged puzzled looks. Something was very wrong. Was this the fiend who had gone down as one of the arch-villains of history?

"I must confess to being somewhat bemused," Kunz heard the English voice whisper behind him. "He seems to be quite a decent sort of chap, really."

"Yeah," the Brooklyn voice breathed in reply. "Dis ain't de way I hoid it. Dat guy's okay."

Kunz frowned, trying to make sense of the situation. He'd seen the newsreels and read the speeches. He recalled Magus's warnings about Hitler's cunning, and the skillful way he deceived his opponents to lull them into a false sense of security. Then it came to him suddenly that it was all a trap. He looked around at the rows of placid faces, some nodding unconsciously as they listened. They were falling for it, all of them—soaking it up.

But not Time Commando Kunz!

He looked away, and saw that the policeman who had quietened the pair behind was still standing a mere couple of feet from Kunz's seat. The policeman's arms were folded, and he was off guard as he listened. He was wearing a belt over his greatcoat, and hanging from the belt on the side nearest to Kunz was a revolver in a holster. The flap of the holster was unfastened. Kunz looked furtively around. Everyone's attention was on what Hitler was saying. And then Kunz's hand was reaching out stealthily toward the butt of the revolver. He was aware of it in a strangely detached kind of way, as if his arm had initiated the motion of its own accord, with the rest of him a spectator. And before he had fully realized it he was on his feet and leveling the gun between both hands. He was dimly aware of voices shouting and heads turning in alarm, and then Hitler was staring straight at him through the sights, white-faced and openmouthed. . . . He didn't remember firing, or the blow on the back of his head after the third shot.

The next thing Kunz knew was that he was stretched out in his seat, and his head hurt. There were policemen on either side of him and in front of him, and a pandemonium of blurred voices all around. He raised his head, and several hands immediately clamped down on his shoulders from behind.

Up on the stage, two medics in white smocks were in the process of lifting an inert form covered by a sheet onto a stretcher. The officials who had been sitting behind were gathered in a huddle, wringing their hands in consternation and talking nervously. Two shiny black jackboots protruded from beneath the sheet as the medics lifted the stretcher and carried it off the stage. As Kunz's head cleared, the voices of the officials floated through into his consciousness.

"Stone dead—no doubt about it . . ."

"Oh dear, oh dear . . ."

". . . three bullets, dead center. Didn't have a chance. . ."

A tired but triumphant smile crept onto Kunz's face. It was done! It didn't matter what happened to him now. The future was saved.

"He was doing such a splendid job of restoring the nation's pride and self-confidence after Versailles and everything. . . . We can't let the people know that this has happened."

"Oh no! That would ruin everything."

"And especially after his achievement today . . ."

"We mustn't let anyone know."

"Then there's no choice. We'll have to use the double."

"But he's so unstable. Do you really think—"

"We have to risk it. There's no choice."

"He's on his way here now."

Kunz sat bolt upright in his seat as the meaning percolated through.

Double?

And then the tramp of jackboots on cobblestones and orders being barked sounded from the court outside. Moments later, two lines of storm troopers entered and surrounded the auditorium, while from the midst of the group of uniformed officers who had appeared inside the entrance, a figure of familiar appearance emerged and strode purposefully down the center, up the side steps onto the stage, and across to the lectern. But not of totally familiar appearance, Kunz saw as the figure glowered out over the hushed audience. The features, forelock, and mustache were similar, but the mouth was grim and determined, and the eyes held a fierce, tempestuous rage.

"Führer, we have decided—" one of the officials began, but the newcomer shut him up with a curt wave of his hand.

"*You* no longer decide anything. This babbling has gone on long enough. We have work to do and a lot of lost time to make good." He raised his head to address the officers at the rear and indicated the audience around the room with a wave.

"Get this rabble out of here for a start and lock them up, and clear away all that junk in the Tiergarten. Then we have the last ten years of records to rewrite. Oh yes, there is much to do, indeed." A wild gleam came into his eyes. "*Ein Reich! Ein volk! Ein führer!*" he shrieked.

"*Sieg Heil!* the storm troopers chanted.

"Oh shit!" Kunz groaned.

MINDS, MACHINES
AND EVOLUTION

If a "machine" is any kind of system created by man, and "think" means everything we normally mean when we use the word, will a machine ever be able to think?

This question is asked a lot these days. It actually implies two different questions, and much of the confusion on this subject results from a failure to distinguish between them. The first asks if the suggestion is possible in principle, and might be rephrased: Given that a human brain is a system which thinks, is there any reason to suppose that no man-made system, as opposed to one that happens to have evolved "naturally," can be capable of doing likewise? The second asks if it will ever be achieved in practice. My experience from sitting on many artificial intelligence panels at science-fiction conventions has been that writers tend to answer the first question, and researchers in the field, the second—which usually leads to two separate dialogues between groups who aren't talking about the same thing. Since there is no question to be asked about the practicability of something that's impossible on principle, the first question is the one to start with in a discussion of the subject. It's also the more intriguing philosophically.

The question of whether man-made intelligence is possible in principle amounts to asking if "mind" can be adequately accounted for by the principles of physics, and nothing else. If it can, then there's no compelling reason to suppose that a man-made system—which would operate by the same principles—shouldn't be able to emulate it. If it can't, then we must conclude that the phenomenon of self-aware consciousness possesses something "extra"—some qualitative difference that sets it above being explainable by the same laws that explain everything else in the universe, and that therefore it will forever be beyond our ability to duplicate.

The first reaction of many people is to insist that something as intricate as "mind" could never arise solely from arrangements of molecules, neural circuits, and the other things we find inside the human brain. It violates their subjective notions of what makes sense. But this kind of intuition is dangerous and has littered the trail of human discovery with the wreckage of all kinds of "proofs" that something or other was impossible. It pays to be open-minded. Ever since primitive man found himself hard put to account for the sun, the moon, the winds, the tides, and so forth, dismissing unexplainable phenomena as "supernatural" has provided many with a quick and easy alternative to expanding their powers of explaining. The "vitalists" of the nineteenth century were similarly convinced that the laws of physics were insufficient to account for living matter, and proposed the existence of a "life force," which set it apart from the inanimate world. Today, life processes can be satisfactorily accounted for in terms of molecular chemistry. The vitalist argument has not gone away as a consequence, however, but has simply shifted levels and reappeared in a new disguise: instead of between the living and the nonliving, it now searches for some fundamental difference between the thinking and the nonthinking, between mind and body.

A basic principle of science asserts that the safest hypothesis to adopt is the simplest one that explains all the facts. In the present context, this asks if there is any way in which the things we observe *could* account for mind in a way that's at least possible. If there is, then the simplest explanation will have sufficed and there will be no need or justification for introducing additional influences.

There is effectively no limit to the number of different books that have been written or could be written. We might describe our impression of one that we've read as "inspiring," "passionate," "entertaining and witty," and so on. Similarly a symphony might strike us as "majestic," or "somber." Well, where in such creations do properties like these exist?

At its elementary level every book consists of letters drawn from the same, very limited, alphabet. Clearly it would be ridiculous to look for such qualities as "inspiration" or "passion" at that kind of level. A letter of the alphabet can be one of only twenty-six possibilities, and hence the amount of information it can convey is very limited. But the act of stringing letters together to form words can convey enough different concepts to fill all the dictionaries of all the world's languages, plus form all the strings of letters that might have been words, but which, as it happens, aren't. Just this simple raising to a higher level of organization brings about an increase in the richness and variety of possible expression that is staggering. And beyond that, words can be arranged into sentences, sentences into paragraphs, until at higher levels it becomes possible to express every shade of thought and meaning from *Alice in Wonderland* to Kant's *Critique of Pure Reason*.

Language is organized as a hierarchy of increasing complexity, in which the variety of possible expression increases by a stupendous degree over even a few levels. New orders of meaning and relationship come into existence that cannot be expressed as properties of the elements that form the building blocks at a given level, but which arise as *emergent properties* of the way the elements are put together. In the same kind of way, every musical composition is built ultimately from the same set of notes, and every chemical substance from the same three subatomic particles. We see nothing remarkable in any of this, and while we might be astonished by the diversity than can arise from combining simple elements in different ways, we feel no need to invoke supernatural agencies to explain it.

The same applies to an even more striking degree in the process of biological evolution, in which more complex systems of organization emerge from simpler ones under the influence of selection. Originally, simple inorganic compounds gave rise to more complicated substances, which in the course of time evolved self-replication and progressed through single-celled organisms to the advanced, multicellular life forms of today. Again we see a hierarchy of progressively increasing organizational complexity, and at each successive level new properties become manifest which exist only in the context of that level, and which can't be described in terms of the subsidiary components. Thus, a single molecule does not possess any attribute of "elephantness"; a sufficiently large number of them, however, when put together in the right way, do.

Now, if the laws of physics, plus selection, a lot of time, and nothing more are sufficient to produce *physical forms* as sophisticated as the nose of a bloodhound or the airframe of a humming bird, isn't it to be expected that the same processes should result in similarly sophisticated patterns of *behavior*? After all, survival is what matters in evolution, and behavior.— how an organism interacts with its environment—is just as important to its survival as its physical attributes, and frequently more so. Having big teeth isn't much good without the capacity to recognize a threat and the motivation to defend yourself. Interacting with an environment consists of acquiring information from that environment, evaluating it, and responding in some way, all of which is performed by the nervous system. It follows that improvements to the nervous system as part of the general evolutionary process would confer significant survival benefits. It's interesting to see that when we trace the sequence that such improvements are believed to have followed, we see emerging the qualities most people would consider essential to characterizing that which we call "mind."

Primitive life-forms such as sponges evolved special cells that reacted to stimuli in the environment to trigger responses that, for example, increased the chances of capturing food. In later organisms like jellyfish these cells developed into simple neural networks capable of coordinating the movements of the entire animal to make possible such revolutionary strategies as directed mobility, with all the attendant advantages. In higher forms still, these networks developed concentrations of neural tissue which eventually acquired the structure and organization of the modern mammalian brain, and with it the ability to apply steadily more sophisticated processing techniques to the information gathered by the senses.

Here, then, is another example of a hierarchy of increasing complexity taking shape. And as was the case with the structure of language, the evolving nervous system forms a hierarchy of increasing information-processing complexity. With language, the concepts dealt with become more abstract at higher levels of organization—farther removed from the "mechanical" low-level world of alphabet and syntax. Different units of information operate at different levels of the hierarchy. Similarly, the units of information being processed at higher organizational levels in the nervous system become more distant from the raw-data world of the stimuli that impinge on the senses. Thus, we have the beginnings of a mechanism for assembling sensory data into higher-level symbols, and manipulating aggregates of symbols into a model of the world outside—a model inhabited not by wavelengths and energy quanta, but by objects, attractions, aversions, goals, and all the other factors that affect a higher-level entity interacting with a higher-level perceived environment.

Models that reflected the real world more accurately would enhance an organism's survival chances and hence be favored selectively for further improvement. In creating progressively more elaborate world models, the evolving brain would learn to synthesize a representation of the three-dimensional space in which it moved, the other objects inhabiting that space, and the interactions taking place between them. A crucial need in a survival-dominated environment would be the ability to distinguish the "self," whose survival is at stake, from the rest of the world around it. Assigning a special status to the focal zone of sensory impressions mapped into the world model gives rise to a *self-model*, which makes possible the emergence of directed action toward the goal of self-preservation, superseding purely automatic reflexes.

Given the ability of the brain to manipulate conceptual symbols that mimic the world that actually exists, it doesn't seem such a gigantic step to go on to manipulating the same symbols into representations of worlds that *could* exist. This would enable, for example, scenarios of a potential danger to be constructed from previously accumulated experiences and played through in advance, before it became a reality, allowing timely action to avoid it—or in a word, the faculty of *anticipation*. And once we're in a position to play with models of worlds and situations that don't exist, surely we're well on the way to displaying *imagination* and *creativity*.

This is all very well, but it won't do very much for our evolving organism's survival prospects if it gets so wrapped up in its internal fantasizings that it loses track of reality and fails to notice the tiger coming at it down the hill. Hence, this variety of complex activity going on inside the brain requires some kind of overseeing function to monitor its own processes, evaluate their relative importance, and decide which should take priority over which from moment to moment. This implies a degree of *awareness*. Being aware of the images being manipulated in the mind, and aware of the preferences that arise from evaluating their implications, adds up, does it not, to experiencing *feelings* (emotions, if you will) and exercising *judgment*. And when coupled to the self-model that we already have, it yields *self-awareness*.

Do we really mean any more than this when we talk about mind and consciousness? I'm not at all convinced that we do. The brain's ability to think requires no supernatural ingredient, but arises purely as an emergent property of its organizational complexity. What led to the phenomenon we call mind was the fact of an adaptive system being operated on by selection. The selection happened to be "natural," and the adaptive system happened to be biological, but those weren't the significant factors in yielding an intelligent, self-aware end product. Therefore there's no reason to suppose that other systems of comparable complexity shouldn't be capable of doing likewise. Hence man-made intelligence ought, in principle, to be possible.

That being so gives a point to the second question that we asked: What, then, is the likelihood in practice? The question these days is usually asked with reference to computers.

The appearance of human intelligence enabled selection to be guided by choice instead of by the unconscious processes that had operated previously; speech and written language transmitted new information through populations virtually instantaneously compared to genetic encoding. This has enabled the development and spread of human culture at the staggering rate that history has recorded. But we have merely accelerated the evolutionary process, not altered it in essence. Whether we're producing a better political system, a Boeing 747, or a bigger and tastier tomato, we apply the same basic method that nature used to turn jelly into vertebrates and vertebrates into us: We experiment with variations of the themes we've got, forget the ones that don't work so well, and try further variations of the ones we decide are worth keeping. That's evolution—by artificial selection. And we are applying it vigorously to systems that are designed to do just what nervous systems evolved to do, namely process information and vary their behavior in response: computers. This is what sets computers apart from other, earlier technologies that have been offered as models of the brain. Perhaps, too, our familiarity with computers has helped make "mind" less mysterious than it used to be.

Of course, I'm not trying to suggest that what goes on inside even the most powerful of today's computers constitutes "thinking," or even comes close. But they do seem to be off to the right start, and only decades after their inception are mimicking in intriguing ways the reflexive, yet sometimes surprisingly elaborate, behavior of primitive nervous systems. I find it hard to believe that a jellyfish can think either; but obviously there was nothing to prevent it—or at least, something akin to it—from evolving into something that could.

For a start, computers possess a comparable hierarchical organization, in which the units of information being processed take on progressively more abstract meaning as we ascend through higher levels. The lowest level is that of the physical hardware, where the circuit chips lead a somewhat monotonous life shuffling binary digits through registers and combining them according to totally mechanical rules. At the higher levels of software activity which this traffic supports, the "bits" combine into codes that represent numbers, characters, instructions, and command strings to convey meaning at the more symbolic level in which programmers, rather than hardware engineers, think. And at higher levels still, these entities in turn are subsumed into programs, files, display formats, and so forth, which have lost all connection with electronics, and relate instead to things like bank accounts, airline flights, Adventure games, and the rest of the world of human affairs.

A common objection to the suggestion that this could ever lead to intelligence is that a computer, however elaborate, is still by nature a "machine," operating according to rigid, mechanical rules that will always cause it to respond to the same inputs in the same, predictable manner. Whatever tricks might be built into it to give an illusion to the contrary (such as deriving some input from internal randomness generators), it can still only do what it's programmed to do. Nothing that qualifies as "thinking," which ought to exhibit some element of free choice, or even capriciousness, could ever result form it.

It is true that at its elementary level a computer system is constructed from components that function mechanically and repetitively. But the same could also be said about us. The DNA, RNA, enzymes, and other constituents of the cells that make up our bodies function in ways that are quite mechanical and repetitive. The neural hardware that supports our mental "software" consists of bewildering interconnections of an enormous number of neurons, each of which behaves predictably. If the signals applied to a neuron add up in such a way as to exceed its activation threshold, it will fire; if they don't, it won't. The neuron doesn't go through agonies of indecision trying to make up some microscopic mind about what to do. At its level there isn't any property of "mind" to make up. The decision is made according to fixed rules, just like the decision of a computer logic circuit to generate an output.

The earth's atmosphere consists of a vast number of interacting elements, each of which is very simple in itself and behaves completely mechanically. At the microscopic "hardware" level, each molecule responds to a combination of forces exerted by its neighbors in a way that can be calculated precisely. But at the macroscopic level, totally new *emergent properties* manifest themselves as storm centers, cloud banks, rainfall, and other phenomena that cannot be expressed in terms applicable to molecules. Instead, we describe them in macroscopically meaningful terms, such as temperature and pressure—statistical measures of the composite effects of huge numbers of molecules whose individual motions can never be known with certainty. In the process we define a qualitatively new set of concepts which lose the precision and predictability that characterize the lower-level activity, and which in the process acquire an increasing degree of uncertain, "whimsical" behavior.

The fallacy with the objection is that it compares the activities taking place at the brain's highest, most abstract level with those at a computer's lowest, most mechanical level. It's a bit like saying that tree shrews could never evolve into humans because humans can build cities and write symphonies, whereas a tree shrew is just a collection of nucleic acids and proteins that are obviously incapable of such feats.

It's interesting to note, however, that the qualities of unpredictability and "whimsy" that many people insist on as indispensable prerequisites for intelligence are in fact beginning to appear in computer systems, too. A large "real-time" system, for example—perhaps for controlling an industrial plant or a communications network—typically contains hundreds or even thousands of different programs for carrying out various tasks that need to be performed at different times and in different circumstances. It would also contain a list of priorities, specifying which task is the most important at any given time and should therefore run if it is ready to, which task is second priority and should run if the first is held up, and so on. Through thousands of input signals coming in from sensors around the plant, or from the network, the system constantly monitors and reacts to the changing conditions, perhaps by suspending the operation of one task to allow a higher-priority response to a critical situation somewhere, or by activating lower-priority fill-in jobs when there's nothing more pressing to attend to. The result can be a bewildering activity pattern of different programs being started, interrupted, waiting to execute, of interrupting programs themselves being interrupted by higher priorities still, all interlaced with the operations of supervisor programs to keep track of what's going on and orchestrate the other programs. Since this activity is all being driven by unpredictable events unfolding in the outside world, it's impossible to say in advance what state such a system will be in or what, precisely, it will be doing at any particular time (unlike a "batch" system, where it's always possible to say, for instance, that payroll is run on Thursday mornings.)

Hence it's not really true, even today, to say that a computer system will always respond in the same way to the same set of inputs. Its response will depend not only on the information coming in through its sensors from the outside world, but also on its own internal "state" at the time, and this in turn will depend on its earlier history, i.e., its "experiences." What's programmed in is the *potential* to react to various external stimuli in different ways, without any specific large-scale behavior being predefined—just as is true of sponges, jellyfish, tree shrews, and with much broader ranges of variability, people.

Because a human brain is far more complex than these systems, the number of different internal states that it can assume is vastly greater. So if it's true that even with today's large computer systems the same external inputs do not elicit the same responses, it will be much more true of the brain. In fact, the brain can never revert exactly to any state that it was once in previously; however close it gets, the very fact of having once been in the earlier state will have left impressions—not necessarily conscious—that weren't there the first time, and hence the state that exists later must be different by at least that much. I find this a far more plausible basis for the variability of human behavior than attempts to derive it from random quantum mechanical effects at the molecular level. Variability of behavior implies a degree of correlation of our responses to the macroscopic realm that we perceive, and this is a different thing from randomness. As Schrödinger conjectured, the reason we evolved to be so much bigger than atoms could be precisely because with objects at the macroscopic level, the uncertainties that dominate the quantum realm are swamped out. In other words, only at higher scales of magnitude does a predictable and repeatable world in which rational intelligence can evolve become possible. Linking our mental activities to the quantum fluctuations of neural atoms would appear to put us back where we started—literally.

The highest-level activity of our brains, our experience of awareness, doesn't extend down to the operations taking place at the lowermost neural hardware level. We think and communicate in terms of persons, places, ideas, and things, with no innate knowledge of the streams of electrical impulses swirling around in our heads, or the chemical codes by which various cells and organs in our bodies exchange messages. They, at their own levels, communicate in their own languages; we, at our level as conscious totalities, communicate in ours.

It's not difficult to see why consciousness should have become shut off in this way from lower-level processes. The simple act of raising an arm involves the coordinated action of something like forty muscles, each of which needs a discrete neural signal to tell it to contract by the right amount at the right time. Such muscular sequences are controlled by fixed "microprograms" hardwired into the brain, which are triggered by high-level commands that we initiate voluntarily. If we had to monitor every step of such sequences consciously, our brains would be constantly saturated with mundane detail. Leaving such routine chores to a subconscious realm frees up our voluntary and conscious abilities for more valuable problem solving.

Again, the beginnings of the same kind of thing are evident in today's computer systems. At the basement level, the machine's elementary operations are controlled by microcode embedded in the hardware. Microcode is the language of circuit chips and hardware designers. At the first software level, a single "machine instruction," typically written in alphanumerics—to execute and ADD operation, for example—triggers a whole sequence of microcode functions, and such instructions form the units in which "machine-language" programs are written. The machine-language programmer does not have to understand microcode to write a program, or even have to be aware that it exists. However, a machine-language program does reflect the architecture of the machine it's designed for, hence its name. A step further removed from the hardware are "high-level" languages, consisting of commands that initiate sequences of machine instructions, which make it possible, for example, for researchers to write programs directly in scientific and mathematical terms, without having to learn machine language. And at higher levels still we find "system" and "user" commands which control the operation of entire programs and are meaningful in real-world terms, without the user having to know or care if what exists behind the buttons is electronics, clockwork, or black magic. Indeed, it's difficult to see how it could be very much different. If every user had to understand microcode to check a bank balance or play Adventure, the computer industry wouldn't have gotten very far.

Designing any kind of system involves tradeoffs. Some of the requirements that the system has to meet will always conflict with others, and improving the design in one direction invariably extracts penalties in others. Thus a toaster is great for making toast but not much good as a blender; F-15s wouldn't be the right buy for Pan Am, and so on. "General purpose" systems offer a compromise by fulfilling a number of roles moderately well without excelling at any of them, for example, the family car or a home computer. You could say that these trade off excellence for versatility. The human nervous system is probably the best example of versatility that we know. It can do practically anything to a degree, but its performance in any given area is limited. So we supplement it with all kinds of specialized accessories such as microscopes, high-speed calculators, and long-range communications equipment, each of which outperforms it by orders of magnitude in its own field, but is useless for anything else.

Conceivably, if we ever did produce a system of comparable versatility to the brain, we might find that one of nature's basic trade-offs is that thinking wide and thinking narrow are mutually exclusive. In return for versatility, we could find that we have to sacrifice many of the features that we associate with the highly specialized machines of today. In the same way that our consciousness operates without any awareness of what its neurons are doing, or even that it has any, a man-made electronic (or photonic, or biosynthetic, or whatever) intelligence might find itself shut off from the substrate levels at which its fast and mathematically precise activities were taking place. Perhaps, therefore, it wouldn't be able to perform astronomic calculations in seconds, or recall word for word a conversation that it had a week ago, or make a decision without wrestling with all kinds of imponderables. So what would it do if it wanted to know pi to a few thousand decimal places? Well, I suppose it would have to either build itself a computer or buy one. And that's a good reason to suppose that long before then we'd have started calling it something else.

It's funny how the right people have a knack of popping up at just the right time. I became interested in writing a book about machine intelligence at about the time I moved to the U.S.A. with my second wife, Lyn, in late 1977. I'd developed a few thoughts and ideas, but before getting serious, I felt I needed to bounce them off somebody who knew a lot more about the subject. One Saturday morning over breakfast I said, "Who do we know who's an Artificial Intelligence expert?"

She replied, "But we've only just arrived in this country. We hardly know anyone yet"—which was about all that could be said on that.

And then, the very next morning, Sunday, the phone rang and a voice said, "Hi, my name is Marvin Minsky. We haven't met, but I'm director of the AI department at MIT. Nobody has written a good book about AI yet. I read *Inherit the Stars* and liked it, and I think maybe you could. How would you like to come along and take a look at what we're doing here, and talk about ideas for fiction?"

I got to know Marvin and his family, and the outcome of our talks about ideas for fiction was *The Two Faces of Tomorrow*, which was published in the summer of 1979.

Perhaps the sign of when artificial systems have become smarter than we are will be when they start making up ethnic jokes about people:

"How many humans does it take to change a light bulb?"

"How many?"

"One hundred thousand and one."

"How come?"

"One to change the light bulb. The rest as biological ancestors to produce him. How inefficient can you get?"

DISCOVERING
HYPERSPACE

Another question that writers are always being asked is where they get their ideas from. In my experience, the ideas that finally turn into books often result when thoughts that complement each other, but which have never connected together in your mind before, suddenly click together like jigsaw puzzle pieces. While I was writing *Inherit the Stars*, I found myself thinking from time to time about the "hyper-drives," "warp drives," and other exotic propulsion systems that we come across in S.F. It seemed to me that they had become something of a cliché, tacitly accepted by writers and readers alike as merely a device to shortcut Einstein by moving characters from here to there fast to get on with the story. . . . But wait a minute. We're talking about a capability that transcends not only any technology imaginable today, but also our most fundamental theoretical beliefs. Never mind getting across the galaxy to save the blonde or deliver the villain his comeuppances—how did they *discover* "hyperspace" to begin with? Surely, there's a much more interesting story right here, which we were about to gloss over. What experiments in labs gave strange results? What body of new theory and speculation did this open up? How were the ideas tested?

How did things progress from there to proven, working engineering? Nobody I talked to had seen a story about how hyperspace came to be discovered. I played around with some extrapolations of physics that provided a plausible theoretical framework, but that doesn't make a novel.

Another subject that I talked about with friends sometimes was the interstellar warships that we saw in books and movies. As usual, I was complaining. It didn't make sense for a vessel that could cross light-years of space in an instant, with the staggering level of technology that implied, to peel off into a dive when it got there, like a World War II Stuka—and usually with a pilot driving it from a World War II cockpit—and drop a bomb on something. After all, what does a bomb do? It concentrates a lot of energy on a target. Well, if you can send a spaceship there through hyperspace, why not just send the energy? Just imagine being able to materialize the equivalent of a fifty-megaton bang out of nowhere, instantaneously, without warning, and with no way for an enemy to know where it came from. That sounded more like a weapon worthy of a futuristic technology. By comparison, sending a spaceship to drop a bomb would be like inventing gunpowder to blow holes through castle walls, but trundling it up to the wall with a horse and cart instead of thinking to invent a cannon. But that doesn't add up to a story either.

These two thoughts existed in separate compartments in my head for a long time. Then one day, the obvious eventually struck me: Perhaps the new physics that our characters stumble on isn't recognized as the way to a hyperdrive at all, to begin with. Perhaps they could be investigating its promise of a revolutionary weapons system—which happens all the time in real life. And only later, maybe, the line of new discoveries takes an unexpected turn which leads to spacecraft drives. The two ideas fitted well together, and that was how *The Genesis Machine* came to be written. It's the book that seems to generate the most questions about where the idea came from.

TILL DEATH US
DO PART

The apartment looked out from high above London's fashionable Knightsbridge, across Hyde Park toward where the green sea of treetops washed against white cliffs of elegant Park Lane buildings that had not changed appreciably in the last hundred years. Spacious, light and airy, and opulently draped and furnished in contemporary style, the residence was not the kind that came with the income of the average Londoner of 2056; but then, the four people whom Harry Stone had come from Las Vegas to meet there that morning were hardly average Londoners, and their income was what he had come all that way to talk about.

For tax purposes the apartment was owned by a nebulous entity registered as *Zephyr Enterprises Limited,* and described as a business property retained for the use and entertainment of clients and customers visiting the capital. The company rented it for ten months of the year at a nominal sum to Nigel Philiman and his wife Delia, who, it turned out, happened to be managing director and company secretary respectively of the holding company that had set up Zephyr. To comply with the minimum required by law, the Philimans spent two months of each year abroad or elsewhere while the apartment was being used by clients. The clients often turned out to be friends who needed somewhere to stay while mixing a considerable amount of pleasure with a modicum of business in the course of a visit to the city, but that was purely coincidental.

Nigel was in his late forties, suave, athletic, suntanned and silver-haired, and always immaculately groomed and dressed. Delia was only a few years younger, but she had a countess's bearing and a movie star's looks, and knew just how to choose slinky, body-clinging clothes that enhanced the latter without detracting from the former. The couple went well with the apartment's image of luxury and high living, and Harry Stone was well aware that the image was no hollow sham.

Where their money came from was none of Harry Stone's business. Being a professional, he had done some discreet checking on the side, however, and he knew that Zephyr had obscure links to a string of loan companies that seemed to specialize in financing such operations as escort agencies, various types of modeling agencies, an employment agency that hired waitresses and hostesses, and home or hotel visiting massage services—in short, anything to do with girls. The girls employed by such enterprises always worked according to a strict code of ethics written into their contracts, and they accepted payment only in the form of checks or credit cards that could be verified by accredited auditors. But like any man of the world, Harry knew that the girls were seldom averse to cultivating friendships further in their own free time, and that any additional such transactions were strictly cash. Where a portion of that cash might wind up and how it might get there were interesting questions.

Clive Philiman, Nigel's younger brother by ten years or perhaps slightly more, ran a group of agencies that specialized in handling rented apartments on the west side of London. Out of curiosity Harry had purchased a selection of the kinds of magazine that younger, single women tended to read, and had found a number of Clive's companies taking prominent advertising space in several of them. He could imagine that Clive, with his dark-brown eyes, classically Roman features, tight curls of short black hair, and sympathetic manner, might be just the kind of person that a girl just in from the country and looking for somewhere to live might find easy to talk to, especially when she learned that he just happened to have the right contacts to give her a job. And of course, making money might become her main problem when she discovered that the great bargain which had brought her into the office had been rented just an hour before she showed up.

Barbara Philiman, Clive's slim and petite, auburn-haired wife, had a good as well as a pretty head on her shoulders; she was director of a personnel selection agency off Wigmore Street which procured managers and senior executives for a wide spectrum of companies and corporations ranging from manufacturers of plastic labels to builders of space stations. This position gave her numerous social contacts throughout the capital's commercial world, and, Harry thought, were she so inclined, she would be the ideal person for somebody who perhaps was interested in arranging some entertainment for an important visitor to know. Furthermore, the agency would have been able to supply a tax-deductible invoice to cover the costs of screening a lot of nonexistent job applicants for positions that had proved unsuitable. It was just a thought.

All Harry Stone knew officially was that the Philiman family wished to convert a substantial inflow of cash from sources they chose not to disclose into a legitimate form of income the British Inland Revenue would be obliged to accept— despite any suspicions they might harbor—as justifying a life-style built around diamonds, personal flymobiles, à la mode gowns from Paris, and jetliners chartered for mid-Atlantic orgies thinly disguised as parties. In the capacity of financial and legal consultant, he had spent the morning explaining how he thought an American institution known as *Neighbors in Need*, with which he happened to have "personal connections," might be able to help solve their problem. Essentially, the organization managed the investment of large sums of money collected by charities of one kind or another, and distributed the proceeds among various worthy causes it was pledged to support. This service was rendered in return for a moderate commission on the amounts handled, plus expenses. Harry's proposition involved setting up a British chapter of the operation.

The British subsidiary would be guaranteed to attract a massive response to the quite moderate program of advertising Harry had outlined. The response—mainly in the form of anonymous donations—was guaranteed because the so-called donations would be almost completely made up of the Philimans' own hot money mailed to themselves after conversion into money orders and travelers' checks bought with cash all over the country. The packages would be opened and the contents registered by certified accountants, thus providing unimpeachable proof of where every penny of the chapter's assets had originated.

"Twenty percent stays here for salaries and expenses, which is the maximum allowed under British law," he said when he summed up the main points. He was speaking easily and confidently as he sat in an armchair of padded purple and chrome that looked as if it belonged in some eccentric millionaire's sculpture collection. The rings on his fingers glittered in the sunshine streaming through the window as he made an empty gesture in the air. "The remaining eighty is tax exempt and goes to the States as your gross contribution to the fund. Obviously you're all charitable-minded people, and there's no reason why you shouldn't add in a personal donation of your own or some deductible contributions from your companies' profits. Four times a year they pay you back a commission that they list as foreign expenses, which brings your effective total revenue back up to fifty percent; you pay tax on only three-fifths—that is to say, the thirty that's fed back. The remaining fifty covers the actual input to the fund, the parent company's commission, and U.S. domestic expenses. I guess that's about it." He sat back in his chair, steepled his fingers below his chin, and studied the four faces before him.

Nigel, looking relaxed in the chair opposite, took a measured sip from the glass of sherry in his hand and savored the taste with an approving nod before replying. "You're still talking about a full half of it," he said. His voice was calm, registering curiosity rather than surprise or indignation. "Allowing for the portion that's taxable over here, we'd end up with the minor share. That does seem rather overambitious, wouldn't you agree?"

Harry knew Nigel knew better than that. He spread his arms expressively. "Most of their half has to go through to the fund. It's a respectable fund management operation, and it's got its payments to make. The rest helps them make a living, something we all have to do.''

"What percentage goes into the fund net at the end of it all?'' Barbara asked from where she was sitting on the sofa to one side, next to Clive.

"What I've described is the deal,'' Harry replied evenly, avoiding a direct answer. "They're not asking where the donations would be coming from at this end.''

"It's still a big chunk whichever way you look at it,'' Clive said. He rubbed his nose dubiously, then looked across at his brother. "The money's clean on their side from the moment it enters the country,'' he pointed out. "We run all the risks over here. That's a difference that should be reflected in the split. I'm for this scheme in principle, but not for settling as it stands.''

"Your money is also hot, and that's another side to the same difference,'' Harry countered smoothly. "It's unspendable, and therefore might as well not be there. Half a loaf is better than no loaf. Your risk is balanced out by their doing you a favor that you need, which squares things back at fifty-fifty.''

A short silence fell. Delia walked back from the window where she had been listening and stopped behind Nigel's chair. "I presume, Mr. Stone, that this matter would be subject to a written contract confirming all these figures and terms,'' she said, speaking in a precise English society accent that was marred only by a slight tendency toward being shrill.

Harry's brow furrowed into a pained look. "Of course,'' he told her. "Everything would be legal and aboveboard. They wouldn't do it any other way. They've got a valuable reputation to protect.''

Nigel sniffed pointedly, but made no comment. Harry smiled to himself and marveled at the mental gymnastics that enabled somebody in Nigel's position to be capable of a gesture implying moral disapproval. Although the bargaining had been tough in places, his instinct made him confident the deal would go through. The Philimans had politely but firmly argued him down from his opening proposal of seventy-five/twenty-five, which he hadn't expected them to accept for a moment, and declined his original suggestion of a one-year-deferred commission, which would have given the U.S. side of the organization the exclusive benefit of a substantial sum accrued as interest. But the negotiations had all been very gentlemanly and a refreshing change from the kind Harry was used to. Furthermore, everybody would be able to have dinner in a civilized manner afterward with all business matters forgotten.

Harry admired and envied the ability of these people to keep different parts of their lives in the proper compartments, and the tradition that enabled them to smile apologetically while they twisted the knife in deeper for the last ounce of flesh. This was the way of life he meant to become part of before much longer, and he recognized in the present situation not only the prospect of some lucrative business but also an opportunity for some social investment that could pay handsome dividends later. Anybody who was just smart could make money, but to really fly high in the circles that mattered, you needed something extra that people like this had. Harry Stone knew that he had it, too, and he was going to prove it.

Nigel kept his face expressionless as he turned toward Clive with an almost imperceptible raising of his eyebrows. Harry could feel a warm surge of jubilation inside as he read the signals, but kept his own face just as straight. Clive's jaw stiffened a fraction, his eyebrows dropped, and he moved his head in a slight sideways motion.

"Sixty-forty," Nigel said, looking back at Stone.

It was what Harry had been expecting, but he frowned intently at the floor in front of him and went through the motions of wrestling with figures in his head. "It's scraping the bone," he said dubiously when he finally looked up. "But since we're talking pretty big dollars, I'd be prepared to try them for another three points. I'm sure we'd be wasting our time if I pushed for anything past that."

"Not enough," Nigel said flatly. "Make it another two. We'll meet you at fifty-five."

That gave Harry forty-five, which clinched the deal because his bottom limit had been forty-three. Nevertheless, he played through some more mental agonies and then asked guardedly, "Would we have a deal if I managed to get them to go for that? No more strings. You'll okay a contract if they beam it through later today?"

Nigel looked over at his partners, and one by one they returned faint nods. "Very well, Mr. Stone," he agreed. "You have a deal. Provided that the terms are as discussed and that our lawyer finds nothing amiss with the details, you may consider the matter settled."

Harry waited for a couple of seconds and then nodded. "I'll see what I can do," he said. "I'll probably be able to call you later this afternoon. Will you be at home?"

"Until about six," Nigel told him. He looked around him to invite any final comments, but there were none. "Very well, we'll consider the subject closed until I hear further from you." The Englishman set his empty glass down and braced his arms along the side of his chair. "There was another matter that you wished to finalize today, I believe," he said.

Stone nodded and reached inside the jacket pocket of his suit for an envelope containing a bank check for forty thousand pounds. He had purchased it two days before in Las Vegas with unlaundered cash bought at a substantial discount, and arranged for it to be wired on to London for collection on his way to the Philimans' apartment that morning. "One hundred thousand dollars, less twenty percent for handling as agreed," he said as he leaned forward to hand the envelope to Nigel. "It gives me a much better break than the standard rate. We're throwing it in as a goodwill gesture."

"*We?*" Nigel looked mildly surprised. "I thought you said this was a private matter."

"A figure of speech," Harry told him with a grin. "Okay, *I'm* throwing it in as a goodwill gesture. I think you'll find everything in order."

Nigel opened the envelope and took out the check, examined it briefly, and nodded. "Excuse me for a moment, please," he said, and with that got up and left the room.

Clive stood up from the sofa and brought his arms up level with his shoulders to stretch gratefully, his action echoing the more relaxed atmosphere that had descended to mark the end of the day's primary business. "It's a beautiful day for seeing some of London if you're not intending to return straightaway," he remarked, glancing across at the window. "The weather must be the best we've had so far this year."

"I am staying over tonight, but I've got other things to

do," Harry said. "I'll have to schedule that in for some other time."

"Perhaps you would care to join us for lunch," Delia suggested. "A new French restaurant has opened in the plaza downstairs. I'm told the cuisine is excellent."

Harry turned his hand palm upward and smiled regretfully. "I'd love to, but I only got in from Vegas this morning and it's a full day. I promise I'll allow for it next time."

"You must live a very busy life," Barbara murmured, leaning forward on the sofa and looking at him with a hint of intrigue that he felt she was not in the habit of displaying toward everyone. He was flattered, and he wondered for a moment if the look in her eyes might be an oblique invitation to get in touch sometime when his schedule was less crowded.

"Always busy, but never too busy," he said, winking in a way he knew could be read as not completely playful, and pretending not to notice Clive's stiffening posture out of the corner of his eye. "You know how it is with Americans— work hard, but play hard, too, huh? Who needs ulcers?"

"I presume you travel Arabee," Clive said in a voice cooler than before. Though speaking to Harry, he glanced down at Barbara pointedly. "There were some things I was hoping to discuss, but I don't think this would be a good time. Could we fix something for a day next week, perhaps?"

Harry realized he had been getting carried away. "Yes," he replied, dropping his smile and producing a pocket vipad from his jacket as he turned to look up at Clive. He activated the unit and studied the information that appeared on its miniature screen. "Sure, I've got some free slots next week. When do you want to make it?"

"Before Thursday," Delia said, looking at Clive. "Don't forget we're due for a long weekend with Maurice and Brigitte in Cannes."

Clive took his own unit from his shirt pocket, compared his schedule with Harry's, and eventually they settled for a Tuesday morning meeting to be followed by lunch. They had just finished dictating the details into the two vipads when Nigel returned with a flat leather briefcase. He set it down on the side table next to Harry, then opened it to reveal bundles of used one-hundred-pound notes.

"Fifty thousand," Nigel announced, at the same time

handing Harry a white envelope he had been carrying. "Here is the promissory note and some ID that you will have no trouble with."

Harry checked the contents of the envelope and then leaned over the table to spend the next minute or two counting the cash. His canceled bank check plus a copy of the promissory note from Zephyr Enterprises to repay the "loan" would satisfy the British authorities that forty thousand pounds had been invested in the company from legitimate sources. Thus through the two transactions that he had made in two days, Harry had converted fifty thousand dollars he had borrowed on a short-term basis into the equivalent of one hundred thousand dollars in illicitly obtained cash. That left him with the problem of translating the profit into personal assets that couldn't be questioned, but he would take advantage of his visit to London as an opportunity to solve that.

At last he pronounced himself satisfied, closed the briefcase, and exchanged final farewells as he stood up to leave. Nigel and Clive began talking about some office space that was available in Piccadilly, leaving Delia and Barbara to escort Harry to the door. Just as she was about to close the door behind him, Barbara said in a low voice, "It might be fun to find out what you're really like, Harry."

"I'm planning on moving over permanently not long from now," he murmured. "Maybe when I do, I'll give you a call at the office. I still need somebody to show me this city."

"Do that," she whispered, smiling a promise, then eased the door shut. Harry tightened his grip on the briefcase and began whistling jubilantly through his teeth as he turned and walked in the direction of the elevators.

The first thing he did after he came out of the main entrance to the apartments was call the States and arrange for a contract to be beamed through to Nigel Philiman in accordance with the terms agreed. The terms were immediately accepted as Harry knew they would be, but not wanting to give the impression that things had been too easy, he postponed calling Nigel back until later. After that he had a snack lunch consisting of an unchilled beer and a ham sandwich in a pub at the top end of Sloane Street, and then took an autocab eastward toward the center of the city.

He found the premises of Melvin & Cooper, Dealers in Rare Stamps, Coins, and Curios, in a side street off Charing Cross Road. It was one of those quaint old London establishments that had barred windows guarding its displays, and solid brasswork its portal, and gave off the impression of having stood there since the street was first laid down way back in whatever century and of boasting the same venerable and dignified staff that had unlocked the doors on its opening day. Inside, Harry spent almost another hour discussing and examining postage stamps, eventually selecting a modest collection dating back twenty years. The complete purchase came to just short of fifty thousand pounds, and Harry paid in cash. The dealer dutifully recorded the details of the transaction and the date along with the name and address of the buyer, the latter of which he took from the document that Nigel Philiman had provided.

From there he took a cab to Marble Arch, where he locked the briefcase containing the collection in a bank deposit box rented for twenty-four hours under his assumed name, after which he called Nigel as promised and advised him that, after a lot of haggling and effort, he had persuaded his associates in the States to go with the figures that Nigel had asked for. That issue having been resolved satisfactorily, he spent thirty minutes in a corner house unwinding and congratulating himself over a cigarette and coffee. It had been a good day's work, and the time was three-thirty, just right for him to get to Bayswater by four to meet Sandra. Now business was really over, and for the rest of the evening, not to mention the night, he would be able to abandon himself totally and with unashamed selfishness.

As he drained the last of his coffee he paused to check back over the day's events for any last detail he might have forgotten. Then, finding nothing, he stubbed his cigarette, smiled to himself in satisfaction, rose from the table, paid the bill, and left.

Feeling ecstatically content, Harry Stone lay back against the silky softness of the pillows admiring the rear view of Sandra's perfect body as she stooped provocatively in front of the vanity to straighten her hair in the mirror. "Wow!" he murmured approvingly.

Sandra smiled over her shoulder in the mirror. "Feeling better?"

"Fantastic! If this is only the beginning, hey, are we gonna have some good times. I never went much for that crap about people being made for each other, but you know something—it's true."

"You, a romantic? I'd never have believed it." Sandra smirked wickedly. "I'm starting to get hungry, Alex. How about eating dinner early? Then maybe we could go on to a club for a couple of hours and still have plenty of night left. I have to be away early in the morning."

"Oh, how come?"

"I promised I'd go to an art show with a couple of the girls from the health club I told you about."

"The place with all the loaded man-hungry widows and debutantes on the prowl for rich husbands?"

"Uh-huh."

Harry shrugged. "Sounds good to me . . . especially the last part. We could go to that place in the park again by the bridge."

"Great." Sandra moved over to the door and slipped on a robe she took off a peg on the back. "I need to shower," she said. "Don't run away, Alex." She left the room, leaving the door open behind her, and disappeared into the bathroom in the hallway. The sounds of cabinet doors being opened and closed and bottles being set down trickled back into the bedroom. Harry stretched out an arm to pick up his cigarettes and lighter from the bedside table, lit one, tossed the pack and lighter down again, and settled back to relax.

There was nothing especially remarkable about bumping into a fellow American overseas, but to have decided for no particular reason to have lunch in the same restaurant as this American three months before had been a rare and unexpected stroke of good fortune, even for somebody like Harry, who made it his business to be lucky. Sandra had come to England three years ago as the wife of a vice-president of a Texas-based construction company who had moved over temporarily to set up a British division of the firm. Her husband had become infatuated with an English girl and taken her back to the States with him at the end of his stay after offering Sandra a generous settlement in return for an easy divorce. Since then she had continued living a life of ease and leisure in London, cultivating the circle of social acquaint- ances that her husband's position had brought her into contact with, but always managing to be free when "Alex" was due to stay in town.

But what he liked most was that she was the same kind of person as he—a born winner. She knew what she wanted and played hard for it, and acknowledged the fact realistically without hiding behind apologies or pretense. Without doubt she was his kind of woman. They both understood the rules of the game and would play it together for as long as they both had something to gain; if that ever changed, then that would be it, with no dues, debts, or recriminations either way. So nothing was guaranteed, but his prospects were looking pretty good, and all the signs indicated that when Harry finally moved over to London as planned, he'd have everything set up and waiting for him. Success, in all its aspects, had never smelled sweeter.

The sounds of shower water were replaced by the low hum of the hot-air dryer system. "When are you going back home to Surrey, Alex?" Sandra called through the doorway.

"Not until later tomorrow," he replied, making his tone not very enthusiastic. "I'll let myself out if you have to get away. I've got to see a couple of guys from a broker's in the city, but not until around lunchtime."

"Which ones are those—the Australian nickel or the Brazilian coffee beans?"

"Something different. We tied up both those deals this morning," he told her.

"So how many millions was that worth?"

"Oh, you know how it is," he drawled carelessly. "A couple here and a couple there. I figure the commission on it should take care of the dinner check tonight."

"So what is it? Tell me."

"Ocean-ridge mining. A new treaty's been drafted by the U.N. that's pretty well bound to go through. It's the right time to be taking out options."

A short pause ensued. Then Sandra remarked in a more

sober tone, "You didn't sound too happy about going home tomorrow. Is she being a bitch again?"

Harry scowled and blew a stream of smoke across the bed. "Yes, but I don't want to talk about it. Why spoil a nice evening? Anyhow, it's not as if it was going to be for much longer."

The hum of the dryer stopped, and Sandra reappeared through the doorway, her robe on again. For the first time that afternoon her expression was serious and her manner tense. "You are still sure you want to go through with it?" she said. "You haven't changed your mind?"

Harry hesitated for just a second, then nodded once decisively. "I don't change my mind," he told her, stubbing the butt of his cigarette in the ashtray by the bed and looking up. "Did you get the . . . *things*?"

"Do you really want to talk about that now?" she asked. "Why not leave it until we get back?"

He shook his head. "Let's get it over with and out of the way now. Then we'll be able to enjoy dinner without it hanging around in the background. . . ." He grinned crookedly. "Not to mention afterward."

Sandra nodded and, keeping her face cool and expressionless, walked over to the wall closet. She slid open the door and reached up to the shelf inside for a padded brown mailer. She drew out a small white package, replaced the mailer on the shelf, and came over and sat down on the edge of the bed. Harry watched as she opened the white package to reveal a preformed plastic container—flat and about two inches square—of the kind used for holding one-shot medical infusers. She flipped the lid open with her thumbnail and uncovered slender metal tubes lying side by side in three of the container's slots, the remaining two slots being empty. Each tube was a little longer and slightly thicker than a match, and was tipped by a glass bead at one end. Two of them had a tiny dot of red paint on the outside about halfway along; the third was plain. Sandra selected the plain one and lifted it from the container. She handled it delicately but surely, her movements telegraphing a cool determination that Harry found momentarily chilling.

"Anyone would think you're unwrapping candy or something," he murmured. "Doesn't this bother you at all?"

"Objective thinking," she said, glancing up at him from under her long, curling eyelashes. "It doesn't have to be like this, Alex. You could always walk out and get a divorce. I thought *you* wanted it this way."

Harry inhaled deeply and was surprised to feel his breath coming shakily. "And get screwed out of every penny I'm worth to keep her in Scotch and hippie boyfriends who don't have the brains to earn their own suppers?" The sound of the bitterness in his own voice steeled his resolve; he nodded curtly. "Yes, I do want it this way. Come on, explain it again and show me how this thing works."

Sandra held up the tiny tube she had taken from the plastic container. "This is a standard medical infuser for injecting drugs as an atomized jet straight through the skin," she said. Harry nodded. Though he was not on any course of medication that required their use, he knew about them, since such devices were not uncommon. Sandra indicated the container in her other hand. "Those other two, with the dots on, are not filled with anything prescribed by any doctor. They're a special kind you can get if you know the right people, and they contain a volatile nerve toxin that's lethal within seconds of becoming active. You'd use one of them like this." She put the container with the two "special" infusers in it down on the bedside table and pulled a cigarette out of the pack lying beside it. Then she snapped the glass bead off the end of the tube she was still holding and touched it lightly against the side of the cigarette just below the end. Nothing happened for about a second, and then the tube began emitting a faint hissing sound. As soon as the hiss started, Sandra drew the tube smoothly and slowly along the length of the cigarette, timing her movement such that it just reached the filter as the sound died. "It takes four or five seconds," she told him. "Make sure you get rid of the glass tip. A few people are doing long stretches because they got careless over that."

Harry took the cigarette from her fingers and examined it curiously. There was nothing on its surface to indicate anything abnormal. Actually he did know about "squirts," as the lethal brand of infusers were called in the underworld, which was where they were usually procured. In fact he could have obtained some himself from Max or Tony or a couple of his other less salubrious acquaintances in Vegas; but there had been no point in risking leaving a trail that might lead back to him there, where he was known, especially not after Sandra had suggested such a solution independently and offered to obtain the stuff for him. But too much familiarity with such matters would not have gone with the image of Alexander Moorfield, commodity broker and investment banker from Maryland, currently living in Surrey, England. So he pretended to be fascinated and just a little nervous.

"That's all you have to do," Sandra said, watching his face. "Then there'll be no alimony to worry about, and you'll be able to afford some nice flowers out of the life insurance."

"Wouldn't I taste anything funny when I smoked it?" he asked, looking up at her with a mild frown that was fitting to his role.

Sandra shook her head. "The poison enters the bloodstream through the lungs and doesn't become active until about half a day," she said. "Then, when it reaches a certain center in the brain, it works almost immediately. It's quite painless. You get hit by a sudden feeling of tiredness that lasts maybe a couple of seconds, and then it's all over. The molecules break down into residues that are indistinguishable from waste toxins produced naturally in the body, so there's no way that anything could show up in an autopsy."

"What about the butt?" Harry asked. "Wouldn't a lab be able to find traces in that?"

"That's possible, but you'd have to be really unlucky," Sandra replied. "Just remember to clean out all the ashtrays before anybody has a chance to think about getting suspicious."

He met her eyes for a second. They were calm and unwavering, and seemed to be challenging him to prove he was everything he said he was by not backing down at the last minute. He drew a long breath to give the impression of a respectable citizen bracing himself to take an irrevocable plunge and found that the nervousness he tried to feign was coming naturally. "Okay," he said from somewhere down in the back of his throat. "It looks simple enough."

Sandra closed the plastic container and returned it to the white package, then took it across the room to the closet and slipped it into a jacket pocket of his suit. When she came back to the bedside table, she picked up the glass bead, the empty infuser, and the cigarette that she had treated, and carried them through to the kitchen where she dropped the lot into the garbage incinerator.

"Where the hell did you get those?" Harry asked as she came back into the bedroom.

"You don't really expect me to answer that," she said reproachfully. Her manner was becoming more teasing now that they had the worst of that particular subject out of the way. "Let's just say I've got friends, and they're not all pillars of virtuous society."

"Did you have to go to bed with someone?" he asked. His voice was matter-of-fact, but his eyes were studying hers curiously as he spoke.

"If I did, would it bother you?"

"Aw, come on . . ." Harry spread his hands appealingly. "We're both grown-up people. If that's what you have to do, it's what you have to do."

Sandra hesitated for a split second, then said, "Yes, I did."

With her chin raised a fraction, she was looking at him defiantly. Harry had the feeling that her answer was meant to test his reaction. "Hey, stop glaring at me as if that's supposed to cut any ice," he told her. "I've been around too much for that." He lay back against the pillows and grinned. "Anyhow, what's new? I already knew you were a bitch. That's why we're right for each other. Boy, are we gonna go places together when all this is over!"

"So when will that be?" Sandra asked, moving a step nearer. "Have you worked something out yet?"

Harry nodded. "I've got a business meeting scheduled at one of the banks in town for Tuesday morning," he said. "I'll take care of it sometime just before I leave. That'll give her all day with me out of the way, and I could see you here in the afternoon to celebrate."

"And after that, are you still planning on selling up the house in Surrey and moving into town?" He detected a trace of disappointment in her voice. "It sounds such a nice place."

"Hell, I wouldn't want you in there," Harry said, pulling a face. "I could use a break in town for a while. After that—aw, there are plenty of nice places."

Sandra nodded in resignation. "How long do you think it'll take?"

"Who knows?" Harry spread his palms. "But there's no reason why I couldn't move out right away—the end of next week, maybe. So if you owe any outstanding payments on those little babies, you'd better get 'em cleared up pretty quick."

Sandra brought her hands up to her hips and stared down at him accusingly. "You really are a bastard," she told him. "You don't give a damn how I got them, do you?"

Harry clasped his hands behind his head and grinned up at her. "You said I shouldn't ask about that, and I believe you. Anyhow, now tell me you don't like bastards."

"Mmm . . . maybe there are one or two around that I could find time for," she said, breaking into a smile.

Sandra had been gone for a few hours by the time Harry emerged from the apartment late the next morning, the white package zipped securely in an inside pocket of his jacket. He went to Marble Arch and retrieved the briefcase from the deposit box, added the package to its contents, and then took the briefcase to a store in Edgware Road that handled a variety of lines including packaging materials. For a small fee one of the assistants boxed and wrapped the briefcase in a manner suitable for mailing, and Harry then took the parcel to the Marble Arch post office, where he consigned it to himself under a box number in Las Vegas. After that he walked half a block along Oxford Street and into the central London branch of Remote-Activated Biovehicles (U.K.), Limited.

The girl at the reception desk greeted him with a warm smile of recognition. "Good morning," she said. "Was your trip enjoyable?"

"Very enjoyable, thanks," Harry told her. "I need another reservation for Tuesday. Any problems?"

"The same model?" the girl inquired, activating the computer terminal beside her.

"Oh, yes. It's very important."

The girl scanned quickly down the table of information that appeared on the screen and began tapping a string of commands into the touchpad with deft motions of her fingers. "No problem," she announced brightly. "The reservation is made, and you can pick up the confirmation in Las Vegas."

She looked up from the screen. "Are there any problems to report?"

"Maybe a few minor scratches and blemishes," Harry said with a wry grin. "Nothing that some rest and a high-protein transfusion won't cure by tomorrow. You might get some complaints about a few aches and pains if you let it out again today, though."

The girl smiled knowingly. "We'll take care of that, Mr. Stone. I'll put it down for a full checkup, regeneration, and recuperation." She entered some more instructions into the terminal. "Will you require the same accessories on Tuesday or will there be any changes?" she inquired.

Harry thought for a second. "Maybe a thinner suit now that the weather's warming up. How about a light blue with a fine silver pinstripe? I'll leave the matching of the necktie, cuff links, and tie clip to you."

"Jewelry, wallet, cigarette lighter, pocket vipad, and cash?" she asked.

"Fine as they are. Make the cash five hundred pounds, one hundred of it in tens."

"Is there any cash to be credited to the account?"

"It's not worth the messing around. I'll lock it up and pick it up again on Tuesday."

"As you wish." The girl completed her operations at the terminal and smiled over at him again. "If you'd like to go on through, cubicle number six is free. We'll see you again on Tuesday, Mr. Stone."

"Take care."

Harry walked through a door at the back of the reception foyer and into a corridor flanked by a dozen or so doors on either side, all bearing numbers. He entered the one numbered "6" and found himself in a small, cheerfully decorated and warm room that contained little apart from a comfortable leather-upholstered recliner and a small table upon which was an open metal strongbox. He emptied the contents of his wallet onto the table, added the personal items from his pockets, and then placed them all in the box, after which he closed the lid and scrambled the combination lock. Just as he was finishing, a knock sounded on the door and an attendant in a light brown tunic entered.

"Good morning, sir," he said cheerfully. "Lovely day for traveling. Is everything ready?"

Harry pushed the strongbox across the table toward him. "Hi, we're all set. This is for the vault."

"Anything to be forwarded on?"

"No, that's it."

"Very good, sir." The attendant produced a vipad from a pocket of his tunic and activated it to display the format of a standard R.A.B. (U.K.) Ltd. deposit-box receipt already filled in with details that the girl had entered at the reception desk outside. He added the identification number of the strongbox in the space provided and passed the vipad to Harry, who verified the transaction by tapping in a memorized personal code. The attendant took back the vipad, picked up the box, and left the room. Harry made one last check of his pockets and person, then sat down in the recliner and allowed his body to sink back into its soft, enveloping contours.

"Everything is ready, Mr. Stone," a pleasant voice said after a few seconds from a concealed speaker above the door. "Are you ready to leave?"

"All set," Harry murmured absently.

"Thank you. Have a good day."

The helmet that had been covering his head all the way around and down to the level of his chin slid smoothly away and retracted to its storage position above and behind him. He opened his eyes and lay waiting in the darkness. After a few seconds the lighting came on and increased to a low level revealing details of another small cubicle, this one including the usual wall of panels and electronics that he had never understood. He blinked a couple of times, then sat up slowly and sat for a moment on the edge of the couch to give his lungs and circulation time to adjust back to a normal level of activity. Then he stood up carefully, did his best to smooth two days worth of creases from the open-necked shirt and casual slacks that he was wearing, and moved toward the door. He felt cold and a little bit stiff, but that was nothing abnormal.

The first thing he did in the corridor outside was visit the men's room, always first on the list of priorities after coming back. He emerged five minutes later and walked out the door at the end of the corridor that led through to the desk.

The young man at the desk had been expecting him. "Hello, Mr. Stone," he said. "How was London?"

"Just fine. It's been cold there, but it's getting warmer. Do you have my charge made up?"

"Right here." The clerk pivoted a flatscreen display around to face Harry, who ran a cursory eye down the details of the account, then verified the charge with his personal code. "And you have another reservation in London for next Tuesday morning." The clerk handed across a white plastic document holder. Harry checked the details, grunted, closed the document holder, and slipped it into the back pocket of his slacks. Then he bade the clerk good day, walked out of the front entrance of the Las Vegas branch office of R.A.B. Inc., and went to have an early-morning breakfast at the all-night restaurant a short walk up the street.

All Harry really knew was that you walked into a cubicle in Las Vegas or somewhere, they put a thing on your head, and a few seconds later you were walking out of another cubicle in London or wherever, inside another body that was yours for the duration of the trip.

Somebody had explained to him once that the bodies rented out at the far end were not legally classified as people because they were grown under the control of synthetically manufactured DNA, designed to produce a physical human form complete with all the lower brain functions that took care of subconscious monitoring and regulating of respiration, circulation, and the like, but with no cerebral cortex or any of the higher faculties the law decreed to be essential ingredients of personality. The unused part of the skull contained instead a microelectronics package that collected the information coming in through the nervous system and transmitted it to the nearest R.A.B. office, from where it was relayed across the world by satellite and somehow injected into your brain by the thing they put on your head in a way that shut out the input from your own body. Also, the signals from your brain to control voluntary movements and so forth were short-circuited off from your own body and transmitted back in the reverse direction. So you could see, hear, feel, and move around by remote-controlling a body that was five thousand miles away while your own self stayed in Las Vegas. Harry wasn't sure of the details, but traveling now took no time at all, and it sure beat the hell out of being jammed into tin cans for hours on end and having to fight to airports and back again. It was expensive, especially if you went for the deluxe models that came with best quality clothing and accessories, but the business community found it a much better investment than physically shipping executives around the world on short visits and having to handle all the accompanying problems.

Remote-Activated Biovehicles, or R.A.B., had the lion's share of the world market and was referred to popularly as "RentABody," or more frequently, "Arabee." Breakdowns in the system were rare but did happen occasionally, in which case an Arabee walking around somewhere would usually tense up suddenly and keel over. The company had an efficient system for dispatching recovery teams swiftly to deal with such emergencies, and the public had come to accept an Arabee crash as just another part of living that they might have the privilege of witnessing and being amused by one day. In fact there had been a few unfortunate instances in the early days when a case of genuine illness had received less than prompt attention because somebody had misinterpreted the situation. Since then the company had installed warning systems that activated automatically in the event of a malfunction to enable anyone who happened to be nearby to recognize the true nature of the event. All in all the system worked well and proved popular, and problems were few.

Harry never relished the prospect of having to return to the particular brand of domestic bliss that came from being married to Lisa, so he had announced that he wouldn't be back from New York until late that night, intending to spend the day in town. However, his mind had enjoyed little rest, even if his body had been immobile, and he realized over breakfast that he was sleepy. Thus he changed his plans and steeled himself to the dismal thought of confronting his wife early in the morning. So, dismissing fond memories of London from his mind for the time being, he took an elevator up to the roof and boarded a cab to fly the ten miles to his home on the north side of the city.

As the cab descended toward the house minutes later, Harry looked down and saw Max's purple-and-pink flymobile parked in front of the garage. There were no lights showing in any of the windows of the house. Harry groaned to himself and decided he was in no mood for a fight. He told the driver to take the cab back up and head for the Holiday Inn a couple of miles back toward town.

"For Christ's sake, I've got important business scheduled for today," Harry fumed across the breakfast table in the kitchen. "I need a clear head. I can do without this kind of stupidity every time I have to take a trip someplace. Why don't you give growing up a try sometime?"

Lisa stared back at him sourly over her coffee. The skin below her eyes was showing signs of getting dark and slack, and her hair hadn't been touched since she got up. Women had no right bitching and whining when they let themselves turn into a mess like that, he told himself as he looked at her distastefully.

"What's the matter?" she demanded. "Can't wait to get back to your little pussycat in New York?" His expression darkened further, and she leered. "Oh, don't tell me that isn't what all this is about, Harry. It's Tuesday and you have to go back to New York already when you were there only last Friday. And you have to stay over again? What do you think—my head's full of rocks or something?"

"Take a look in a mirror and try listening to yourself, then tell me you'd be surprised if I was," he retorted. He glowered down at his eggs, decided he wasn't hungry, and tossed his fork down on the plate with a clatter. Indignation boiled up inside, and he threw out an arm to take in the whole of the house. "You get looked after okay. Isn't a guy supposed to expect anything back the other way? What do you want—body, soul, and checking account with no strings? If I fool around, it's because I've got enough reasons."

"All I wanted was a man," she threw back. "But I ended up with a small-time slob who thinks he's another Rockefeller." Her face twisted into a sarcastic smile. "Is your pussycat in New York another little innocent who fell for the same line about Malaysian rubber deals and Zambian copper stocks that I did? Mister Big Wheel again, huh? Bah! Everything about you makes me sick."

"At least that's one honest thing you've said," Harry

grated. "Big money was all you ever did want. So, you've got it. Why is it a rough deal all of a sudden? I don't remember you complaining when you were peeling your clothes off for five hundred a week and probably making it up with extras after hours."

"I like money, sure," she spat. "Who doesn't? I don't like where it comes from or the 'friends' that come with it."

Something in Harry's chest nudged close to boiling point. "What about my friends?" he hissed in a voice that was suddenly icily brittle.

"Is that what you call them? They'd gamble away their own mothers' medical checks."

Harry's grip tightened on his coffee mug. "If that's how you feel, what was Max's flymo doing here at six in the morning?" he shot back. Lisa's eyes blazed furiously, and her mouth tightened into a thin line. He leveled a finger across the table at her. "I came back early on Friday but changed my mind about coming in. So don't you try any more of that crap on me, understand?" His eyes had narrowed, and his voice had taken on the mean note that said he had reached his limit.

Lisa slammed her mug down on the table, got up, and turned away toward the window. "Any attention is better than no attention," she snarled without turning her head. "At least he doesn't make me sound like dirt every day of the goddamn week."

"Why should he? He's making out okay."

"Why don't you just get out of here and on your way," she seethed hatefully.

Harry's knuckles whitened around the mug as he heard himself being ordered out of his own house, but he resisted the impulse to hurl it across the room. All he wanted to do was get out, but there was one more thing to be taken care of first and it needed a clear head. He looked down at the table and saw Lisa's pack lying half open with three cigarettes in it. He knew they would be gone within the hour. He picked the pack up and threw it back down on the table with a loud slapping sound. "Don't we have any of my brand in this goddamn house?" he raged. "Jesus, is that too much to ask as well?"

"There are some in the den," Lisa told him coldly without looking around.

He waited, but she made no attempt to move. "I never know where in hell you hide anything," he said, forcing a note of menace into his voice. He stayed put, and in seconds the tension rocketed to breaking point.

"Oh, for Christ's sake, I'll get 'em," Lisa exploded, and stormed out of the room.

Harry waited a few seconds to make sure that her footsteps were fading away, then reached in his pocket and drew out an unsealed envelope containing an opened pack of Lisa's brand with two missing, and the two that he had treated half an hour earlier, in the way that Sandra had shown him, wrapped separately in a piece of tissue. He unwrapped the treated cigarettes, switched them for two of the three in the pack on the table, put the two he had taken back in the envelope along with the tissue, and returned the envelope to his pocket.

The switch had taken only a few seconds but it had seemed like a slow-motion nightmare; in that short time his heart had started pounding and a sick, heavy feeling had formed in his throat and stomach. He clenched his fists and tried to force himself to calm down. There's nothing to it, he told himself. It's done now. Christ, why wouldn't his hands stop shaking?

He heard the door of the bathroom along the hall outside the kitchen close and lock, and breathed a silent prayer of thanks for the extra minute or two it gave him to pull himself together. He wiped his palms on his thighs, forced himself to take a series of slow, deep breaths, then got up and switched on the wall terminal in TV mode. A blonde with disgustingly perfect teeth was talking about a space colony or something somewhere. It didn't interest him, and he watched without hearing the words until the sound of flushing amplified suddenly by a door being opened jerked his attention away from the screen. Lisa came in and threw a pack down on the table.

"Only two?" Harry grumbled darkly as he fumbled one to his mouth and lit it. "What are we, destitute or something? Don't we have any full ones left?"

"Well, I can't find any," Lisa told him irritably. "Get some more when you go out. I'll put a carton on the grocery order when I send it off."

"Why do you always have to wait until we run out?" Harry snapped. "Didn't it ever occur to you to do something when they're getting low? Why don't you try thinking with your head for a change instead of giving it?"

The side of his jaw was still throbbing twenty minutes later as he looked down from a cab on his way to downtown Vegas. But by that time the air around him tasted fresh and free, and the feeling of everything he had just left being about to become a closed chapter in his life was exhilarating. When he next saw that house his troubles would all be over, and there would be only the formalities to attend to before he could begin the new life in London that was his by right because he had earned it. Sometimes making that decision to go for the jackpot and seeing it through was tough, but for the exclusive elite who had what it took, the reward was the moon. And Harry Stone had now proved that he was one of them. It was a good feeling.

Sandra lay back in the bed with the sheet covering her up to her waist and beads of perspiration still dotting the skin around her navel.

"I've been keeping a little surprise for you," Harry said. "What would you say to a bit extra on top of the insurance—like maybe a hundred grand, less the death taxes?"

"Sounds good," she cooed. "Tell me about it." Harry began sliding his hand down over her body toward the sheet. She caught his wrist and giggled. "I need to get my breath back, Alex. What's the extra?"

"Well, our friends back home in Surrey will be surprised to learn that my wife has been a stamp collector for years," he said. "I knew, naturally, but I was never that interested, and I don't know much about it. So I'll be as surprised as anybody when they tell me that she left some very valuable items among her collection. Maybe she never realized what they were worth either. Who knows?" He shrugged. "I guess we'll never find out."

Sandra emitted a delighted laugh. "Alex, you're too much! So what did you do—plant them somewhere? Were they to soak up some cash you had lying around that you didn't want anyone asking questions about?"

Harry brought a finger up to his face and tapped it

meaningfully against the side of his nose. "Let's just say that even if they do a lab test on the glue, they'll find it's genuine and has been there for years. It's the little details like that that amateurs trip up over."

"But not Alexander Moorfield, huh?" she said, turning her head and gazing at him admiringly.

Harry lay back and folded an elbow under his head. "How long will it take you to understand that I'm a real professional, baby? When I do things I do 'em right, and I go for the big stakes. That's what you have to do to survive in this world."

"And you sure know how to survive." She moved closer and rested her face on his chest.

"I guess so."

Sandra nuzzled against his neck and nibbled playfully at the lobe of his ear. "You really are a bastard, Alex," she teased softly. "And it's just what a bitch like me needs."

He thought to himself for a while and then asked casually, "What would you say if I told you I've been a *real* bastard?"

She moved her face back a short distance to peer at him curiously, but her eyes were still twinkling with laughter. "I wouldn't be a bit surprised," she told him. "Why? What have you been doing?"

Harry hesitated for a moment, wondering if perhaps he had misjudged the moment, but the half smile dancing on her lips was disarming. He sighed and grinned apologetically. "Honey, I guess you have to know this sooner or later—I'm not really me. I'm an Arabee."

Although he kept his voice relaxed and easy, inwardly he was prepared for her to be shocked, insulted, or indignant, to cry, sulk, throw a tantrum, or do any one of a dozen other things that would have made things difficult. But she didn't do any of them. Instead she stared at him in disbelief for a second or two, then smiled, and then threw back her head and laughed. "You *are* a bastard!" she exclaimed. "All this time and you never told me? Christ, I admire the sheer balls of it!"

"You don't mind?" he asked, not really believing that his luck could be holding out like this.

"You're still the same to me," she replied. "In fact it's

quite exciting. Meeting the real you will be like being se-
duced by a new lover all over again. I like the whole idea."

"Suppose I turn out to be fat, bald, and fifty," he said.
"Wouldn't you care about that? You'd better say you would;
otherwise I might start thinking you're only interested in the
bread. I wouldn't want that much of a bitch. I've only just
finished getting rid of that particular brand of problem."

"Of course not," she said. "So now go ahead and tell
me it's just as well, because it was only a line anyway."

"No," Harry tossed out a hand carelessly. "It was
straight, but I'm getting out of that business. I've got some
personal enterprises that I want to develop."

"I knew it," Sandra said, sounding happier. "And I
don't believe you are fat, bald, and fifty. It wouldn't go with
your personality." She sat up and turned toward him with an
intrigued look on her face. "What are you like?"

"Oh, a year or two older than this, maybe, but just as
handsome. I've got a little bit of gray at the temples, too.
Does that sound okay?"

"Very distinguished," Sandra pronounced. She traced
her fingers lightly across his chest. "And what about all these
beautiful muscles? Are you as good as that, too?"

"Better," he told her. "I used to do a lot of athletics.
And I've got a much deeper tan than this." It was all too
good to be true, and as the last shreds of apprehension flowed
away, he found himself starting to laugh uncontrollably. His
laughter triggered Sandra's, and soon they were both writhing
helplessly with tears pouring down their cheeks.

"What about those dimples on the sides of your face?"
she asked between sobs.

"I've got one on my chin, and it's just as cute." They
burst into another paroxysm of weeping. "And don't worry
about the rest," he managed between heaves of his chest
which was beginning to ache. "It's best American stud."

After a while Harry began to calm down, but Sandra was
still clutching her stomach and laughing, if anything, more
loudly than ever—almost insanely. He watched and grew
puzzled, and as her laughter continued with no signs of
abating, his puzzlement changed to concern. "Hey, Sandy,
it's not *that* funny," he said. "Cool it, for heaven's sake.
You'll get hysterical if you carry on like that."

Sandra wiped her face with the sheet and shook her head as she fought for breath. "It's okay, Alex. I'm not getting hysterical," she gasped. "It's just that you don't—you don't understand how funny this really is."

She wasn't making any sense. Harry frowned and shook his head. "What the hell are you talking about?"

"Alex—you see, it's—" She erupted into another spasm of sobbing laughter and bunched part of the sheet to her mouth in a futile attempt to stifle it. Harry's amusement turned to irritation as he began getting the feeling that he was being made a fool of somehow, and his mouth clamped tighter as he waited. "You see, Alex, it's funny because—because—" But she never finished the sentence. Her mouth froze half open, her eyes widened in sudden alarm, and she slumped weakly back against the pillows.

"Sandy, what is it?" Harry forgot his anger at once. "What's the matter? Are you sick?"

"I . . . don't know, Alex." Her voice was a dreamy whisper. "Sleepy . . . just hit me . . . Can't keep . . . my eyes . . . op—"

"Sandy? Sandy, say something!" Harry's voice was close to panic. But Sandra made no further sound. She lay with her eyes glazed and her mouth gaping as it had stopped in mid-syllable, with every trace of life and movement gone from her body. Harry stared at her, horrified, and instinctively drew away and stood up. After a few seconds, a monotonous synthetic voice began speaking from somewhere in the region of her head.

"Please do not be alarmed. This is a malfunction of a remotely animated, nonhuman surrogate owned by Remote-Activated Biovehicles (U.K.), Limited. We regret any inconvenience. A recovery team is already on its way to you. If you need further assistance, please call 01-376-8877. Thank you . . . Please do not be alarmed. This is a malfunction of . . ."

But Harry didn't hear any more. He backed away in wide-eyed horror, unable to tear his eyes from the lifeless figure draped across the bed. It wasn't the knowledge of what she was that was terrifying him; it was the *way* it had happened, and *when*.

Surely to God it was impossible. He gnawed at his knuckle and forced himself to calm down and think. There had to be some way of being sure. Then as his shoulder touched the closet door, he remembered the padded mailer.

He turned toward the closet, opened the door, and reached up to feel along the shelf. The mailer was still there. He took it down and read the address on the front: Sandra Parnell, 2754 Cunningham Court, Bayswater, London W.2., U.K. His hands started trembling when he saw that it had been stamped and mailed in the U.S.A. He turned the mailer over and read on the back:

Sender: Mrs. Lisa Stone
          Box 3683
          Las Vegas
          Nevada 89109

A strangled moan escaped his lips as the mailer dropped to the floor. But his anguish was not due to remorse over Lisa or the realization that Sandra didn't exist. It was due to pure terror.

For all of a sudden he knew why Sandra was always away, but always managed to be free when he himself was away from home, and he knew why she had needed to leave early on Friday, what Max's flymobile had been doing outside the house, and where the infusers had come from. But what was worse, he knew now why Lisa had stopped off in the bathroom on her way back from getting his cigarettes from the den, and why there were only two left when he *knew* there had been some full packs around the night before.

"You bitch!" he breathed as it all became clear in its gruesomeness. And then a senseless rage welled up at his own predicament and helplessness, and he hurled himself across the room and began pounding furiously at the unfeeling face and body. *"Bitch! Bitch! Bi—!"* he screamed. But the words died in a gurgle in his throat as a wave of tiredness and heaviness swept suddenly over him. His body collapsed in a limp heap on top of the other. After a few seconds, another voice began speaking to fill the room with a macabre canon of out-of-phase intonations.

"*. . . We regret any inconvenience. A recovery team is already on its way. . . . Please do not be alarmed. This is a malfunction of a remotely . . .*"

*   *   *

Two lamps were flashing to accompany the emergency tone sounding from a monitor panel in the control room of the Las Vegas branch of Remote-Activated Biovehicles, Inc. "Hey, Al," the operator called over his shoulder to the day manager, who was coming out of his office to investigate. "I've never even seen one crash all the time I've been here. We've got two at the same time, and in adjacent cubicles. What odds do you think the guys in town would give against the chances of something like that?"

Sometimes ideas come from talking to people. The following is more a thought than a story, but it illustrates what sometimes happens. It resulted from a conversation over breakfast one morning with a computer wizard called Charles Curley, during a convention in Sacramento at which I was guest of honor.

It also cost me twenty dollars. I didn't know how thick a postcard was for the example that I use in the opening sentence, and nobody I called on the phone could tell me. So I went into the hardware store next door to my office and bought a micrometer to measure one (it's 0.013 inch to save anyone who's insatiably curious twenty dollars). Perhaps this also says something about how science-fiction writers think. Ideas come from asking questions, and to ask questions you have to be curious.

FORTUNE COOKIE

One year is to 4.5 billion years as a cent is to 45 million dollars, or as the thickness of a postcard is to the distance between New York and the Mississippi.

That long ago, the earth formed as one of several accumulations of matter falling together in a spinning pancake of dust and gas that had condensed from the exploding debris of an earlier generation of stars. As the final meteorite bombardment died away and the planetary smelter processed and separated its rocky slags into mantle and crust, rain fell from the hot outgassings to become the first oceans.

There, in shallows and pools invigorated by young radionuclides and a raw, unshielded sun, a new chemistry began of molecules too elaborate to have come together in the rarified depths of space, and impossible in the plasma maelstroms of stars. Colliding, fragmenting, and recombining at quantum-mechanical speeds, billions of different combinations came and went during every second of hundreds of millions of years. Some of them proved stable and remained intact, and were able to grow into progressively more elaborate structures by further additions from the molecular constructor-kit soup. Eventually a few, or possibly only one, hit upon a configuration that would act as a template for parts to come together in the right way to form a copy of itself. Self-replication had appeared.

In their resource-rich primeval surroundings, the replicating molecules proliferated at an exponential rate and soon extinguished the feeble competition put up by their crude predecessors. The copies were not always accurate—mutations occurred, each yielding its own line of offspring, and the competition came to be between different designs of replicators, all experimenting with different survival strategies. A potent strategy came with the invention of chemical warfare, which some varieties used to physically dismantle their rivals—it reduced the competition and increased available resources at the same time. In reply to this, the replicators that survived learned to build themselves protective molecular coatings. Defense stimulated new methods of attack, which resulted in improved defenses. . . .

In the billions of years that followed, the primitive molecular coats evolved into huge, elaborate survival machines which the replicators continue to control by remote programming from secure command bunkers deep inside. When a particular survival-machine begins wearing out and slowing down, the replicators—virtually immortal experts at survival—copy themselves through into a new one. On their way down through the ages, acting through their progressively improving sequence of robot proxies, they have continued to invent new technologies that have opened up new realms of survival-enhancing resources. Early on, the blue-green algae freed themselves from dependency on food produced through slow, abiotic processes, by patenting the chlorophyl molecule and photosynthesis, which opened up the entire ocean surface as a resource. Even greater ingenuity turned the ensuing planetwide catastrophe—its inundation with the toxic, corrosive waste, oxygen—into an opportunity by evolving metabolisms which not only tolerated it, but thrived on it and harnessed it as fuel for better engines. Double-stranded instruction tapes enabled error-correction for accurate copying of the vast amounts of information necessary to build multicellular organisms; the sexual mixing of instructions from the growing information pool produced new combinations much faster than coincidences of mutations ever could; and the invention of the spacesuit in the form of the amphibian egg led to the colonization and exploitation by animals of a completely new, initially hostile, alien environment.

The progression led on through warm-blooded metabolisms, mammalian reproduction, and upright posture to binocular vision, opposable thumbs, and bigger brains. Eventually the species that represented the culmination of the process became self-aware, and learned to make tools and build artificial, inorganic survival-facilitating environments around the organic survival machines. That same self-awareness caused him to wonder where he had come from and why. He used his intelligence to construct enormous instruments, with which he scanned the remote reaches of the cosmos in search of a sign from his creator.

Eventually he found his creator in the opposite direction—at the other end of a proton microscope. And at last he decoded the sign he had been seeking, which had been written into the creation: HELP! I'M A PRISONER IN A DNA FACTORY!

MORE ON REPLICATION

I mentioned earlier in *Minds, Machines and Evolution* that contemporary science is satisfied that such phenomena as the emergence of life and conscious mind can be adequately explained by the laws of physics and the principle of evolution, without needing any additional guiding powers. Given variability and selection, the rest follows mechanically. Thinking about this got me intrigued by the thought of a story involving a world inhabited by a naturally evolving biosphere made up of machines. The problem was, I couldn't think of a way to get it started. We can see how abiotic molecules could assemble themselves into structures that eventually came to exhibit self-replication and life, but with machines it's not so simple. As Taya insisted in *Silver Shoes for a Princess,* something had to *make* the first machine.

Then in 1982, Rodger Cliff, an AI scientist with NASA, invited me to take part in a one-week seminar at the Goddard Space Center which NASA was arranging to examine the role of computers in future space missions. The group included people from NASA, from the academic world, and from industry. One of the possibilities we talked about was an idea for a self-replicating lunar factory—an initial package of robots and machines to be landed on the Moon, which would grow exponentially and transform the entire lunar surface into an automated mass-production facility dedicated to supplying Earth's needs for products and materials. The implications were staggering. From an initial one-hundred-ton "seed" system, the annual output after ten years of unrestricted, self-reproducing growth would be a million tons, and by twenty years it would exceed the entire yearly output of today's human civilization!

I'm a rather slow thinker, which is perhaps why I chose to be a writer and not a talker. The connection didn't occur to me until I was on the plane back to California. Of course! Here, possibly, was the means I'd been looking for to get a machine biosphere started. Suppose, for example, that long ago an alien civilization sent out seeds like that on an interstellar scale, and one of them had mutated and gone out of control for some reason.

This must have been genuine inspiration, because I began typing *Code of the Lifemaker* the very next day. Since then, a number of readers have written or told me that the prologue alone was worth the price of the book.

So, hoping among other things that it might sell a few more copies, I thought I'd include it here.

CODE OF THE LIFEMAKER: PROLOGUE

THE SEARCHER

1.1 Million Years B.C.; 1,000 Light-Years from the Solar System

Had English-speaking humans existed, they would probably have translated the spacecraft's designation as "searcher." Unmanned, it was almost a mile long, streamlined for descent through planetary atmospheres, and it operated fully under the control of computers. The alien civilization was an advanced one, and the computers were very sophisticated.

The planet at which the searcher arrived after a voyage of many years was the fourth in the system of a star named after the king of a mythical race of alien gods, and could appropriately be called Zeus IV. It wasn't much to look at—an airless, lifeless ball of eroded rock formations, a lot of boulders and debris from ancient meteorite impacts, and vast areas of volcanic ash and dust—but the searcher's orbital probes and surface landers found a crust rich in titanium, chromium, cobalt, copper, manganese, uranium, and many other valuable elements concentrated by thermal-fluidic processes operating early in the planet's history. Such a natural abundance of metals could support large-scale production without extensive dependence on bulk nuclear transmutation processes—in other words, very economically—and that was precisely the kind of thing that the searcher had been designed to search for. After completing their analysis of the preliminary data, the control computers selected a landing site, composed and transmitted a message home to report their findings and announce their intentions, and then activated the vessel's descent routine.

Shortly after the landing, a menagerie of surveyor robots, equipped with imagers, spectrometers, analyzers, chemical sensors, rock samplers, radiation monitors, and various manipulator appendages, emerged from the ship and dispersed across the surrounding terrain to investigate surface features selected from orbit. Their findings were transmitted back to the ship and processed, and shortly afterward follow-up teams of tracked, legged, and wheeled mining, drilling and transportation robots went out to begin feeding ores and other materials back to where more machines had begun to build a fusion-powered pilot extraction plant. A parts-making facility was constructed next, followed by a parts-assembly facility, and step by step the pilot plant grew itself into a fully equipped, general-purpose factory, complete with its own control computers. The master programs from the ship's computers were copied into the factory's computers, which thereupon became self-sufficient and assumed control of surface operations. The factory then began making more robots.

Sometimes, of course, things failed to work exactly as intended, but the alien engineers had created their own counterpart of Murphy and allowed for his law in their plans. Maintenance robots took care of breakdowns and routine wear and tear in the factory; troubleshooting programs tracked down causes of production rejects and adjusted the machines for drifting tolerances; breakdown teams brought in malfunctioning machines for repair; and specialized scavenging robots roamed the surface in search of wrecks, write-offs, discarded components, and any other likely sources of parts suitable for recycling.

Time passed, the factory hummed, and the robot population grew in number and variety. When the population had attained a critical size, a mixed workforce detached itself from the main center of activity and migrated a few miles away to build a second factory, a replica of the first, using materials supplied initially from Factory One. When Factory

Two became self-sustaining, Factory One, its primary task accomplished, switched to mass-production mode, producing goods and materials for eventual shipment to the alien home planet.

While Factory Two was repeating the process by commencing work on Factory Three, the labor detail from Factory One picked up its tools and moved on to begin Factory Four. By the time Factory Four was up and running, Factories Five through Eight were already taking shape, Factory Two was in mass-production mode, and Factory Three was building the first of a fleet of cargo vessels to carry home the products being stockpiled. This self-replicating pattern would spread rapidly to transform the entire surface of Zeus IV into a totally automated manufacturing complex dedicated to supplying the distant alien civilization from local resources.

From within the searcher's control computers, the Supervisor program gazed out at the scene through its data input channels and saw that its work was good. After a thorough overhaul and systems checkout, the searcher ship reembarked its primary workforce and launched itself into space to seek more worlds on which to repeat the cycle.

Fifty Years Later

Not far—as galactic distances go—from Zeus was another star, a hot, bluish white star with a mass of over fifteen times that of the Sun. It had formed rapidly, and its life span—the temporary halt of its collapse under self-gravitation by thermonuclear radiation pressure—had demanded such a prodigious output of energy as to be a brief one. In only ten million years the star, which had converted all the hydrogen in its outer shell to helium, resumed its collapse until the core temperature was high enough to burn the helium into carbon, and then, when the helium was exhausted, repeated the process to begin burning carbon. The ignition of carbon raised the core temperature higher still, which induced a higher rate of carbon burning, which in turn heated the core even more, and a thermonuclear runaway set in, which in terms of stellar timescales was instantaneous. In mere days the star erupted into a supernova—radiating with a billion times the brightness of the Sun, exploding outward until its photosphere enclosed a radius greater than that of Uranus's orbit, and devouring its tiny flock of planets in the process.

Those planets had been next on the searcher's list to investigate, and it happened that the ship was heading into its final approach when the star exploded. The radiation blast hit it head-on at three billion miles out.

The searcher's hull survived more-or-less intact, but secondary x-rays and high-energy subnuclear particles—things distinctly unhealthy for computers—flooded its interior. With most of its primary sensors burned out, its navigation system disrupted, and many of its programs obliterated or altered, the searcher veered away and disappeared back into the depths of interstellar space.

One of the faint specks lying in the direction now ahead of the ship was a yellow-white dwarf star, a thousand light-years away. It too possessed a family of planets, and on the third of those planets the descendants of a species of semi-intelligent ape had tamed fire and were beginning to experiment with tools chipped laboriously from thin flakes of stone.

Supernovas are comparatively rare events, occurring with a frequency of perhaps two or three per year in the average galaxy. But as with most generalizations, this has occasional exceptions. The supernova that almost enveloped the searcher turned out to be the first of a small chain that rippled through a localized cluster of massive stars formed at roughly the same time. Located in the middle of the cluster was a normal, longer-lived star which happened to be the home star of the aliens. The aliens had never gotten round to extending their civilization much beyond the limits of their own planetary system, which was unfortunate because that was the end of them.

Everybody has a bad day sometimes.

One Million Years B.C.

One hundred thousand years after being scorched by the supernova, the searcher drifted into the outer regions of a planetary system. With its high-altitude surveillance instruments only partly functioning and its probes unable to deploy at all, the ship went directly into its descent routine over the first sizable body that it encountered, a frozen ball of ice-encrusted rock about three thousand miles in diameter, with seas of liquid methane and an atmosphere of nitrogen, hydrogen, and methane vapor. The world came nowhere near meeting the criteria for worthwhile exploitation, but that was of no consequence since the computer programs responsible for surface analysis and evaluation weren't working.

The programs to initiate surface activity did work, however, more or less, and Factory One, with all of its essential functions up and running to at least some degree, was duly built on a rocky shelf above an ice beach flanking an inlet of a shallow methane sea. The ship's master programs were copied across into the newly installed factory computers, which identified the commencement of work on Factory Two as their first assignment. Accordingly, Factory One's Supervisor program signaled the ship's databank for a copy of the "How to Make a Factory" file, which included a set of subfiles on "How to Make the Machines Needed to Make a Factory," i.e., robots. And that was where everything really started to go wrong.

The robots contained small internal processors that could be reprogramed via radiolink from the factory computers for each new task to be accomplished. This allowed the robots to proceed with their various jobs under autonomous local control and freed up the central computers for other work while they were waiting for the next "Done that—what do I do now?" signal. Hence many software mechanisms existed for initiating data transfers between the factory computers and the remote processors inside the robots.

When the copying of the "How to Make a Factory" file from the ship to Factory One was attempted, the wrong software linkages were activated; instead of finding their way into the factory's central system, the subfiles containing the manufacturing information for the various robots were merely relayed through the factory and beamed out into the local memories of the respective robot types to which they pertained. No copies at all were retained in the factory databank. And even worse, the originals inside the ship managed to self-destruct in the process and were irretrievably erased. The only copies of the "How to Make a Fred-type Robot" subfile were the ones contained inside the Fred-types out on the surface. And the same was true for all the other types as well.

So when the factory's Supervisor program ordered the Scheduler program to schedule more robots for manufacture, and the Scheduler lodged a request with the Databank Manager for the relevant subfiles, the Databank Manager found that it couldn't deliver. Neither could it obtain a copy from the ship. The Databank Manager reported the problem to the Scheduler; the Scheduler complained to the Supervisor; the Supervisor blamed the Communications Manager; the Communications Manager demanded an explanation from the Message Handler; and after a lot of mutual electronic recriminations and accusations, the system logging and diagnostic programs determined that the missing subfiles had last been tracked streaming out through the transmission buffers on their way to the robots outside. Under a stern directive from the Supervisor, the Communications Manager selected a Fred from the first category of robots called for on the Scheduler's list, and beamed it a message telling it to send its subfile back again.

But the Fred didn't have a complete copy of the subfile; its local memory simply hadn't been big enough to hold all of it. And for the same reason, none of the other Freds could return a full copy either. They had been sprayed in succession with the datastream like buckets being filled from a fire-hose, and all had ended up with different portions of the subfile; but they appeared to have preserved the whole subfile among them. So the Supervisor had to retrieve different pieces from different Freds and try to fit them together again in a way that made sense. And that was how it arrived at the version it eventually handed to the Scheduler for manufacture.

Unfortunately, the instruction to store the information for future reference got lost somewhere, and for each batch of Freds the relevant "How to Make" subfile was promptly erased as soon as the Manufacturing Manager had finished with it. Hence when Factory One had spent some time producing parts for Factory Two and needed to expand its robot workforce to begin surveying sites for Factory Three, the Supervisor had to go through the whole rigmarole again. And the same process was necessary whenever a new run was scheduled to provide replacements for robots that had broken down or were wearing out.

All of this took up excessive amounts of processor time, loaded up the communications channels, and was generally inefficient in the ways that cost accountants worry about. The alien programmers had been suitably indoctrinated by the alien cost accountants who ran the business—as always—and had written the Supervisor as a flexible, self-modifying learning program that would detect such inefficiencies, grow unhappy about them, and seek ways to improve things. After a few trials, the Supervisor found that some of the Freds contained about half their respective subfiles, which meant that a complete copy could be obtained by interrogating just two individuals instead of many. Accordingly it made a note of such "matching pairs" and began selecting them as its source for repeat requests from the Scheduler, ignoring the others.

Lost along with the original "How to Make a Fred" subfiles were the subsubfiles on "Programs to Write into a Fred to Start It Up After You've Made It." To make up for the deficiency, the Supervisor copied through to the Scheduler the full set of programs that it found already existing in the Freds selected to provide reproduction information, and these programs, of course, included the ones on how to make Freds. Thus the robots began coming off the line with one half of their "genetic" information automatically built in, and a cycle asserted itself whereby they in turn became the source of information to be recombined later for producing more Freds. The method worked, and the Supervisor never figured out that it could have saved itself a lot of trouble by storing the blueprints away once and for all in the factory databank.

The program segments being recombined in this way frequently failed to copy faithfully, and the "genomes" formed from them were seldom identical, some having portions of code omitted while others had portions duplicated. Consequently, the Freds started taking on strange shapes and behaving in strange ways.

Some didn't exhibit any behavior at all but simply fell over or failed during test, to be broken down into parts again and recycled. A lot were like that.

Some, from the earlier phase, were genetically incomplete— "sterile"—and never called upon by the Supervisor to furnish reproductive data. They lasted until they broke down or wore out, and then became extinct.

Some reproduced passively, i.e., by transmitting their half-subfiles to the factory when the Scheduler asked for them.

A few, however, had inherited from the ship's software the program modules whose function was to lodge requests with the Scheduler to schedule more models of their own kind—program modules, moreover, which embodied a self-modifying priority structure capable of raising the urgency of their requests within the system until they were serviced. The robots in this category sought to reproduce actively: they behaved as if they experienced a compulsion to ensure that their half-subfiles were always included in the Scheduler's schedule of "Things to Make Next."

So when Factory One switched over to mass-production mode, the robots competing for slots in its product list soon grabbed all of the available memory space and caused the factory to become dedicated to churning out nothing else. When Factory Two went into operation under control of programs copied from Factory One, the same thing happened there. And the same cycle would be propagated to Factory Three, construction of which had by that time begun.

More factories appeared in a pattern spreading inland from the rocky coastal shelf. The instability inherent in the original parent software continued to manifest itself in the copies of copies of copies passed on to later generations, and the new factories, along with their mixed populations of robot progeny, diverged further in form and function.

Material resources were scarce almost everywhere, which resulted in the emergence of competitive pressures that the alien system designers had never intended. The factory-robot communities that happened to include a balanced mix of surveyor, procurement, and scavenger robots with "appetites" appropriate to their factories' needs, and which enjoyed favorable sites on the surface, usually managed to survive if not flourish. Factory Ten, for example, occupied the center of an ancient meteorite crater twelve miles across, where the heat and shock of the impact had exposed metal-bearing bedrock from below the ice; Factory Thirteen established itself inside a deep fissure where the ice beneath was relatively thin, and was able to melt a shaft down to the denser core material; and Factory Fifteen resorted to nuclear transmutation processes to build heavier nuclei from lighter ones frozen in solution in the ice crust. But many were like Factory Nineteen, which began to take shape on an ill-chosen spot far out on a bleak ice field, and ground to a halt when its deep-drilling robots and transmutation reactors failed to function, and its supply of vital materials ran out.

The scavenger and parts-salvaging robots assumed a crucial role in shaping the strange metabolism that was coming into being. Regardless of what the Schedulers in the various factories would have liked to see made, the only things that could be assembled readily were the ones for which parts were available, and that depended to a large degree on the ability of the scavengers to locate them, or alternatively to locate assemblies suitable for breaking down—"digesting" —and rebuilding into something useful. Factory Twenty-four was an extreme case. Unable to "metabolize" parts directly from any source of raw materials because of the complete failure of its materials-procurement workforce, it relied totally on its scavengers. Factory Thirty-two, on the other hand, could acquire raw materials but couldn't use them since it had been built without a processing facility at all. Its robots delivered instead to Forty-seven, which happened to produce parts for some of the scavengers being manufactured by Thirty-two, and the two factory-robot organisms managed to coexist happily in their bizarre form of symbiosis.

The piles of assorted junk, which shouldn't have accumulated from the earlier phases of the process but had, were eaten up; the machines that broke down were eaten up; and the carcasses of defunct factories were eaten up. When those sources of materials had been exhausted, some of the machines began to eat each other.

The scavengers had been designed, as they had to be, to discriminate between properly functioning machines and desirable products on the one hand, and rejects in need of recycling on the other. However, as with everything else in the whole, messed-up project, this function worked well in some cases, not so well in others, and often not at all. Some of the models turned out to be as likely to attempt the dismantling of a live, walking-around Fred as of a dead, flat-on-its back one. Many of the victims were indifferent to this kind of treatment and soon died out, but others succeeded in developing effective fight-or-flee responses to preserve themselves, thus marking the beginnings of specialized prey and predators in the form of "lithovores" and "artifactovores."

This development was not always an advantage, especially when the loss of discrimination was total. Factory Fifty was consumed by its own offspring, who began dismantling it at its output end as soon as they came off the assembly line, and then proceeded proudly to deliver the pieces back to its input end. Its internal repair robots were unable to undo the undoings fast enough, and it ground to a halt to become plunder for marauders from Thirty-six and Fifty-three. The most successful factory-robot organisms protected themselves by evolving aggressive armies of "antibody" defenders, which would recognize their own factory and its "kind" and leave them alone, but attack and attempt to destroy any "foreign" models that ventured too close. This gradually became the dominant form of organism, usually associated with a distinct territory which its members cooperated in protecting collectively.

By this time only a few holes in the ground remained at opposite ends of the rocky shelf to mark where Factories One and Two had once stood. They had failed to keep up with the times, and the area had become the domain of Factory Sixty-five. The only trace left of the searcher spacecraft was a long, rounded depression in the ice beach below, on the shore of the liquid methane sea.

The alien engineers had designed the system to enjoy full planetary communications coverage by means of satellites and surface relays, but the idea hadn't worked too well since nothing had been put into orbit and surface relays tended not to last very long. This enabled some of the organisms without strong defenses to remain protected, for a while, from the more metal-hungry empires by sheer distance. But, to allow for communications blackouts and interference, the aliens had also provided a backup method of program and data exchange between robots and factories, which took the form of direct, physical, electrical interconnection. This was a much slower process than using radiolinks, naturally, since it required that the robots travel physically to the factories for reprograming and reporting, but in a self-sustaining operation far from home the method was a lot better than nothing. And it kept the accountants happy by protecting the return on the investment.

With defects and deficiencies of every description appearing somewhere or other, it was inevitable that some of the organisms would exhibit partial or total communications breakdowns. Factory Seventy-three, built without radio facilities, was started up by programs carried overland from Sixty-six. None of its robots ever used anything but backup mode, and the factories that it spawned continued the tradition. But this very fact meant that their operating ranges were extended dramatically.

So the "defect" turned out to be not so much of a defect after all. Foraging parties were able to roam farther afield, greatly enlarging their catchment areas, and they frequently picked up as prizes one or more of the territories previously protected by geographical remoteness. Furthermore, selective pressures steadily improved the autonomy of the robots that operated in this fashion. The autodirected types, relying on their comparatively small, local processors, tended to apply simple solutions to the problems they encountered, but their close-coupled mode of interaction with their environment meant that the solutions were applied quickly: they evolved efficient "reflexes." The teledirected types, by contrast, tied to the larger but remote central computers, were inclined to attempt more comprehensive and sophisticated solutions, but—as often as not—too late to do any good. Autodirection thus conferred a behavioral superiority and gradually asserted itself as the norm, while teledirection declined and survived only in a few isolated areas.

The periodic instinct to communicate genetic half-sub-files back to their factories had long become a universal trait among the robots—there could be descendants only of ancestors who left descendants—and they responded to the decline of radio as a means of communication by evolving a compulsion to journey at intervals back to the places whence they had come, to return, as it were, to their "spawning grounds." But this method of reproduction had its problems and posed new challenges to the evolutionary process.

The main problem was that an individual could deliver only half its genome to the factory, after which the Supervisor would have to store the information away until another robot of the same type as the first happened to show up with a matching half; only then could the Supervisor pass a complete copy to its Scheduler. If, as frequently happened, the Supervisor found itself saturated by a peak workload during the intervening period, it was quite likely to delete the half-subfile and allocate the memory space to other, more urgent things—bad news for the Fred that the data had come from, who would thus have enacted the whole reproductive ritual for nothing. The successful response to this problem came with the appearance of a new mode of genetic recombination, which, quite coincidentally, also provided the solution to an "information crisis" that had begun to restrict the pool of genetic variation available for competitive selection to draw on for further improvement.

Some mutant forms of robot knew they were supposed to output their half-subfiles somewhere, but weren't all that sure, or perhaps weren't too particular, about what they were supposed to output it into. Anything with the right electrical connections and compatible internal software was good enough, which usually meant other robots of the same basic type. And since a robot that had completed its assigned tasks was in a receptive state to external reprograming, i.e., ready for fresh input that would normally come from the factory system, an aspiring donor had little trouble in finding a cooperative acceptor, provided the approach was made at the right time. So to begin with, the roles adopted were largely a matter of circumstance and accidental temperament.

Although the robots' local memories were becoming larger than those contained in their earlier ancestors, the operating programs were growing in size and complexity, too, with the result that an acceptor still didn't possess enough free space to hold an entire "How to Make a Fred" subfile. The donor's half, therefore, could be accommodated only by overwriting some of the code already residing in the acceptor. How this was accomplished depended on the responses of the programs carried inside the various robot types.

In some cases the incoming code from the donor was allowed to overwrite entire program modules inside the acceptor, with the total loss to the acceptor of the functions which those modules controlled. This was usually fatal, and no descendants came into being to repeat such mistakes. The successful alternative was to create space by trimming nonessential code from many modules, which tended to leave the acceptor robot with some degradation in performance—usually manifesting itself as a reduction in agility, dexterity, and defensive abilities—but at least still functioning. The sacrifice was only temporary since the acceptor robot would be reprogramed with replacement modules when it delivered its genetic package at the factory.

But in return for these complications and superficial penalties came the immense benefit that the subfiles presented at the factories were complete ones—suitable for dispatch to the Schedulers without delay and the attendant risk of being deleted by overworked Supervisors. The new method thus solved the reliability problem that had plagued the formerly universal "asexual" mode of reproduction.

The information crisis that it also solved had developed through the "inbreeding" caused by the various Supervisors having only the gene pools of their respective "tribes" available to work with, which made recombination difficult because of the restrictive rules imposed by the alien programers. But the robots swapping genes out on the surface were not always averse to adventuring beyond the tribal limits, knew nothing and cared less about programers' rules, since nothing approaching intelligence or awareness was operative yet in what was unfolding, and proceeded to bring half-subfiles together haphazardly in ways that the aliens' rules didn't permit and which the Supervisors would never have imagined. Most of the offspring resulting from these experiments didn't work and were scrapped before leaving the factories; but the ones that did radiated functionally outward in all directions to launch a whole new, qualitatively distinct phase of the evolutionary process.

The demands of the two sexual roles reinforced minor initial physical differences and brought about a gradual polarization of behavioral traits. Since a female in a "pregnant" condition suffered the loss of some measure of self-sufficiency for the duration, her chances of delivering (literally!) were improved considerably if her mate happened to be of a disposition to stay around for a while and provide for the two of them generally, thus helping to protect their joint genetic investment. Selection tended, therefore, to favor the genes of this kind of male, and by the same token those of the females who mated preferentially with them. As a consequence a female trait emerged of being "choosy" in this respect, and in response the males evolved various repertoires of rituals, displays, and demonstrations to improve their eligibility.

The population had thus come to exhibit genetic variability and recombination, competition, selection, and adaptation— all the essentials for continuing evolution. The form of life— for it was, wasn't it?—was admittedly somewhat strange by terrestrial standards, with the individuals that it comprised sharing common, external reproductive, digestive, and immune systems instead of separate, internal ones . . . and of course there were no chains of complicated carbon chemistry figuring anywhere in the scheme of things. . . . But then, after all, what is there apart from chauvinism to say it shouldn't have been so?

THE REVEALED
WORD OF GOD

In connection with a creationist lawsuit that I read about awhile ago in California, the creationists' lawyer was quoted as saying to a reporter, "They'd better be able to prove that evolution is right." Thus, if evolution cannot be proved beyond question to be fact, the lawyer was saying, then it's just as much a theory as creationism, and if one deserves to be called scientific, so does the other. Now, I certainly wouldn't dispute the right of anyone to believe what they choose and to express those beliefs freely. But when attempts are made to pass those beliefs off as *science*, when they're nothing of the kind, and to force them on the educational system as such, that's another thing entirely.

The fallacy with the above claim is its assumption that all degrees of uncertainty are equal—by the same logic we could argue that since George Washington can't be proved absolutely and conclusively to have existed, then the case for Santa Claus is just as solid. But more interesting is the cause this gives to reflect a little on the differences between science and other belief systems. For everything that I read of the public debate surrounding the case succeeded only in missing the point of the issue entirely, which has nothing to do with whether evolution or creationism—or neither, for that matter—is right or wrong. The issue is understanding what it is that makes a belief genuinely "scientific."

Science never claims anything to be finally and absolutely proved. So in that sense every scientific belief is "just a theory." A demand for evolution to be proved beyond question to be fact is an absurdity that fails to comprehend what science is all about. Although we speak loosely of a theory being "proved by experiment," philosophically this is impossible. The best that an experiment can hope to do for a theory is *fail to falsify* it. An experiment does this when *all* of the results agree with the theory, and *not one* observed, incontestable fact contradicts it. Even this doesn't prove a theory true—the agreement could still be a coincidence due to other, perhaps totally unsuspected causes. All that can be said is that the theory wasn't shown to be wrong.

The difference sounds like hairsplitting, but it's crucial. It means that in science your theoretical boat must be watertight everywhere—one hole is enough to sink it. For example, experimental results and astronomical observations accumulated before the late nineteenth-century all accorded with Newtonian mechanics. Later measurements, however, such as of the speed of light in different directions and of the precession of Mercury's orbit, contradicted its predictions and were sufficient to invalidate it as a general model. Since then, of course, relativity has accommodated the new facts while continuing to explain the old; but this no more proves relativity to be "true" than Newton's unification of terrestrial and cosmic motion proved the earlier ideas true. As was the case with the Newtonian system for almost three centuries, relativity has so far survived all attempts to find a flaw. It skates on the same pond.

One of the most important criteria that science demands for a theory to be acceptable as a serious candidate for consideration is that it be falsifiable. It was precisely the fact that it *could* be tested and shown to be false that made Newton's a genuinely scientific theory. Whether it ultimately survived or failed the tests is not the point. This is why the contention that "some UFOs might be alien spacecraft" is not answerable by scientific inquiry. Yes, some of them might be, and however many specific instances are shown not to be, the speculation can never be shown to be untrue. It is unfalsifiable. (The inverse theory—that *no* UFOs are alien spacecraft—can very simply be proved untrue, but not by any of the claims submitted to date as evidence.) And creationism is unfalsifiable, since every fact, every new discovery that might be made, any result of any test that might be imagined—can all be dismissed with the assertion that "it was created that way." Hence, even before any debating or appeals to evidence, creationism fails the most basic test. It is not "scientific," and no amount of legal semantic juggling can make it so.

Science has never made any claim to infallibility. What makes a belief scientific isn't whether it turns out to be true or not, but the *process* by which it is arrived at. It seems ironic that those who preach knowledge of absolute truths tend to be the first to accuse scientists of being arrogant.

How does creationism measure up against other criteria by which a belief is judged as being scientific? Well, in the first place science seeks to be objective, which means having no preconceived notions about how things ought to be—no advance commitment to any holy book, sacred doctrine, or political, social, or economic ideology that has to be upheld as a first priority. Science is an open system based on skeptical appeal to evidence, and uses inductive logic to formulate general principles from specific observations. A pseudoscience—of which creationism is an example—is a closed system based on uncritical appeal to doctrine, and uses deductive logic to infer specific accounts of how the world must be to conform with its inviolate principles. The goal of science is to discover what the reality out there *is*. To this end its conclusions are always open to revision—or might even be abandoned completely—in the face of new evidence: the belief structure follows the facts. But a pseudoscience contrives to uphold a belief structure that exists before any evidence is considered, and to maintain itself subsequently, it must deny or distort any facts that it finds inconvenient. Darwin did not set out to prove evolution because it reflected any ideas he might have had about how societies should function, or because he found it emotionally appealing. He ended up proposing it because it best explained the facts available to him. Like an explorer, which it is, science charts new territory as it finds it, and while at times it might base its choice of direction on hunches, it draws its maps from the reality that it encounters. It accepts that whatever is true will remain so, with complete disregard for the intensity of human convictions or the number of people who can be persuaded to share them. Is this creationism?

When science has amassed its facts, it attempts to construct a theory to explain them. A successful theory must be consistent with all the facts, contradicted by none, and survive experiments aimed at proving it false. It sometimes happens that two or more rival theories meet all of these requirements, which poses the problem of having to choose between them. The guideline in a situation like this is "Occam's razor," which says, in effect, go for the simplest explanation— the one that accounts adequately for all the facts and requires the fewest assumptions. It won't guarantee that we'll never have to change our minds later, William of Occam warns . . . but it's the way to bet.

This means that explanations based on familiar, well-understood principles are to be preferred over far-out fancies— true, a poltergeist might have upset the cookie jar, but the presence of a three-year-old in the household suggests a more promising line of inquiry. Ideas which are compatible with existing, well-supported bodies of knowledge and experience take precedence over ones that aren't. Thus, when a disciple of the maharishi shows a photograph of somebody allegedly levitating, the onus is on him to prove that the picture is genuine (easily done by staging a repeat performance before witnesses), not on us to accept it. Extraordinary claims require extraordinary proof. Hence the skepticism of most scientists toward, for example, claims of ESP abilities—there is nothing in the realm of undisputed, demonstrable fact that can't be accounted for more simply by such familiar mechanisms as carelessness, self-deception, or deliberate fraud, which we know happen. Introducing "paranormal" phenomena to explain any of it is neither necessary nor justified. A new, more elaborate theory is called for *only* when facts have been shown, incontestably, to be true, which cannot be reconciled with the simpler, already existing model. Relativity was accepted because it explained observations that Newton's system couldn't; quantum mechanics arose from the failure of measured results to support earlier models of thermal radiation.

Evolution does indeed offer a consistent and comprehensive interpretation of facts accumulated from a whole range of disciplines that include paleontology, geology, zoology, botany, embryology, biochemistry, comparative anatomy, anthropology, and behavioral psychology, to name just some. It establishes a common framework within which observations collected from many fields of investigation and tested independently all fit together and have reason for being the way they are—as geneticist Theodosius Dobzhansky put it, "Nothing in biology makes sense except in the light of evolution." The facts are explained. But is the evolutionary explanation the simplest? Although the assertion may appear strange to some at first sight, yes, it is—it's the simplest that can be offered for the facts available at the present time. Simplicity here has nothing to do with the shelves of books devoted to the theory of the years of study necessary to comprehend it. It has to do with assumptions—how much has to be taken on faith. The less that is assumed, the simpler the theory. And evolution requires very little: merely the laws of physics and probability—introduced, moreover, not on an ad hoc basis to prop the theory up, but as derived independently within the entire body of scientific knowledge.

What can be said in this respect of creationism? First, it offers no reasons why—why the anatomy of different species should show any relatedness at all; why the fossil record should show its progressive accumulation of change; why embryos of different species should be more alike at earlier phases of growth, why isolated populations should diverge. . . . The inevitable rejoinder that "it was made that way" merely aquiesces to the fact; it explains nothing. We could say the same about anything and add not one scrap to our understanding of it. But on the other hand, creationist theory requires the assumption that a creator exists, that a supernatural judge of morals exists who is concerned about the day-to-day affairs of people on this planet, that both these beings are one and the same, that it communicated its motives to chosen writers of ancient books, that those writers were correct, and honest, in interpreting the source of their inspiration, that later translators were equally infallible . . . and a long list of similar premises that no physicist would entertain for a moment as a basis for constructing a theory. The property insurance would be pretty expensive to cover an edifice built on foundations like that.

A scientific theory explains most and assumes least. Creationism explains nothing and assumes everything.

Lastly, the value of a scientific theory is judged by its power to predict—not in the sense of "psychic" predictions headlined by supermarket tabloids, but in the sense of predicting further experimental results. One failed prediction is enough to torpedo a theory. Success with every prediction, on the other hand, means only that it has survived everything thrown at it so far. So, if evolution is valid, the newer discoveries made since its inception ought to be consistent with it. Apart from some haggling among specialists over relatively minor details, this has turned out to be overwhelmingly the case. Darwin and others predicted the essential properties of inherited genetic units, even though genes and chromosomes were unknown at that time. From evolutionary theory, DNAs from different species should exhibit a branching pattern that reflects the same time sequence of divergence as is deduced by other methods; they do. The primitive metabolic chemistry of ancestral organisms should be discernible in today's organic cells; it is. There shouldn't be much difference in the genetic code inherited by all organisms; there isn't. And so it goes.

And of the predictive power of creationism? Can it predict which band in a series of tree rings should indicate the same age as a given mix of carbon isotopes? Or the tidal record that ought to be found written into fossil corals by the moon's orbital motion of several hundred million years ago? Does it have anything to say about the composition of the early atmosphere and the kinds of minerals that would be formed as a consequence—their chemical nature, where they should be located, and at what depths we should expect to find them today? Can creationism, in fact, give a hint of any future finding? Not a one. It operates with hindsight only. Because of its built-in unfalsifiability it can cobble together an explanation of anything at all—but only after the fact as established by other means. As a method of prediction it is sterile.

In its demand to be recognized as a science, therefore, creationism not only fails all the basic tests, but from the credentials that it presents shows no comprehension of what constitutes a science. It should be taught in schools, certainly, to those who wish to study it—students of religion, of philosophy, of history, of the development of human thought. But there can be no trying to pass it off as a science. The suggestion of "scientific creationism" is a self-contradiction.

If one chooses to think in terms of the revealed word of a God, then surely whatever God has to say is written in the language of life, the world, and the physical universe around us. This is a form of scripture that comes direct from the source, leaving no room for doubts about authenticity, suspicions of forgery, or uncertainties over translation. And the Word that the processes of physics, biology, geology, astronomy, and cosmology are revealing is that the universe and everything in it have been evolving for as far back as it's possible to track time. I think that EVOLUTION IS THE REVEALED WORD OF GOD would make a good bumper sticker.

Such thoughts lead to stories like *Making Light*. . . .

MAKING LIGHT

In his spacious office atop the Headquarters Building of the Celestial Construction Company Inc., the General Operations Director hummed to himself as he sat at his desk and scanned over Contract 15,000,000,000 B.C. The contract document was brief and straightforward and called for the creation of a standard Mark IV universe—plenty of light; the usual suns, planets, and moons; a few firmaments here and there with birds and animals on the land; fish-filled waters around the land. There was an attached schedule for accessories, spares for renewable resources, and some supporting services. Deadline for the contract was seven days—a piece of cake, the GOD told himself. Design Engineering Department's final proposal for the bid lay to one side of the desk in the form of a bulky folder that constituted the Works Order Review Document. Until final approvals were granted, the W.O.R.D. would be all that existed of the universe . . . but it was a beginning.

What promised to make this project a little different from the previous Mark IV's, and somewhat more interesting, was the optional extra that Design Engineering had tagged on in the *Appendix* section of the proposal: *people.*

Unlike the species that made up the usual mix of Mark IV animal forms, which simply consumed resources and multiplied until they achieved a balance with the environment, the people would have the capacity to harness fire, make tools, and generally think about how they could be better off. This would produce an awareness of needs and the motivation to do something about satisfying them. Eventually the people would discover that, as their numbers and their demands increased, they would no longer be able to satisfy their needs with the resources that came readily to hand. At that point, the computer simulations indicated, they could simply give up, they could fight over what they had until it ran out and then be obliged to give up anyway, or they could develop the intellectual potential inherent in their design and apply it to discovering the progression of newer resources hidden around them like the successively more challenging, but at the same time more rewarding, clues of a treasure hunt. The way out of the maze lay in the third alternative.

Wood, growing all over the surface of the planets, would be the most obvious fuel following the taming of fire, but it would not prove adequate for long. It would, however, enable the more easily mined metal ores—conveniently scattered on top of the crusts or not very far below—to be smelted and exploited to make the tools necessary for digging deeper to the coal. Coal would enable an industrial base to be set up for producing machines suitable for drilling and processing oil, which in turn would yield the more highly concentrated fuels essential for aircraft and rudimentary space vehicles. The scientific expertise that would emerge during this phase would be the key to unlocking nuclear energy from crustal uranium, and the fission technologies thus brought into being would pave the way into fusion—initially using the deuterium from the special-formula oceans premixed for the purpose—and hence out to the stars and on to the advanced methods that would render resources effectively infinite for the lifetime of the universe. On planets set up for them in that way and with brains that ought to be capable of figuring the rest out for themselves, the people would have a fair chance of winning the game.

What the purpose of the game was, Design Engineering hadn't said. The GOD suspected that it was more for their own amusement than anything else, but he hadn't objected since he was quite curious himself to find out how the people would handle the situation. A modicum of applied precognition could no doubt have revealed that, but somehow it would have spoiled things.

He was still browsing over the last page of the contract when the phone rang with a peal of rising and falling chimes. It was Gabriel, the Vice President of Manufacturing. He sounded worried. "It's proposal number fifteen billion B.C.," he said. "I think we might have problems."

The GOD frowned. "I was just going through it. Looks fine to me. What's the problem?"

"Somebody from Equal Employment Opportunities Creation has been onto the Legal Department. They're objecting to DE's proposal for the people on the grounds that it would discriminate unfairly against the animals. I think we ought to get the department heads together to talk about it. How are you fixed?"

"Pretty clear for the next few millennia. When did you want to do it?"

"How about right now, while the large conference and congregation room's free?"

"Sure. Get the others over and I'll see you there in, say, ten minutes."

"Leave it to me."

The GOD replaced the phone, slipped the contract document inside the WORD folder, tucked the folder under his arm as he stood up from the desk, and began walking toward the door. Outside in the corridor he paused to pat the pockets of his suit and found he was out of holy smokes, so he made a slight detour to get a pack from the machine by the ascension and descension elevators.

"The EEOC says that we can't endow one species with that kind of intelligence," the Head of the Legal Department explained across the gilt-edged conference table a quarter of an hour later. "Doing so would confer such a devastating advantage that the animals would be guaranteed permanent second-class status with no opportunity to compete, which would constitute an infringement of rights."

"And we've been looking into some of the other implications," another of the lawyers added. "The people would eventually assume a uniquely dominant role. That could set us up for an antitrust suit."

All heads turned toward the Chief Design Engineer. "Well, we can't take the intelligence away from the people," he objected. "The physiques that we've specified don't give them any other means of survival. They'd have no chance. Then we'd still be in trouble with EEOC but with everything the other way around." He threw his hands out impatiently. "And besides, it would defeat the purpose of the whole exercise. It was the addition of intelligence that was going to make this project more interesting.

"Why not make *all* the species equally intelligent?" somebody suggested.

The CDE shook his head. "We planned the ecology so that the animals would do most of the work for the people in the early phases and provide a lot of their food. If we made them equally intelligent, the situation would qualify as slavery and exploitation. We'd never get it past the Justice Department."

"And on top of that they'd all become eligible for education, sickness benefits, and retirement pensions," the CDE's assistant pointed out. "HEW would never accept the commitment. They couldn't handle the load."

That was true, the GOD admitted as he thought about it. Already the Department of Harps, Eternity-pensions, and Wings had insisted that all guarantees of benefits be deleted from the proposal. And that had been just on account of the projected numbers of people, never mind all the animals. "So why can't we change things so the people don't have to depend on the animals at all?" he asked, at last looking up. "Let's make them strong enough to do all the work themselves, and have them just eat plants."

"Not that easy," the CDE answered, shaking his head dubiously. "They'd have to be at least the size of elephants on an input of vegetable protein. Then food-gathering would become such a problem that they'd never have any time left over for mental development, which puts us back to square one." He thought for a second or two, then added, "Though it might work if we redesigned the food chain somehow."

The GOD looked over at the Head of Research. "What do you say to that?" he asked.

The scientist didn't appear too happy as he pinched his nose and reflected upon the question. "We'd have to figure it out again all the way down to the bacteria," he replied after a while. "You're talking about a complete redesign, not just a few modifications. Setting up a whole new ecology and running it through the simulator is a long job. I don't think we could finish before the closing date on the bid, and that doesn't allow for having to rewrite the proposal from scratch. If we could use the new Infallible Biological Modeler we might have had a chance, but we can't. It's not up and running yet."

"I thought the IBM was supposed to have been installed last week," the GOD said, sounding surprised.

"It was, but the systems angelists haven't handed it over yet," the Research Chief replied. "They're not through exorcizing the bugs."

The GOD frowned down at the table in front of him. "Hell," he muttered irritably.

"Er . . . we don't say that here," Gabriel reminded him politely.

"Oh, of course." The GOD made an apologetic gesture and then cast his eyes around the table. "Does anyone else have any suggestions?" he invited. No one had. He sighed in resignation, then looked at the Chief Design Engineer. "I'm sorry, Chief, but it sounds as if we're stuck. I guess there's no choice but to drop the extras and revert to a standard Mark IV."

"No people?" The CDE sounded disappointed.

"No people," the GOD confirmed. "It was a nice thought, but it's out of the question on the timescale of this contract. Keep working on it with Research, and maybe you'll have it all figured out in time for the next bid, huh?" The CDE nodded glumly. The meeting ended shortly thereafter, and the Vice President of Sales went back to his office to begin drafting a revised *Appendix* section to be delivered to the customer by winged messenger. So the project wasn't going to be so interesting after all, the GOD reflected with a pang of regret as he collected his papers. But at least that meant there was less risk of overrunning on time and incurring penance clauses.

The Chief Design Engineer was on the phone shortly after lunch on the following day. "Have you heard?" he asked. He sounded distressed.

"Heard what?" the GOD answered.

"Feathers, Aviation, and Aquatics have been onto our legal people. They're trying to tell us that our birds and fish aren't safe."

"That's ridiculous! They're the same ones as we've always used. What's wrong with our birds and fish?"

"According to FAA regulations, all flight-control and navigation systems have to be duplicated," the CDE said. "Our birds only have a single nervous system. Also, we're allowing them to fly over water without inflatable life jackets."

The GOD was completely taken aback. "What's gotten into them?" he demanded. "They've never complained about anything like that before."

"They've never really bothered to check the regulations before, but the controversy over the people has attracted their attention to this project," the CDE told him. "Our legal people think they're all at it—all the angelcies are brushing the dust off manuals they've never looked at before and going through them with magnifying glasses. We could be in for some real hassles."

The GOD groaned. "But what do they want us to do? We can't go loading the birds up with all kinds of duplicated junk. Their power-weight ratios are critically balanced. They'd never get off the ground."

"I know that. But all the same it's regulations, and the FAA won't budge. They also say we have to fit bad-weather landing aids."

The GOD's patience snapped abruptly. "They don't fly in bad weather," he yelled. "They just sit in the trees. If they don't fly, why do they need aids for landing? It'd be like putting life jackets on the camels."

"I know, I know, I know. But that's what the book says, and that's all the FAA's interested in."

"Can we do it?" the GOD asked when he had calmed down a little.

"Only with the penguins, the ostriches, and the others that walk. I called the FAA guy a couple of minutes ago and told him that the only way we could equip all the birds for bad-weather landing was by making them all walk. He said that sounded fine."

"I've never heard of anything so stupid! What's the point of having birds at all if they're only allowed to walk? We can't have planets with walking birds all over the place. The competition would die laughing."

"I know all that. I'm just telling you what the guy said."

A few seconds of silence went by. Then the GOD asked, "What's wrong with the fish?"

"The shallow-water species don't have coastal radar."

Pause.

"Is this some kind of joke?"

"I wish it were. They're serious all right."

The GOD shook his head in disbelief and slumped back in his chair. "Maybe we might just have to go along without birds and shallow-water fish this time," he said at last. "Would the rest still work?"

"I'm not so sure it would," the CDE replied. "The birds were supposed to spread seeds around to produce enough vegetation to support the herbivores. If we reduce the quotas of herbivores, we'd have to cut back on the carnivores, too. And without the birds to keep down the insects, we'd have the Forestry Cherubim on our backs for endangering the trees. With the trees in trouble and no shallow-water fish to clean up the garbage from the rivers, the whole ecosystem would break down. None of the animal species would be able to support themselves."

The GOD sighed and wrestled with the problem in his head. The CDE himself had precipitated the current crisis by introducing the idea of people in the first place, but there would be nothing to be gained by starting rounds of recriminations and accusations at this point, he thought. What was important was to get the proposal into an acceptable form before the closing date for the bid. "The only thing I can think of is that if the animals become unable to support themselves, we'll have to put them all on welfare. If I call HEW and see if I can fix it, would that solve the problem?"

"Well . . . yeah, I guess it would . . . if you can fix it." The CDE didn't sound too hopeful.

The GOD phoned the HEW Director a few minutes later and explained the situation. Would HEW accept a commitment to supplying welfare support for the animals?

"No way!" was the emphatic reply.

"What in he— heaven's name do you expect us to do?" the GOD demanded, shouting in exasperation. "How can we meet anybody's regulations when they always conflict with somebody else's?"

"That's not our problem," the HEW Director stated bluntly. "Sorry."

Another meeting was called early the next morning to discuss the quandary. After all avenues had been explored, there seemed only one solution that would avoid all the conflicts: an azoic universe. *All* forms of living organisms would have to be deleted from the proposal. The meeting ended on a note of somber resignation.

The Environmental Protection Angel was on the line later that afternoon. Her voice was shrill and piercing, grating on the GOD's nerves. "Without any plants at all, the levels of carbon dioxide, nitrogen oxides, and sulfur compounds from volcanic activity would exceed the permitted limits. The proposal as it stands is quite unacceptable. We would not be able to issue operating licenses for the volcanoes."

"But the limits were set to safeguard only living organisms!" the GOD thundered. "We've scrapped them—all of them. There *aren't any* living organisms to be safeguarded."

"There is no clause in the regulations which specifically exempts lifeless planets," the EPA told him primly. It was too much.

"What kind of lunatics are you?" the GOD raged into the phone. "You don't need a specific exemption. What do you need protective regulations for when there isn't anything to be protected? How stupid can you get? Any idiot could see that it doesn't apply here—any of it. You're out of your mind."

"I'm simply doing my job, and I don't expect personal insults," came the reply. "The standards are quite clear, and they must be met. Good day." The line went dead.

The GOD conveyed the news to Design Engineering, who discussed it with Research. Without the volcanoes there wouldn't be enough planetary outgassing to form the atmospheres and oceans. Okay, the atmospheres and oceans would have to go. But the volcanoes were also intended to play a role in relieving the structural stresses and thermal buildups in the planetary crusts. How could that be taken care of without any volcanoes? Only by having more earthquakes to make up the difference, the CDE declared. The GOD told him to revise the proposal by deleting the volcanoes and making the crustal formations more earthquake-prone. Everybody agreed that the problem appeared at last to have been solved.

The Department of Highlands, Undulations, and Deserts called the GOD a day later with an objection. "I'm dreadfully sorry, old chap, but we seem to have run into a bit of a problem," the man from HUD told him. "You see, the mountain ranges you've proposed don't quite come up to the standards set out in our building codes for the increased level of seismic activity. We'd have no choice but to condemn them as unsafe, I'm afraid."

"What if we do away with the mountains, then?" the GOD growled sullenly.

"That would be perfectly satisfactory as far as we're concerned, but I rather suspect that you might still have a problem in getting it passed by the Occupational Safety and Health Angelcy. All those fissures opening up and landslides going on all over the place . . . it would be a bit hazardous for the animals, wouldn't it?"

"But we've already gotten rid of the animals," the GOD pointed out. "There won't be any."

"I see your point," the man from HUD agreed amiably, "but it is still in the jolly old rules. You know how finicky those OSHA types can be. Just a friendly word in your ear. Frightfully sorry and all that."

The GOD was past arguing.

Design Engineering's response was to make the planets completely inactive. There would be no mountains, no fluid interiors, no mobile plates—in fact, no tectonic processes of any kind. The planets would be simply featureless balls of solid rock that could never by any stretch of the imagination be considered potentially hazardous to any living thing, whether one existed or not.

The Great Accounting Overseer didn't like it. "What do you need them for?" a GAO minion challenged a day later. "They don't serve any useful purpose at all. They're just a needless additional expense on the cost budget. Why not get rid of them completely?"

"They've got a point," the CDE admitted when the GOD went over to Engineering to talk about it. "I guess the only reason we put them in is because that's the way we've always done it. Yeah . . . I reckon we should strike them out. No planets."

But the Dispenser of Energy wasn't happy about the idea of a universe consisting of nothing but stars. "It might be budgeted to last for billions of years, but it's still finite nevertheless," an assistant of the DOE declared in a call to the GOD "We are trying to encourage a policy of conservation, you know. This idea of having billions of stars just pouring out all that energy into empty space with none of it being used for anything at all . . . well, it would be terribly wasteful and inefficient. I don't think we could possibly approve something like that."

"But it's just as we've always done it," the GOD protested. "The planets never used more than a drop in the ocean. The difference isn't worth talking about."

"Quantitatively, yes, but I'm talking about a difference in principle," the DOE assistant replied. "The waste was high in the earlier projects, but at least there was a reason in principle. This time there isn't any, and that does make a difference. We couldn't give this universe an approval stamp. Sorry."

A day later Design Engineering had come up with a way to conserve the energy: Instead of being concentrated into masses sufficiently dense to sustain fusion reactions and form stars, the stellar material would be dispersed evenly throughout space as clouds of dust and gas in which the small amount of free energy that remained would be conserved through an equilibrium exchange between radiation and matter. The DOE was satisfied with that. Unfortunately the EPA was not; the clouds of dust and gas would exceed the pollution limits.

With two days to go before the closing date for the bid,

the GOD called all the department heads and senior technical staff members together to discuss the situation. The ensuing meeting went on all through the night. After running calculations through the computers several times, they at last came up with a solution they were sure had to be acceptable to everybody. Sales forwarded a revised final proposal to the customer, and the company waited nervously for the responses. Miraculously the phone on the GOD's desk didn't ring once all through the next day. The proposal was approved, and the final contract was awarded.

Out at the construction site, Gabriel watched despondently as the project at last got under way. All that was left of the original plan was a pinpoint of exotic particles of matter, radiation, space, and time, all compressed together at a temperature of billions of degrees. The bizarre particles fell apart into protons, neutrons, electrons, muons, neutrinos, and photons, which after a while began clustering together through the radiation fluid as he watched. After the grandeur of the previous projects he had witnessed, the sight was depressing. "I guess we just write this one off, forget all about it, and file it away," he murmured to the GOD, who was standing next to him. "It's not much to look at, is it? I can't see this even getting a mention in the report to the stockholders." He turned his head to find that the GOD's eyes were twinkling mischievously. "What's funny?" he asked, puzzled.

The GOD tipped his yellow hard-hat to the back of his head and grinned in a conspiratorial kind of way as he scratched his forehead. "Don't worry about it," he said quietly. "We've worked out a new method. It'll all come out just the way we planned . . . everything."

Gabriel blinked at him in astonishment. "What are you talking about? How do you mean, *everything*? You don't mean the stars, the planets, the oceans, the mountains . . ." His voice trailed away as he saw the GOD nodding.

"And the birds, and the fish, and the animals, all the way through to the people," the GOD told him confidently. "It'll turn out just the way we planned it in the original proposal."

Gabriel shook his head, nonplussed. "But . . . how?" He gestured at the expanding fireball, in which traces of helium and a few other light nuclei were beginning to appear. "How could it all come out of *that*?"

The GOD chuckled. "The research people developed some things called 'Laws of Physics' that they buried inside it. The angelcies will never find them. But they're in there, and they'll make it all happen just the way we planned. We ran the numbers through the IBM last night, and they work. You wait and see."

Gabriel looked over his shoulder at the site supervisor's hut and then gazed back at the embryo universe with a new interest and respect. "I was going to go inside for a coffee," he said. "But this sounds interesting. I think I'll hang around a little longer. I don't want to miss this."

The GOD smiled. "Oh, that's okay—you go get your coffee," he said. "There's plenty of time yet."

HOW LONG SHOULD A
PIECE OF STRING BE?

Aspiring writers often ask me if they should begin with short stories and work up from there toward full-length novels. I think this is the wrong question to ask. How long a work needs to be depends on what the writer wants to say. Some crushingly tedious books have resulted from padding out to hundreds of pages the single idea that ought to have been a short story; and many shorter works have suffered from jumbling together too many interesting thoughts which deserved the space to be developed. Hence I don't care very much what lengths are supposed to constitute a short story, a novella, a short novel, and so on. Whatever best expresses what I have to say is the length it needs to be, and others can worry about what category it belongs to. Writing shouldn't be a Procrustean bed that ideas are cut or stretched to fit.

Assassin was the first thing I wrote that came out as a short story (or novella, or whatever). That was in late 1977, after I'd written three novels—which answers the question about having to write short fiction first. Judy-Lynn Del Rey called from New York soon after we'd arrived in the U.S. to say that she was putting together the fourth in her *Stellar* series of anthologies, and had reserved a slot in it for me.

"So write something, Hogan," she ordered. Reflecting back, I don't doubt that this was her way of making sure I kept up the writing habit, before excuses about having just arrived in a new country and started a new job had any time to take root. One of the things that made Judy-Lynn such a good editor was that she never allowed authors to get lazy by deciding to take breaks between books—which can easily turn into those "blocks" you hear about that last for years. As soon as she received the manuscript for that latest novel, she'd be on the phone demanding an outline for the next. It didn't matter if the outline was half-baked and full of unresolved problems, or even if we ended up abandoning it completely—the wheels that would eventually produce the next story had been kept turning.

The problem with *Assassin,* though, was that I *had* just moved to a new country and begun a new and very demanding job with Digital Equipment—and on top of that had blown all my spare time by getting involved in restoring the house. So I wrote it by going to the office three hours early every morning and using my secretary's typewriter. As with many first attempts at shorter fiction, it was too wordy and rambling. The version included here—reread eight years later—has been pruned mercilessly.

I think this tells us something about writing technique. The purpose of a first draft is to capture every thought and get it down on paper before it evaporates (I still print out first drafts, even though I now use a word processor). The art of developing it from there is knowing what to cut—and in my opinion, the more ruthless the process, the better the end product tends to be. "When in doubt, leave it out" is a good maxim to follow.

ASSASSIN

Even before the conscious parts of his mind realized that he was awake, his reflexes had taken control. The slow and even rhythm of his breathing remained unbroken; not a muscle of his body stirred. To all appearances he was still sound asleep, but already his brain, now fully alert, was sifting the information streaming in through his senses.

There were no alarm bells ringing in his head—no half-remembered echo of perhaps the creak of a shoe, the rustle of a sleeve, or the barely audible catching of breath that would have betrayed the presence of somebody in the room. He could detect no change in the background pattern of sound and smell that he had registered and filed away in his memory before falling asleep.

Nothing abnormal then. Just the routine beginning of another day.

He opened his eyes, allowed them to sweep around the darkness of his hotel room probing for anything irregular, then rolled over and switched on the bedside light. He yawned, drawing the first clean breath of the new day deep into his lungs, and then stretched, long and luxuriously, allowing the energy that accumulates through eight hours of complete rest to charge every nerve and fiber of his body. After holding the position for perhaps ten seconds, the man who currently called himself Hadley Krassen relaxed, and returned fully to wakefulness.

His watch told him it was 6:35 A.M. He leaned across to the bedside console and flipped a switch to activate a voice channel to the hotel computer.

"Good morning." A synthetic bass-baritone voice issued from the grille near the top of the console panel. "Can I help you?"

"Room service," Krassen replied.

"Room service." The machine was now speaking in a rich, New England, female voice.

"Cancel my call for seven hundred hours. Also, I'd like a room breakfast at seven thirty—two eggs, bacon, tomatoes, toast, coffee. Okay?"

"Okay."

Pause.

"That's all."

"Thank you." *Click.*

Krassen flipped off the switch and interlaced his fingers behind his head as he settled back to reflect on the events of the past ten days. Experience had taught him that this was the time to catch any danger signals that might have been thrown up by his subconscious data processing during the night. Once whatever the new day had in store had begun to unfold, they would be lost forever.

His voyage from Mars—as a regular fare-paying passenger aboard the *Sirius*-class photon-drive ship *Percival Lowell*— had passed without incident. Upon his arrival at the Earth-orbiting transfer satellite, the passport and papers identifying him as Paul Langley, structural design engineer, citizen of the Federation of Martian City-States, visiting Earth for two weeks' vacation, had passed the scrutiny of the immigration officials. Nothing to worry about there—everything had gone smoothly.

The shuttle from the transfer satellite had brought him down thirty miles north of Oklahoma City limits at Roosevelt Spaceport, where, as prearranged, he had collected a package from the information desk at the east end of the arrivals terminal. The package had contained the key to a baggage locker, and inside the locker he had found a black briefcase.

The briefcase had provided the items that he would need for the assignment, including a complete set of personal documents relating to one Dr. Hadley B. Krassen, in whose affairs he had already been thoroughly schooled. Also, there were the keys to Krassen's personal airmobile, located three hundred miles away in the public parking area at Kansas City International Airport.

Who the "real" Hadley Krassen was the Assassin didn't know and probably never would. Hadley Krassen was a sleeper—an agent quietly injected into an ordinary, everyday position in American society, possibly years previously, since which time he had maintained banking and credit accounts, acquired ground driver's and airmobile pilot's licenses, and generally performed all the functions expected of a statistical unit in the federal data banks. Whoever had been Hadley Krassen would already have been spirited away to some low-profile existence elsewhere. If, by some inspired piece of detective work, the authorities managed to trace anything that happened subsequently back to Hadley Krassen, it wouldn't matter very much; but that time "Hadley Krassen" would have ceased to exist.

After arriving at Roosevelt and collecting the briefcase, the Assassin had rented an airmobile, still as Paul Langley, and flown it to Kansas City Airport. On arrival there he had confirmed his reservation on a suborbital flight to London in fourteen days time. Then he had switched identities.

He had locked all of Langley's papers, including the ticket to London, inside the rented airmobile and secured the keys out of sight up inside the undercarriage recess. Then, carrying only Krassen's papers and with nothing on him to link him with Paul Langley in any way, he had walked down two levels of the airmobile park, located Krassen's vehicle, and departed on a ten-day hotel-hopping tour of the North American continent. Thereafter he had faithfully acted out the part of a holidaymaker with a surplus of money and time and a shortage of ideas as to how to spend both of them. So far as "his" employers—the Fellerman Chemical Company of Long Island—were concerned, Dr. Krassen had left on two weeks' vacation and was strictly incommunicado. Anybody calling his apartment would have discovered that before leaving he had not programmed his infonet terminal to forward incoming calls.

During those ten days he had detected nothing suspicious. His tortuous meanderings about nearly a dozen cities, back and forth among the ramps, terraces, and walkways of the pedestrian precincts, on and off the autocabs, had failed to reveal any sign of a tail. There had been no unlikely coincidences, such as the same face appearing in two different restaurants a mile apart, or a fellow hotel guest "happening" to choose the same bar as he for an evening drink on the far side of town. His comings and goings had not been watched by curious eyes shielded by newspapers in hotel lobbies; no room that he stayed in had been searched; his vehicle had not been opened during his absence. He allowed himself to arrive at the conclusion therefore that he was, with a high degree of certainty, "clean."

He rose, took a shower, and shaved, moving with the unhurried ease of one conditioned to the notion that haste and disaster go hand in hand. That done, he selected his clothing from piles arranged the night before on top of the room's second, unused bed. The lightweight undervest, made from a foam-filled honeycomb of toughened nylon mesh, would stop a .38 bullet fired from anywhere beyond twenty feet. The trousers were of a strong but flexible material, loose-fitting around the hips and narrowing at the ankles to afford maximum freedom of movement; to go with them he chose a short-sleeved shirt, plain necktie, and conventional jacket. His shoes were soft, light, and nonslip, and would enable a suitably skilled wearer to move noiselessly over almost any surface.

With his single suitcase open on the bed, he sat down at the writing desk alongside and emptied his pockets and his wallet. First he checked Krassen's personal documents, transferring them into the wallet as he did so. The last item among them was a high-security pass folder, about half the size of a postcard, which contained his own photograph and thumbprint, and which, according to the wording carried on its face, had been issued by the Defense Department (NORAM) of the United Western Democracies and signed by James S. Vorner, Secretary to the Director of Military Intelligence. Then he put the wallet in one of his inside jacket pockets and his airmobile keys and a handkerchief in the side pockets, leaving his trousers empty for better mobility. Everything else went into the suitcase along with his spare clothing.

Next he checked the technical papers and research journals that provided legitimate contents for the briefcase, arranged them inside, and finally closed the case and positioned it on the desk in front of him, together with two other items—an ordinary-looking gray ballpoint pen, and a small transparent plastic box containing what appeared to be a common brand of tranquilizer capsules.

The pen came apart rapidly under his practiced fingers, the writing head, ink tube, and tapering portion coming away at one end and the rounded cap at the other, to leave just a plain cylinder of toughened, high-density plastic.

Turning his attention to the briefcase, he located the concealed catch beneath the lock and pressed it, allowing the handle to come away in his hand. The grip was bound with decorative hoops of leather thong. When he took the handle between both hands and flexed it, the grip broke like a shotgun, parting between two of the leather hoops and pivoting about a hinge on the inner edge of the grip; at the same time, a trigger clicked out from a point near the hinge. The handle had hinged into two parts of unequal length: The larger section formed the butt and body of the pistol, while the smaller section, hinged back to curve below his index finger, provided the trigger guard. The gray plastic tube screwed quickly into place to become the barrel.

The weapon fitted snugly in his hand. It was small, lightweight, and smoothly angled, easily concealed in an inside jacket pocket. Formed from plastic components that resembled everyday objects, it could be carried with impunity through the most stringent X-ray and visual security checks.

He squeezed the trigger a few times and felt the mechanism trip smoothly. Then he opened the pillbox and took out one of the yellow-and-blue capsules. What made these capsules different from those that looked the same and could be obtained in any drugstore was that the yellow end was soft and concealed a needle-sharp projectile formed from a fast-acting neurotoxin designed to fragment almost immediately after impact and cause death in under five seconds. The propellant was a charge of highly compressed gas contained in the blue end.

The Assassin drew the magazine slide out from the butt, carefully pressed the capsule into one of the five positions provided, and pushed the slide back in until he felt its restraining spring click into place. Pistol in hand, he rose from the chair, selected a large Florida orange from the bowl of fruit provided by the management, and lodged it firmly in the ashtray standing on the desk. He backed off ten paces, raised his arm, aimed, and fired.

A dull *phutt* from the pistol, a sharper *splatt* from the orange, and the briefest suggestion of a *hiss* from nowhere in particular sounded all at the same time. He walked back to the writing desk to inspect his handiwork.

About an inch off center, the skin of the orange was punctured by a quarter-inch diameter hole surrounded by a thin halo of pulped peel and flesh. The juice oozing out was discolored a greenish yellow. He peeled the skin back and inspected the damage, checking the depth of penetration and looking especially for signs of incomplete fragmentation. If the bullet were from a bad batch, with the center of mass not lying precisely on the spin axis, the ensuing in-flight wobble would cause too much energy to be dissipated in tearing through layers of clothing, preventing effective penetration of the target.

Satisfied, he removed the spent propellant cartridge from the magazine and tossed it down the disposal unit, to be incinerated, along with the orange.

He dismantled the pistol, refitted the briefcase handle, and put the reassembled pen and the pillbox away in zip-protected pockets in his jacket. The chime of the console panel sounded just as he was finishing.

"Krassen," he said, touching a button to accept the call.

"Seven-thirty breakfast, sir. Would it be convenient now?"

"Okay."

"Thank you."

Half a minute later the light above the room's dispensing unit indicated that the tray had arrived.

As he ate his breakfast he made his final mental run-through of the day's planned operation. Normally he preferred to work alone; on this occasion, however, too many specialized skills had been called for, so that had not been possible. But he had satisfied himself that those chosen to make up the rest of the team were all first class in their jobs.

His meal over, he swiveled the console around to face the desk and activated the keyboard. A swift sequence of commands connected him to the continental infonet service and activated an inquiry program already residing in a file established in the system. The program accessed a virtual address in the net and relayed its contents back to the screen on his console. The process was the electronic equivalent of the traditional dead-letter box: messages could be deposited in and retrieved from the virtual address with neither sender nor recipient being known to, or traceable by, the other.

The message read:

> JOHN
> VISIT PROFESSOR AS ARRANGED.
>
> MARY (7:00)

So—everything was *go* up until seven that morning; no last-minute hitches. He finished his coffee, then operated the console once more to access the hotel computer and call up the checkout routine. A record of the transaction appeared from the console's hard-copy unit, accompanied by a message thanking him for his business, expressing the hope that he would choose Holiday Inn again next time, and inviting him to call for manual assistance from the duty clerk if everything had not been to his complete satisfaction.

He loaded his suitcase into the receptacle of the baggage-handling system and left instructions to deliver it to the hotel airmobile park, Level 2, Bay 26. After a final check of the room, he put on his jacket and hat and walked down the hallway to the elevator.

Five minutes later, he settled himself into the pilot's seat of the airmobile, switched on the control console, and flipped the *Manual/Auto* flight-mode setting to *Auto*. The display screen came to life:

ALL SYSTEMS CHECKED AND FUNCTIONING NORMALLY.
FLIGHT MODE <u>AUTO</u> SELECTED.

<u>KEY</u> FOR DESTINATION:

N   NEW
P   PREPROGRAMMED
X   AUXILIARY SERVICES

He pressed the N key.

AUTO FLIGHT-LOG-IN.
SPECIFY DESTINATION REQUIRED.

He bit his lower lip as the first trace of tension began
building up inside him. If disaster was going to strike, it
would surely be within the next sixty seconds. He keyed:

JOINT SERVICES ARMAMENTS RESEARCH ESTABLISHMENT
ANDERSCLIFF
LINCOLN
NEBRASKA

Almost certainly, the destination that he had specified would trigger a response from a surveillance
program running somewhere in the system. Sure
enough:

QUERY
DESTINATION REQUESTED IS TOP-SECURITY LOCATION.
ACCESS PERMITTED TO AUTHORIZED PASS-HOLDERS ONLY.
<u>STATE</u>
NAME, POSITION HELD, PASS CODE/VISITOR CLEARANCE
REFERENCE.

He responded:

DR. HADLEY B. KRASSEN
SECTION A.8, DEPARTMENT 39, PLASMA PHYSICS
$7 \times 8H/927380$. BB

An eternity passed while the characters remained frozen
on the screen. This was the moment of truth.

No Krassen had ever been employed at Anderscliff.

Eighty-seven miles away, a computer deep below the administration building of the Joint Services Armaments Research Establishment scanned the information that he had entered and compared it against the stored records. It located a record pertaining to a Krassen, Hadley B., as described, and verified the pass code. Its verdict was composed into a message and flashed back through the infonet system. In the airmobile, the display changed at last:

AUTHORIZATION POSITIVE.
DESIRED TAKEOFF TIME:

The Assassin felt a surge of jubilation as he replied: IMMEDIATE. The rest of the preflight dialogue took only a few seconds.

ESTIMATED FLIGHT TIME IS 18 MINUTES. DETAILED FLIGHT PLAN REQUIRED?

NO.

FUEL ADEQUATE. ESTIMATED RANGE REMAINING ON ARRIVAL WILL BE 328 MILES. OKAY?

YES.

VEHICLE SYSTEM SLAVING TO TRAFFIC CONTROL. CLEARED FOR IMMEDIATE TAKEOFF.

Five minutes later, the man who currently called himself Hadley Krassen was gazing down from one of the speeding dots in the westbound traffic corridor at ten thousand feet, Route 305, of the Omaha Traffic Area.

Over fourteen hundred miles away, in an office block in the center of San Francisco, the plaque on the door of one of the suites proclaimed it to be the registered business premises of J.J. MARSHALL, INDUSTRIAL FINANCIAL ANALYST. Inside, the offices all looked normal enough. One room at the rear of the suite, however, was different. Inside it, four people—three

men and a woman, all in their late twenties to late thirties—
sat surrounded by an array of consoles, keyboards, and display screens amid a confusion of banks of electronic and
computing equipment. Working in these cramped conditions
over the previous five months, this team had penetrated the
"hyper-safe" integrated communications and database network of the NORAM Defense Department. That, of course,
included the computers at Anderscliff.

From their room in San Francisco, the Martian Federation scientists could extract and alter any data in the Anderscliff
system and monitor the operation of its most highly protected
programs. Also, if they wished, they could insert into the
system, and run, programs of their own devising—the personnel record for Krassen, Hadley B., had not found its way
into the Anderscliff file system through the normal channels.

The woman noted a change in the pattern of symbols on
one of the screens and keyed a command string into her
console. Groups of numbers appeared in columns on another
display.

"The call code and flight-profile data for his airmobile
have just been received from area traffic control, along with
details of a bunch of other vehicles," she announced.

One of the men behind her consulted another readout.
"They'll all be incoming flights," he said. "Morning com-
muters into Anderscliff. Area control is programming the
local ground processors and approach radars at Anderscliff to
handle the landing sequences."

"He must be nearly there, then," somebody commented.

The Assassin gazed down at the expanding sprawl of
office blocks, laboratory buildings, domes, storage tanks, and
girder lattices, all tied together loosely by a triangle of road-
ways and pipelines, that made up the Joint Services Armaments Research Establishment. His vehicle was sinking toward
a rooftop parking area, which he recognized as one of the
staff parking zones from ground plans taken from satellite
pictures; he had memorized it all thoroughly before leaving
Mars.

The vehicle slowed as it descended, finally coming to
hover thirty feet above the next available space along one of
the partially filled rows. The optical scanner presented a view

of the landing spot, and he satisfied himself that the area was clear before okaying the computer to proceed with the final phase of landing.

Three minutes later, briefcase in hand, he was walking toward the rooftop entry gate and checkpoint, through which he would have to pass to enter the Establishment itself. He had timed his arrival to coincide with the morning rush. Ahead of him, a half dozen or so persons, some shouting morning greetings back and forth, were converging on the door that led in to the checkpoint. Nobody took any notice of him as he tagged along behind two men talking shop in loud voices, and followed them through the doorway between two steel-helmeted guards.

Inside, the pair in front passed their hand-baggage to an attendant behind a counter, who in turn passed it through the hatch in the wall behind her for checking. The Assassin followed suit. There was no sign of the spot body-searches for which he had been told to be prepared.

Following the still-chattering duo, he found himself in a short queue shuffling slowly forward toward a desk where passes were being checked. Almost immediately, others lined up behind him. He watched the procedure being followed at the desk, searching for any subtle differences from what he had been briefed to expect. There were none. Whoever had been responsible for research for the assignment had done a thorough job.

Avoiding eye contact with the security officer seated at the check-in desk, he stepped forward, extracted the magnetically coded name-tag from his pass folder, pushed it into the slot provided, and keyed the memorized check digits into the keyboard below. He then pressed his right thumb against the glass plate located next to the slot and recited aloud into the microphone above:

"Krassen, Hadley B. 7X8H/927380.BB."

Elsewhere in the Establishment, a computer located the record and compared the check digits stored with the pass code against the sequence that had just been keyed in at the gate. They matched. The thumbprint and voiceprint profiles held in the record also matched those that had just been input.

"I don't know you, do I?" The security officer at the desk regarded him through narrowed eyes.

"Only started working here a coupla days ago." The Assassin's reply was in a matter-of-fact drawl. His face retained the deadpan stare of the early-morning riser not quite awake yet.

"Your pass folder, please."

The Assassin passed the folder across and stood impassively while the officer ran his eye rapidly down the card, pausing to compare the photograph inside it with the features confronting him.

"Who's your boss?"

"Professor Henderson, Department 39, Plasma Physics."

The security officer surveyed the column of illuminated signs on his console panel, all glowing POSITIVE for the computer checks, then nodded and passed the folder back together with a plastic lapel badge.

"Okay. Hope you enjoy working at Anderscliff, Dr. Krassen."

"Thank you."

The Assassin removed the magnetic name-tag from the slot in front of him, moved a few paces forward, and paused to insert it in the window of the lapel badge and fasten the badge to his jacket. Then he moved on to the counter beyond and retrieved his briefcase, checked and cleared.

For the first time in several minutes he allowed himself to relax a little, drawing in a long, slow breath and exhaling with it the worst of the tension that had built up inside him. He was in. He had penetrated the impenetrable. He knew of course that the real work had been done long before, and represented something like ten man-years of effort.

He took an elevator down to ground level and emerged from the building through a set of glass doors surmounting a flight of shallow steps, where he stopped for a while to study the geography of this part of the Establishment, especially the approaches to the building he had just come out of. Then, guided by his predeparture briefing and the direction signs about the Establishment, he made his way through the maze of buildings and up to the cafeteria on the third floor of the domestic block.

As he progressed from one area to another, detectors above the doorways through which he passed picked up the signal being transmitted by the microcircuit in the lapel badge.

The signal was unique to his pass code, controlled by the magnetic name-tag that he had inserted from his pass folder. Everybody in Anderscliff carried such a badge. All the signals picked up by all the detectors all over the Establishment were monitored by a surveillance computer which continuously compared them against stored tables of which pass codes authorized entry to any particular building, floor, section, or room. An attempt to violate the system of limited access would trigger an immediate alert. The surveillance system thus provided an automatic check of who was entering restricted areas and enabled reports to be printed out, if required, of who had been in any particular place on any given day and at what time.

The surveillance computer was not programmed to track the movements of an individual through the Anderscliff complex, although the data from the detectors would have enabled such a task to be accomplished quite easily. The designers of the system had not seen any purpose in such a function. But the Martian Federation scientists in San Francisco had. Accordingly, they had developed a program of their own that enabled them, from fourteen hundred miles away, to monitor the precise movements of both the Assassin and his victim. They thus possessed all the information needed to guide him to his target.

He settled himself at an empty table by one wall of the cafeteria and consumed a leisurely cup of coffee, allowing the people who were still arriving time to disperse about the Establishment and settle down to their daily routines. After twenty minutes or so had passed, he rose and walked back to the lobby to enter one of the three public infonet booths located near the door. The message waiting for him in the electronic dead-letter box read:

JOHN
PROFESSOR WILL SEE YOU ALONE AT HOME
                                    MARY (9:32)

So—Brozlan was alone in his private apartment suite in the residential sector of Anderscliff, as expected. Weeks of analysis of the data patterns extracted from the surveillance computer had revealed that the professor never left his private quarters before ten-thirty in the morning. Perhaps he was in the habit of working alone for the first part of the morning before going over to the biophysics labs, where he spent most of his time; maybe he was simply a late riser. The reason really didn't matter. The Assassin knew all he needed to know.

He left the booth, returned to ground level, and waited for one of the Establishment's auto-shuttles to take him to the residential sector. Eight minutes later, a porter seated at a desk just inside the entrance door of Residential Block 3 looked up in surprise as a tall, lean, hatted figure carrying a black briefcase marched straight past him, tossing back a curt "Good morning" over his shoulder. The porter just had time to check the ENTRY AUTHORIZATION POSITIVE display on his panel before the figure disappeared into the elevator at the far end of the hall.

The residential sector was a high-security zone, accessible to only a handful of privileged people apart from the scientists and other special-category personnel who resided within the perimeter of Anderscliff. The tables stored in the memory subsystem of the surveillance computer, however, told it that the holder of the pass code assigned to Krassen, Hadley B., could move freely anywhere within the Establishment.

When he came out of the elevator on the second floor, he was carrying the briefcase under his left arm and holding the pistol, assembled and loaded, in his right-hand jacket pocket. He moved slowly along the corridor, walking straight past the door that bore the nameplate BROZLAN without checking his stride or turning his head. At the end of the corridor he stopped, turned, and just as slowly walked back again, scanning the walls and ceiling for any sign of TV cameras. Finding none, he stopped when he came back to the door, listened for perhaps ten seconds, then pressed the ball of his right thumb against the printlock plate set into the doorframe. A click sounded as the lock disengaged.

Records of which prints were authorized to operate which of the thousands of printlocks around Anderscliff were also stored in the surveillance computer. Officially, only four prints had been specified to open the lock of Brozlan's private suite: those of the professor himself, the domestic attendant for Residential Block 3, the manager of domestic services, and the duty medical supervisor. Somehow a fifth print had been added to that set; it was identical to the one stored in the personnel record headed KRASSEN, HADLEY B.

He paused inside the door and closed it softly behind him. One of the other doors leading off from the small entrance hall was ajar, and from behind it came the sound of movement and the rustle of papers. The Assassin moved forward and brought his eye close to the crack at the edge of the door.

The room was a litter of books, papers, and scientific journals, and its far wall consisted entirely of shelves. Sitting at a desk in front of the shelves, a white-haired man, probably in his late fifties, and wearing a plain gray suit, was sorting piles of documents into something approaching order. The Assassin recognized him at once. He stepped quickly and silently around the door. Three catlike paces brought him facing the desk, pistol leveled.

"Keep your hands on the desk. Don't move. Don't make a noise."

The white head jerked up sharply in surprise. Eyes open wide with alarm and disbelief took in the menacing figure confronting them.

"You—you are from the Federation . . ." He had detected the slight Martian accent in the other's voice.

The Assassin nodded expressionlessly. "And you are Professor Malleborg Brozlan—defector from Mars and traitor to the Federation."

Brozlan saw the coldness behind the unblinking gray eyes and knew then that he had no hope. He tried the only gambit open to him.

"Did they tell you why I defected to Earth? Haven't you wondered?"

"Those things do not concern me." The Assassin's tone was final.

"But they concern everybody. Did you realize that—"

A dull *phutt*, a muffled *thud*, and the briefest suggestion of a *hiss* sounded all at the same time. The professor recoiled back in the chair, his eyes wide with shock. His fists clenched as his body stiffened. Then his eyes glazed over and stared sightlessly at infinity. The rim of the small hole that had appeared in his shirtfront, an inch to the left of the breast-bone, began to turn red.

The Assassin waited a few seconds longer, then stepped around the desk and lifted the professor's chin with his finger. The head lolled limply to one side. He reached out and felt the temple for a pulse. There was none. He raised the pistol again, rested the tip of the barrel against the pad of muscle over the carotid artery at the side of the neck, and gently squeezed the trigger again.

Five minutes later he emerged from Residential Block 3 and boarded the next passing shuttle. As the shuttle was pulling away from the pickup point, the wail of a siren heralded the approach of an ambulance moving at high speed. The ambulance screeched to a halt outside the residential block and disgorged three white-clad medical orderlies, who raced in through the door before the last moans of the siren had died away.

The planners of the Assassin's mission could not have known that six weeks before to the day, the professor had suffered a heart attack, and that during the ensuing surgery a microelectronic cardiac monitor had been implanted in his chest. The signals transmitted by the monitor were picked up continuously by detectors similar to those that read the lapel badges, and routed to measuring instruments in the Establishment's medical center. The instruments were programmed to sound an alarm the instant that any irregularity appeared in Brozlan's cardiac waveforms.

The Assassin almost made it. The alarm reached the roof-top checkpoint seconds after he had passed through without incident. As the guards came rushing out of the door behind him, shouting after him to stop, he broke into a run toward the airmobile. The tranquilizer dart hit him squarely in the back of the neck. The dose on it would have stunned an ox.

*   *   *

"Doctor, I think he's coming 'round now." The voice, a woman's, sounded blurred and far away. Coherent thoughts refused to form in his mind. Bright lights and meaningless patches of color swam before his eyes. Two faces seemed to be peering down at him from a million miles away. He passed out again.

*　　*　　*

He was in bed in what could have been a hospital room. Apart from the uniformed guard standing by the door, there were two other men in the room, seated on chairs flanking his bed. The one to his left was aged maybe forty-five and dressed in a navy-blue three-piece suit, white shirt, and silver tie. His hair was graying and his upper lip adorned by a clipped, military-style moustache that seemed to enhance his generally debonair image. His eyes were twinkling, and he seemed to be waiting for the Assassin to fully regain his faculties. The other was younger, dark-haired, swarthy-skinned, and unsmiling.

"Allow me to offer my congratulations," the older of the two said after a few seconds. "Another minute and you'd have got clean away." He was obviously English, probably an army officer, possibly high-ranking. The Assassin said nothing, allowing his thoughts time to coalesce into something approaching organized. The most important thing was that the mission had been successful: He had penetrated one of the most closely guarded places on Earth and carried out his assignment. What happened now was of secondary importance.

He hauled himself up for a better view of his visitors, and the Englishman moved the pillows behind him to prop him up. Silence persisted for what seemed a long time.

"What went wrong?" the Assassin asked at last. His voice was monotonous and resigned . . . but curious.

"Wrong? Actually, nothing, old chap. That is, you didn't do anything wrong. We picked you up through something that you couldn't possibly have known about. Call it an accident. The details of that can wait until later. Right at this moment there are a lot of other things that we'd very much like to know about you."

The Assassin slumped back against the pillows and raised his eyes to the ceiling in feigned boredom. His expression said the rest.

"You'd be surprised how much we know about you already," the Englishman went on, unperturbed. "We know that you're from the Martian Federation, that you came in via Roosevelt Spaceport ten days before Anderscliff, posing as a structural engineer called Paul Langley, and that after assuming the role of Hadley Krassen you spent some time touring around the continent to test your cover. I can give you a list of the places you stayed at if you want.''

The Assassin's face remained blank, but inwardly he felt uneasiness. If they had known this much all along, he would never have gotten within a hundred miles of Anderscliff. On the other hand, how could they have worked it out since his capture? He could think of no obvious flaw in his getaway arrangements.

''But let's start with introductions to prove that we are all civilized people,'' the Englishman continued. ''I am Colonel Arthur Barling—this is Carl May. Our precise functions need not concern us for now. You are . . . ?'' He let the question hang. The Assassin remained silent.

''Never mind. We'll call you Hadley for the time being. Any objections?'' He paused but there was no response. ''Very well, Hadley, now let's get down to business. It's obvious that you were sent here after the most meticulous preparations in order to eliminate Brozlan. Equally obviously, you are just one member of a team that includes some extraordinary talents.'' Silence. ''Just think of it—all that effort, all those people, all that distance . . . just for one man. A man of your undoubtedly high intelligence must have wondered what made him so important. I know that people like you are never told that kind of thing.''

The colonel regarded him silently for a few seconds. Carl May continued to sit frowning, saying nothing. The Assassin guessed that he was the observer, there to study his reactions while Barling did the talking. No doubt a camera was concealed somewhere as well.

The colonel carried on with what the Assassin had already decided was an outwardly nonchalant probing for weak spots.

''It's the old, old problem that separates you and us, isn't it, Hadley—the breakaway pressures of the New World pulling against the restraining influences of the Old. On the one hand there's the progressive new ideology of the former colonial city-states, and on the other the conservative and tradition-bound regimes of Earth.'' Barling made an empty-handed gesture and pulled a face. ''And so we hear the old song about an oppressed people yearning to be free and go its own way. But in reality it's an old story of another kind—a bunch of opportunists who've spotted something that's up for grabs, only this time it's a whole planet. So they feed out the same claptrap that we've been hearing for a thousand years . . . liberty, justice, that kind of thing . . . and the incredible thing is that people like you still swallow it.'' An expression of disbelief spread across the Englishman's face. ''Do you really believe that you'd be a penny's worth of anything better off if Mars did go its own way? I mean . . . Take that bunch that sent you off on your little errand. You can see the kind of methods that they don't think twice about using . . . the sort of scruples that they have. What kind of society do you think they'd make for you if they didn't have to answer to anybody? Is that the great 'cause' that you're all so dedicated to fighting for?''

The Englishman paused and considered the Martian quizzically, but was rewarded only by a stare of indifference. This was the kind of thing that the Assassin had expected. He knew that the mild taunts were intended to be provocative—to lure him into making the mistake of responding before he could think clearly.

Barling tried another angle. ''Anyway, it couldn't possibly work, could it? Mars depends on the industrial capacity and resources of Earth. As long as that remains fact, any talk about Martian independence can be nothing more than an illusion. Without us you couldn't last a month.''

The Assassin's jaw tightened as he fought to repress the indignation welling up inside him. The statement the colonel had just uttered was outrageous. Mars had no natural resources worth talking about. With no biosphere, no hydrosphere, and virtually no atmosphere, the planet had never experienced the processes of erosion, biological activity, and marine deposition that had laid down the treasures of Earth. But the pioneers had not expected to find any. What they had expected to find was freedom— freedom from stifling bureaucracy and legislation, and the freedom to tackle their problems in their own ways. Their first problem had been the horrendous cost of importing every ton of needed material from Earth.

In answer, the scientists of Mars had realized a dream that was centuries old, but on a scale that no alchemist had ever imagined. They perfected techniques for transmuting elements on an industrial scale. The Martian wilderness was no longer a waste. Not only that. Scientists eventually learned how to use the elements that they had created to synthesize increasingly more complex compounds, until virtually anything they required could be derived from a few common, locally available raw materials. Fusion reactors had satisfied the demand for the enormous amounts of energy required by these processes.

The new technology from Mars had transformed the industries of Earth in a few decades; indeed, all the nations of Earth rose to levels of affluence that would have been inconceivable, even to the most optimistic, only fifty years previously. The costs of synthetic compounds from Earth's own processing plants had plummeted so far that it became uneconomical for Mars to develop its pilot installations into fullblown industries and it continued to rely on imports.

And now Barling was turning that same fact around and using it to imply that Mars could never survive alone. But it was Earth that would never have survived without Mars! Mars had paid its debt. It had earned the right to decide its own destiny, alone and without interference. The Assassin continued to say nothing, but his eyes glared his defiance.

"Oh dear. This really isn't getting us anywhere at all," the colonel conceded. If we carry on in this fashion, the conversation is going to be very dull and one-sided. Although I'm sure you'd find the story of why Brozlan came to Earth a fascinating one, I've a feeling I might be wasting my breath if I tried to tell it to you. Therefore, I won't attempt it. Instead, I'll get someone else to tell it to you—someone who, I'm sure you will agree, will be able to make it far more interesting." The colonel nodded briefly to the guard, who turned and left the room. Silence descended, to be broken after a few seconds by the colonel whistling tunelessly to himself through his teeth. The Assassin remained expressionless, but deep inside he was becoming troubled.

Something was wrong. An alarm was sounding somewhere deep in his brain. There was something about the Englishman's tone and manner that didn't fit. The Assassin hadn't expected moral reproaches or accusations of criminal outrage; he had already assessed Barling as a professional at this kind of business. But the Englishman's nonchalance was coming through too sincerely to be contrived. If Brozlan's removal had been so important to the Federation, it followed that it should also have constituted a major disaster to the Western Democracies of Earth. The seriousness of the situation should have been detectable in the way that Barling spoke and acted. It wasn't.

The guard returned, ushering in before him somebody who had presumably been waiting outside. For the first time, the Assassin's iron self-control broke down. His eyes bulged, and he gaped across the room as if he had seen a ghost . . . which was not surprising.

"Good morning," said Professor Malleborg Brozlan.

Time seemed to stand still. For once, the wheels in the Assassin's mind ground to a complete halt. No coherent thought formed in his head; no words came to his lips. This was definitely no illusion . . . but there was no doubt that the man he had left at Anderscliff had been totally, absolutely, unquestionably . . . dead.

"Surprised?" The dryness in the colonel's voice did not conceal a faint trace of amusement.

The Assassin closed his eyes and slumped back against the pillows. "How?" he managed, in a voice that was barely more than a whisper. "How is this possible?"

"So—you're hooked, eh? You've got to know, haven't you? You'll listen to what we have to say?"

The Assassin nodded numbly without opening his eyes.

"Good." A pause. "Professor?"

The guard placed a spare chair at the foot of the bed. Brozlan sat down and began speaking. Clearly he had been following the conversation on a monitor outside the room.

"Maybe there were some hotheads among us." He nodded his snowy head slowly. "But the thought of a truly independent Martian civilization . . . free to benefit from all the lessons and mistakes that are written through the history of Earth . . . without having to inherit any of the consequences . . . A chance to begin again, in a way, but this time to get it right. It was a dream that fired the imagination and raised the passions of practically every young man of my generation." The professor shifted his eyes and regarded the figure lying in the bed. "I'm sure you know the kind of thing

I mean." Despite himself the Assassin found his gaze drawn irresistibly to the apparition sitting a few feet away from him. Brozlan was real; he was warm; he was alive . . . and talking matter-of-factly to the man who, without a moment's thought or hesitation, had killed him.

"How can this be?" the Assassin whispered again.

Brozlan looked at him coldly, but without overt malevolence. When he spoke again, his voice was sad. "You know nothing of the power that exists on Mars today. You allow yourself to be manipulated by people who are interested only in serving their own ends . . . as I myself was once manipulated."

"I . . . don't understand." In spite of his resolve not to be drawn into conversation, the Assassin was unable to restrain the question. "What power are you talking about?"

"Science!" Brozlan replied, his voice trembling slightly with sudden emotion. "The power of science. The domes of Mars contain some of the finest brains that the human race has ever produced. Think back over the last twenty or thirty years. Think of the discoveries and developments that have come from the laboratories of Mars. . . . The whole science of gravitics and the first practicable gravitic drive; economical transmutation of elements on a bulk scale; bulk synthesis of molecular compounds; computer biocommunications; genetic programming . . . The list is long. But do you think for one moment that all the knowledge acquired in those laboratories is public knowledge? Things have happened there, and are still happening, that people have never dreamed of."

The Assassin stared at him incredulously for a few seconds. "Are you saying that you are a reincarnation?" he gasped. "Something like that is really possible?"

Brozlan shook his head briefly. "No, nothing like that. Let me begin at the beginning." He paused to collect his thoughts. "I am a physicist. I specialize in molecular structures. Practically all of the raw materials used in industry today are synthesized from artificially transmuted elements—using techniques originally perfected on Mars." The Assassin nodded, keeping his eyes fixed on the professor. Brozlan did not continue at once, but gestured toward the flask of water that stood on the bedside locker. Carl May filled a glass and passed it to him, while Barling rose from his chair and began pacing to and fro between the bed and the window, his hands clasped loosely behind his back.

"To produce a full range of materials needed on Mars, it was not sufficient to just synthesize unstructured molecules in bulk," Brozlan resumed. "We needed to be able to duplicate, say, the crystal lattice structures of many metal-base compounds, or the polymer chains of organic substances— things that are abundant on Earth but totally lacking back there."

"I'd have thought that that's where you'd use traditional processing methods," the Assassin muttered. He didn't mind talking as long as it was he who was asking the questions. It could only be to his ultimate advantage to know more about what was going on.

"We could have done that." Brozlan nodded. His face creased into a frown. "But we were not satisfied with that idea. We had a virgin planet with no set ways or traditions to uphold. It seemed unsatisfactory simply to follow slavishly the methods that had evolved on Earth. We could have spent fortunes copying all of Earth's industrial complexes on Mars only to find them obsolete before they went into production. We were convinced that there had to be a better way."

The Assassin thought for a moment and looked puzzled. "How?" he asked at last. Brozlan's eyes glinted. He replied:

"Consider any form of component that is used in the construction of a larger assembly . . . the parts of a machine, for example. How is the component made? We take a lump of whatever material we need and cut away from it all the excess to leave the shape that we require. That forms the basis of just about every machining process that is used traditionally."

The Assassin shrugged. "What other way is there?"

"*Deposition!*" Brozlan peered at him intently. "Instead of cutting material away to leave the part, we *deposited* material to build the part up!"

"You mean like electrolytic forming? That's not new."

"The idea isn't," Brozlan agreed. "But the way we were doing it was. You see, electrolytic forming works only with certain metals. We were working with every kind of molecule."

"You mean you could build up something out of anything—any substance at all?"

"Exactly! And it didn't have to be all the same kind of molecule. We could mix them together any way we chose. We could produce a solid block that was phophor-bronze at one end and polythene at the other, with a smooth transition from one to the other in between. It opened up a whole new dimension in engineering design possibilities. The whole process was computer-controlled. A designer could develop a program to create any part he wanted out of any material he chose or any combination of materials—molecule by molecule if he really wanted to go down to that level of detail."

"Molecule by molecule . . ." The Assassin's face registered disbelief.

"Nevertheless, it worked," Brozlan told him. "There have been experimental plants on Mars operating for years now, turning out goods that are higher in quality and cheaper to produce than anything that could ever come out of the factories of Earth—even things normally processed from organically derived substances, such as paper, oils, fats, sugars . . ."

"Oil . . . food . . . paper . . . synthesized from transmuted elements? Why have we never heard of such things?"

"Politics." Brozlan sighed. "By that time there was a different brand of thinking among the higher echelons of the Federation government. Ambitious and unscrupulous men were taking over. They did not see these discoveries as potential benefits for all mankind, but only as a means toward securing full economic autonomy. They began to see themselves as undisputed rulers over a self-sufficient world. That purpose would be served better if Earth were allowed to lag behind. The Federation authorities assumed tight control over our work and placed a strict security blanket over everything. That was why few people knew about what we were doing. That was also where the movement for Martian independence had its origins. Only a handful of individuals stand to gain, and not in the ways that are popularly believed."

"Interesting, isn't it, Hadley?" the colonel came in, spinning on his heel to face the bed. "But if you think that's hard to swallow, wait until you hear the next bit." He nodded at Brozlan, who continued:

"That was just one aspect of the research going on at

that time. Another aspect was Dr. Franz Scheeman's work on structural scanning with neutrino beams. Scheeman developed a method for scanning a material object, inside and out, and for extracting from the transmitted beams a complete encoding of its arrangement of atoms and molecules. It was analogous to the way in which an old TV camera encoded the information contained in a visual scene." Brozlan took a deep breath. "The real breakthrough came when we combined Scheeman's technique with the molecular-deposition process that we have just been talking about."

Silence reigned for a long time while the Assassin digested the professor's words. Then his eyes widened slowly and transfixed Brozlan with a dumbfounded stare. "You're joking . . ." the Assassin breathed at last.

"A solid-object camera!" the colonel confirmed for him. "Yes, Hadley, you've got it. They could scan an object and derive a complete structural code for it. From that code they could generate a computer program to control the deposition process. Result—a perfect analog, a molecule-by-molecule copy of the original. And, of course, if they could make one they could just as easily make as many as they liked. Think of it, Hadley . . . "But think of some of the deeper implications, too. What would happen if somebody suddenly introduced that kind of technology into a complex and established economy like Earth's? Suppose that once you'd built the prototype of, say, a domestic infonet terminal"—he pointed to the bedside console—"you could churn out a million of them, all for peanuts. What would happen to the conventional electronics industry then? What about the components industry that supplies it? What would happen to the industries that supply all the parts—the plugs, sockets, metalwork, moldings, and all that kind of thing? And then, what about the service industries that depend on all those in turn . . . office equipment, furnishings, data processing, real estate, and so on through the list? How could they survive if half their customers and half their business went to the wall?" The colonel spread his arms wide in the air. "All finished, Hadley. Total collapse. How could you cope with ninety-five percent of a planet's population being suddenly redundant? How could a global economy, with its roots buried in centuries of steady evolution, survive an upheaval like that?"

"You see," Brozlan added, "that is exactly what the Federation government wanted to do. They wanted to rush into setting up a huge Martian industrial conglomerate based on the new technology, flooding Earth's markets with goods at giveaway prices."

"Earth would have been ruined," Barling interjected. "Or at best would have faced the prospect of existing as a very second-rate entity, dependent on a new rising star."

The Assassin, however, was not satisfied. "People can always adjust to innovations," he said. "You can't stop progress. What about the Industrial Revolution in England in the nineteenth century, or the way that three quarters of the world jumped straight out of feudal economies into the atomic age in the fifty years after World War Two? Or the Communications Revolution across the West? They all caused problems in their time, but people learned to live with the changes, and ended up better off as a result."

"But those things take *time*, Hadley," Barling answered. "You're right—people can adjust to anything, given time." He made an imploring gesture in the air again. "But that was the one thing the Federation hotheads weren't prepared to allow. They didn't need it. Martian society was small and flexible. Mars could have absorbed the new technology and thrived within a generation; Earth couldn't. Relatively speaking, Earth would have been thrown back into the Dark Ages overnight.

"Fortunately, some of the more levelheaded scientists around at the time, including Brozlan here, talked them out of it. They argued that Earth would have gone all the way to unleashing an all-out interplanetary war rather than let it happen. With the balance of things as it was then, Mars wouldn't have lasted a week." The colonel scowled. "We would have, too," he added with a growl.

Brozlan went on. "For a long time we developed the duplication process in secret, striving to improve its resolution further. After ten years or so, we reached a point where we could consider seriously an experiment that we had conceived right at the beginning—to produce an analog of a living organism!"

"How about *that*, Hadley?" the colonel inquired quietly. "Interesting?"

The Assassin stared back at the scientists in mute incredulity. Nobody spoke for a long time.

"That's preposterous . . ." the Assassin whispered, but the expression on Brozlan's face stifled any further words.

The professor nodded his head solemnly. "We refined the process so much, you see, that we could duplicate not only the spatial arrangement of the molecules in an organism, but also the patterns of electrical activity in its nervous system. We could reproduce, in the copy, all the behavioral habits and memorized information that had been acquired in the lifetime of the original—in other words, all those phenomena which in higher forms of life we term 'intelligence' and 'memory.' We could create an analog of a living organism," Brozlan continued, "that was itself living! The analogs that we created were indistinguishable from the originals by any test that we could devise. We produced analog rats that could readily negotiate a maze that their originals had needed weeks of effort to learn . . . analog dogs that exhibited the same reflexes that we had conditioned into their originals. From the data collected in such experiments, it soon became obvious that there was no reason why the same thing would not work with a human being."

Impossible thoughts that were already forming in the Assassin's head focused suddenly into clarity. His eyes had frozen into a stunned stare directed straight at the figure seated at the foot of his bed. Before he could form any words, the colonel spoke again.

"Think about *that*, Hadley! You can put a person through a harmless scanning process and derive a code that specifies everything about him uniquely—physically and mentally. You can store that code away in a computer, and then use it to generate an identical analog of him. But why stop at one? You could make as many as you like! If what we talked about before was alarming, then what about this?"

He allowed a few seconds for his words to sink in, then went on. "They had some brilliant brains on Mars all right. But suddenly there was no reason why they should have to be content with just *some*; now they could *mass-produce* them!" Barling rested his hands on the back of his chair and leaned forward to peer at the Assassin intently. "What could have been achieved in the twentieth century with a thousand Albert Einsteins?

"How would you fight a war with an enemy that can store his army away in a data bank and simply re-create it every time you wipe it out? Come to that, why should he wait until you'd wiped it out at all? He could make sure you didn't by making his army twice as big to start with . . . or ten times as big . . . or any number you like. What sort of strategy would make sense any more? It all gets crazy.

"Or what about life-insurance companies? Instead of paying out a cash benefit to compensate the bereaved for losing somebody, they could offer an analog to replace him. What kind of premium would they charge for that service?"

The Assassin gaped from Barling to Brozlan and back again as he shrugged to keep pace with it all. This was too much.

"I don't believe all this," he protested. "It's some kind of trick."

"It most certainly is not, I assure you," Barling replied evenly. He pointed toward Brozlan. "Isn't that enough proof for you?"

The Assassin followed the colonel's finger with his eyes and subsided back into silence.

"The things that Colonel Barling has just mentioned are just examples," Brozlan said. "It takes little imagination to realize what chaos could be let loose. The whole of civilized living as we know it would be turned upside down."

"Yes, exactly," Barling agreed.

"And consider this, Hadley—the code that controls the duplication process can be transmitted from anywhere to anywhere by ordinary telecommunications methods. Hence, the part of the machine that scans the original and the part that manufactures the analog don't have to be in the same place. You could send anybody anywhere, instantly! It would be the old science-fiction dream come true, but with a difference—you'd still be left with the original at the sending end." He paused and took in the Assassin's amazement.

"I assure you I'm not joking, Hadley. Never mind economic problems now. How would you cope with the social, moral, and administrative anarchy that would follow if this kind of thing ever got loose? How could anybody stay sane in a world that was proliferating dozens of everybody? That's not technical progress, it's an explosion!'' He paused and looked down.

The other, still stupefied, shook his head weakly. ''I am a Martian,'' he said. ''You can't stop things like that, explosion or not. Man will always find answers. It's his nature.''

''Oh, we can think of answers,'' the Englishman returned breezily. ''Take that instant travel thing I just mentioned, for example. It would be an ideal way to send somebody to Mars or somewhere in a couple of seconds flat . . . if it weren't for the fact that you'd be stuck with two of him afterward—one here and one there. And things would get even worse if the one there decided to come back again the same way. So, why not simply arrange for the transmitting end to destroy the original? After all, the effect as far as the rest of the universe was concerned would be that he just 'went' from here to there, wouldn't it?''

The Assassin shrugged. ''Perhaps.''

The colonel rubbed the palms of his hands together and smiled faintly. ''Ah . . . But that would surely be murder, Hadley,'' he replied. ''Our legal and moral system wouldn't allow it. Let me illustrate the point by asking a simple question. Suppose I were to say that we were going to send you through a system like that, and that in the very near future you were going to walk out of the receiving end in, say, Paris. Now, how would you feel about the idea? Would you be happy about it?'' He paused and watched the change in expression on the Assassin's face. ''Mmm . . . no . . . I thought not. The fact that another individual who happened to look and think like you had come into existence somewhere else wouldn't really be of interest, would it? *You* would still be dead. You can't really accept that there'd be any sense of *continuity* with your analog, can you? It just feels wrong—true?''

Again the Assassin did not reply, but the look in his eyes was enough. Barling nodded but still took the point further. ''See, it wouldn't work. But suppose I were to argue that all we would have done would be to speed up slightly something that happens naturally anyway. Every molecule in your body will be replaced eventually by the normal processes of cell regeneration; the Hadley that will exist in six months' time won't contain one atom of the person lying in that bed right now. So why should you feel any less of a sense of continuity with your synthetic analog than you feel with the 'natural analog' that will be you six months from now? Logically there is no difference. The two processes are the same, but one takes a little longer than the other." The colonel allowed the proposition time to register, then suggested: "But nevertheless something's wrong. The argument wouldn't convince you—right?"

"But one day maybe—" the Assassin began, but Barling cut him off.

"Ah—*one day*, Hadley, perhaps . . . but that's another matter. As you say, man will always find answers. Maybe some day things like that might be accepted as perfectly normal—as normal as embryonic genetic adjustments or artificially grown limbs seem to us today. Maybe someday we'll populate another star system by simply beaming the information to generate a few thousand analogs out to receiving equipment that has already been sent on ahead. Maybe someday we'll send people around the world as easily as we send messages through the infonet. It might become standard practice to back everybody up in data banks so that nobody need be permanently lost at all." Barling spread his arms appealingly. "But not today, Hadley—not in our lifetime. Good God, man, it will take fifty years at least just to plan how to use that kind of thing intelligently. We couldn't just let it loose overnight without any preparation at all."

"You see, that is precisely what the Federation was proposing to do," Brozlan supplied, sitting forward in his chair. "We managed to talk them out of doing anything rash the first time, but after this there was no way of making them listen. Mars was about to break free and find its own destiny. They saw themselves as potential gods—able to create at will and, in a sense, immortal. None of Earth's traditional advantages mattered any more: its military superiority, economic strength, huge population, and abundance of resources . . . all of them counted for nothing. Mars would begin a new era of civilization, and Earth would pale into insignificance in its shadow."

"And you—a Martian—didn't want this?" The Assassin seemed unable to comprehend.

Brozlan shook his head slowly. "I was older by then. I saw the future not in terms of Earth or Mars, but of mankind. I and many of my colleagues decided that if, by this new knowledge that we had discovered, man was to elevate himself to godliness, then he would do so united as one race. This new power would not be used for something that would have amounted to war. We agreed, therefore, that, before the imbalance became any greater, we would bring the new sciences to Earth."

"And so you defected," the Assassin completed for him, nodding.

Brozlan hesitated for an unnaturally long time before replying. "Yes and no," he said at last. The Assassin looked puzzled.

"By the time I was forced to work under conditions of intense and constant surveillance by Federation security. Straightforward defection would have been impossible. So . . ." He took a deep breath. ". . . One of me remained on Mars as a decoy; the other one of me came to Earth."

"Brozlan created an analog of himself," Barling confirmed. "Two years ago one came here while the other stayed there. For reasons he won't go into, he's never told us which was which. Because there was still a Brozlan working on Mars, it took the Federation over a year to find out what had happened."

The Assassin was still confused. He had concluded already that the analog-generation process described by Brozlan was the explanation for the scientist's "reincarnation." But the account that he had just heard went nowhere toward answering the immediate question. One Brozlan was surely dead. The other Brozlan was just as surely still on Mars. So who was the figure sitting at the foot of the bed? He looked from Brozlan to Barling, but before he could utter any words the Englishman told him:

"As insurance, whichever of the two it was that came to Earth brought with him a copy of the program that had been used to generate the analog. Thus, once we had built the equipment at Anderscliff, we would be able to regenerate Brozlan if anything happened to him. Once a week he went through the scanning process to update the program with his latest memory patterns and so on. Hence, if we ever had to use the program, it would only be a week out of date at the most. He must have guessed that once the Federation had figured out the situation they'd stop at nothing to get rid of him . . . as you, Hadley my friend, very well know."

Brozlan lifted his chin and hooked his collar down with his finger to reveal the side of his neck. "No scar, you see," he said. "Yes—I am an analog, generated from the stored program at Anderscliff after you got to the Brozlan who arrived from Mars."

"Don't worry about losing control of your senses or anything like that, old chap," the colonel advised reassuringly. "The Brozlan that you left behind was very dead all right." He smiled wryly and added, "But it wouldn't do you any good to have a crack at this one, too. We'd simply make another one."

The Assassin sank back and closed his eyes as the full meaning of it all seeped slowly into his mind. Futile. The whole mission had been futile. The greatest piece of computer espionage in history—all for nothing.

He lay in silence for a long time. And then his mouth contorted into a faint smile. His chest began to heave with suppressed laughter. He opened his eyes and looked up at the Englishman. "But you've lost, Arthur, old chap," he mimicked in barely more than a whisper. "Don't you see—the Federation knows now that the mission has failed. They'll deduce that Brozlan is still working for Earth and that very soon Earth will catch up in technology. That means that the Federation will be forced to make its move now—while the gap is widest and in their favor—just the opposite of what you want. Earth needs time, Arthur—time to develop the ways of applying Brozlan's know-how. Once Earth has closed the gap, its traditional advantages will tilt the balance and count for something again. Given technical equality, Mars would have to stay in line and stay friendly. Earth could blow it out of the solar system if it had to, and lose nothing." The Assassin laughed again, this time out loud.

"Know what you should have done? You shouldn't have told me any of this. You should have let me escape somehow, still thinking that my mission had succeeded . . . I'd have gone back to Mars and given them a wrong report. Then, afterward, you could have quietly regenerated Brozlan and carried on. That way the Federation would have believed that they had a monopoly and as much time as they liked to set things up. By the time they found out differently, it would have been too late: Earth would have had the time it needed to make itself invincible.'' The Assassin shook his head in mock sympathy. ''That, Arthur, is what you should have done.''

The colonel looked down at him and stroked his mustache pensively. When he spoke, his tone was soft and mildly reproaching. ''But, my dear Hadley, that's precisely what we did do.''

The Assassin's face registered confusion and noncomprehension.

''I must apologize,'' the colonel said. ''I haven't quite told you everything yet.'' He swiveled the bedside infonet terminal around so that the screen was facing the Assassin, and keyed in a sequence of commands. ''Here are some movie records from our files that I think you'll find answer your questions.'' The screen came to life to show a row of airmobiles in a parking area.

''Recognize it?'' the colonel asked casually. ''It's at Kansas City International Airport. We found out you were going there by interrogating the traffic control net to see what designation you'd logged in. We simply had one of our agents waiting on every level to see where you went after you landed. Here you come now—there—in the gray coat. Telephoto shot from five rows back.''

The Assassin's bewilderment increased as he watched the image of himself walk along to one of the vehicles, which he recognized, retrieve the keys from up inside the undercarriage recess, climb in, and depart.

''It didn't take long, of course, for us to trace that that vehicle had been hired out by a Paul Langley at Roosevelt Spaceport,'' the colonel commented. ''From there on it was just routine to establish how Langley arrived from Mars and that he was booked on a flight to London and from there back to Mars via Anglia Spaceport, England.

''British security agents watched you check through the boarding gate for the shuttle up from Anglia—just to make sure there were no hitches. We even had somebody up on the transfer satellite to make sure you didn't miss your ship out to

Mars. There . . ." Barling touched another button, and the picture changed to show a short line of people standing at a check-in gate. "Passengers embarking for Flight 927 to Mars. There you are again—fourth from the front. The ship left on schedule, and that was the last we saw of you, or should I say of Paul Langley." He snapped off the screen and regarded the Assassin challengingly.

The Assassin shook his head wildly from side to side. "But—those pictures—I never did those things. I'm here!"

The Englishman frowned and made a clicking noise with his tongue. "Oh dear, you disappoint me, Hadley. Hasn't it dawned on you yet? Don't you realize? When you were captured, you were knocked out cold, weren't you? You've been out for quite some time now. I'm afraid that during that time we took something of a liberty. . . ."

A look of horror spread across the Assassin's face.

"Ah! I think you've cottoned on at last." The colonel nodded approvingly. "Yes—you've got it. You're not the *real* Hadley—the one who arrived from Mars. That one you've just been looking at on the screen was the real one. You're an *analog* of him.

"He woke up remembering exactly the same as you did—everything that happened right up until he was knocked out on the roof at Anderscliff; that, of course, included the successful elimination of Brozlan. Unlike you, however, he managed to escape. Quite extraordinary, that—wouldn't have thought our security could be so lax. Actually his escape was, shall we say, contrived, but he wasn't to know that. The rest you know. I think Earth has bought the time it needs."

The Assassin had been seized by something akin to acute mental shock. His eyes bulged, and his fingers clawed at the sheets. "But why?" he croaked. Perspiration showed on his forehead. "Why all this?"

"I explained it all at the beginning," the colonel replied in unruffled tones. "You can help us with so many things we'd like to know. We'd like to know a lot more about an organization that can crack one of our top-security computer systems . . . where they got the bogus information from to put in those files . . . how they knew the pass codes . . . you know the kind of thing, Hadley. There's lots more."

"No." The Assassin clenched his teeth grimly. "I am still a Martian. You can expect no help from me."

"Oh dear, Hadley." The colonel shook his head and sighed. "Look, how can I put this?" He paused as if considering how to phrase a delicate matter. "There really is no point at all in being obstinate. Everybody has his weakness. Some people crack up when things get unpleasant; others respond to the friendly approach. Every man can be bought for a price of some kind: money, women, a life of luxury without worries . . . There's always something. The big problem that interrogators have had to contend with in the past has been that they've had only one subject to work with. It was always too easy to ruin any chance of the right approach working by trying the wrong ones first." The Englishman's eyes twinkled.

"But we don't have that problem with you, do we, Hadley? We can go back to the beginning as often as we like by simply generating another of you from the same program that we used to generate you. We're bound to succeed eventually. Maybe we'll learn a little bit from one Hadley, a little bit more from another . . . Sooner or later we'll know all we need to."

He paused as if struck by a sudden, amusing thought. "Come to think of it, you've no way of knowing if you're the first Hadley at all, have you . . . or the only one? We could have ten Hadleys in this building right now for all you know. That day at Anderscliff might have been years ago now, mightn't it?

"Now, as I'm sure you can understand, we are very busy people, and we'd much rather spend our time talking constructively to a sensible Hadley than wasting our time with one that chose to be difficult. It's up to you to decide which you are going to be. It really doesn't make a lot of difference to us; but, as I'm sure you will already have worked out for yourself, it could make an awful lot of difference to *you*."

A moan escaped the Assassin's lips as he slumped back against the pillows. He had been rigorously trained to understand and counter every situation of interrogation in the book. He knew all the tricks.

But they'd never thought of this . . . Nothing like this. . .

GOING FULL-TIME

When, in 1979, I finally quit my regular job to write full-time, everyone wanted to know how much more I'd produce in a year. I told them I didn't think I'd produce any more than I had been. "Why not?" they asked. "How could you not write more with an extra forty hours every week?" I explained that I expected to do other things with the extra time, such as actually be able to sit down and read every now and again, talk to people occasionally, and recover something of a social life. It turned out I was right.

Many of the people at S.F. conventions would like to be writers (sometimes I get the feeling this is true of every other person in the country). The panels on writing topics always generate lots of questions from the audience on personal working habits and methods, as if there were some kind of "insiders' secret" to be divulged. There isn't, of course. My advice is usually to "burn your TV" (I haven't owned one for years), "live within walking distance of a twenty-four-hour restaurant, and after that, do whatever works best for you." It does help to have something worthwhile to say and know how to say it, but amazingly few of the questioners seem very concerned about such irrelevancies. I suspect that a lot of people are in love with the *thought* of writing, not with writing.

As I settled into the U.S., I met people from all sides of the publishing business—editors, agents, writers who were professionals before I was born—some of whom have since become close friends. When I started mentioning that I was contemplating going full-time, one comment I heard time and time again was that the biggest mistake made by new writers was that after selling one book—frequently without even waiting to see any reactions or sales figures—they'd be off yelling, "I've made it! I've made it!" quitting their jobs, getting new cars, and checking the real-estate prices in Hawaii. Almost invariably it didn't work out, and within six months they'd be knocking on the door of their old company, desperate to get back in out of the rain. And more often than not, worse than the financial setback, they had destroyed themselves psychologically.

That was some of the best advice I ever had.

So, I set three conditions that I said would have to be satisfied before I'd consider going full-time. One: I'd have five published books—not signed contracts or manuscripts delivered, but five titles out on shelves in bookstores, and out there long enough for the sales to be evident. Two: Each would have to have done better than the one before. In general, the sales of a book peak in the month or two following its release, and then drop off. What this condition said was that each peak should be higher than the last, indicating a satisfied, growing readership. Three: Enough cash in the bank to last one year—even if all income were to dry up, but expenses continued unabated—and no debts or credit.

People can delude themselves in strange ways when defending their fantasies. I've often heard it assumed that once the earnings from part-time writing equal one's regular salary, then quitting the job won't make any difference. Wrong. Let's say, to take a round number, that somebody's salary is thirty thousand dollars per year. When their part-time writing income equals that, their total income is sixty thousand dollars—simple when you think about it, but so few do. When they quit, they'd better be ready for a 50 percent cut.

The third condition was to cushion against life's "unexpecteds." Not unexpectedly, there were plenty of those, not the least of which was acquiring a third wife and another three children. Since the survival plan was resilient enough for us to muddle through without my having to abandon writing, I feel I can recommend it.

The message, I suppose, is to make sure that your umbrella isn't designed for sunny summer days.

NEANDER-TALE

Artificial fire!? Waddya mean 'artificial fire'? What the hell is artificial fire?'' Ug scowled down from beneath heavy close-knit Neanderthal brows at the tangle-haired, bearskin-clad figure squatting in front of him. Og was leaning forward to peer intently into the pile of sticks and twigs that he had built between two stones in the clearing where the trail from the stream widened on its way up toward the rock terrace fronting the caves. He seemed unperturbed by Ug's pugnacious tone; Ug was standing with his club still slung across his shoulder, which meant that, for once, he was not in a trouble-making mood that day.

"It's the same as you get when lightning hits a tree," Og replied cheerfully as he began rubbing two sticks vigorously together in the handful of moss which he had placed underneath the twigs. "Only this way you don't need the lightning."

"You're crazy," Ug declared bluntly.

"You'll see. Just stand there a couple of seconds longer and then tell me again that I'm crazy."

A wisp of smoke puffed out from the moss and turned into a blossom of flame which quickly leaped up through the twigs and engulfed the pile. Og straightened up with a satisfied grunt while Ug emitted a startled shriek and jumped backwards, at the same time hurriedly unslinging his club.

"Now tell me again that I'm crazy," Og invited.

Ug's gasp was a mixture of terror, awe, and incredulity.

"Holy sabre-cats, don't you know that stuff's dangerous? It can take out a whole block of the forest in the dry season. Get rid of it for chrissakes, willya!"

"It's okay between those rocks. Anyhow, I don't want to get rid of it. I was wondering if we could figure out how to use it for something."

"Like what?" Ug continued to stare nervously at the crackling pile and kept himself at a safe distance. "What could anybody do with it, besides get hurt?"

"I don't know. All kinds of things. . . ." Og frowned and scratched his chin. "For instance, maybe we wouldn't have to kick people out of the caves and make them trek a half mile down to where the hot springs are whenever they start to smell bad."

"How else are they gonna clean up?"

"Well, I was thinking . . . maybe we could use this to make our own hot water right there in the caves and save all the hassle. Think what a difference that would make to the girls. They wouldn't—"

"WHAT!" Ug cut him off with a shout that echoed back from the rocks above. "You wanna take that stuff *inside* the caves? You are crazy! Are you trying to get us all killed? Even the mammoths take off like bats outa hell if they catch so much as a whiff of that stuff. Anyhow, how could you make water hot with it? It'd burn through the skins."

"So you don't put it in skins. You put it in something else . . . something that won't burn."

"Such as what?"

"Hell, I don't know yet," Og yelled, at last losing his patience. "It's a brand new technology. Maybe some kind of stone stuff. . . ."

The sounds of running feet and jabbering voices from just around the bend in the trail above interrupted them. A few moments later Ag, the Vice-Chief, rushed into the clearing, closely followed by about twenty of the tribespeople.

"What's going on down here?" Ag demanded. "We

heard shouting . . . ARGH! FIRE! There's fire in the valley. FLEE FOR YOUR LIVES! FIRE IN THE VALLEY!'' The rest took up the cry and plunged back into the undergrowth in all directions. The trees all around reverberated with the sounds of colliding bodies and muffled curses, while Og continued to stare happily at his creation and Ug watched nervously from a few paces back. Then silence descended. After a while bearded faces began popping one by one out of the greenery on all sides. Ag re-emerged from behind a bush and approached warily.

"What's this?" he enquired, looking from Ug to Og and back again. "There hasn't been a storm for weeks. Where did that come from?"

"Og made it," Ug told him.

" 'Made' it'? What are you talking about—'made it'? This some kinda joke or sump'n?''

"He made it," Ug insisted. "I watched him do it."

"Why?"

"He's crazy. He says he wants to take it inside the caves and—''

"INSIDE THE CAVES?" Ag clapped his hand to his brow and rolled a pair of wide-staring eyes toward Og. "Are you outa your mind? What are you trying to do? Haven't you seen what happens to the animals that get caught when the forest goes up? We'd all get roasted in our beds."

"Nobody's saying you have to sleep on top of it," Og said wearily. "You keep it out of the way someplace. Water pulls up trees when the river floods, but you can still take water inside without having to flood the whole goddamn cave. Well, maybe we can make our own fire and learn to live with it in the same sort of way."

"What's the point?" Ag challenged.

"It could be useful to have around," Og said. "The animals don't like it. It might stop the bears from trying to muscle into the caves every time the snow comes. Things like that . . . all kinds of things. . . .''

Ag sniffed and remained unimpressed. "All the people would have taken off for the hills, too, so it wouldn't do much good," he pointed out.

"What about the smoke?" a voice called out from the

circle of figures that had started to form around the edge of the clearing.

"What about it?" Og asked.

"You can't breathe it. How could people live in a cave full of smoke?"

"You fix it so the smoke goes outside and not inside,"Og shouted in exasperation.

"How?"

"For Pete's sake, I don't know yet. It's a new technology. What do you want—all the angles figured out in one day? I'll think of something."

"You'd pollute the air," another voice objected. "If all the tribes in the valley got into it, there'd be smoke everywhere. It'd black out the sun-god. Then he'd be mad and we'd all get zapped."

"How do you know it isn't a she?" a female voice piped up from the back, only to be promptly silenced by a gentle tap on the head from the nearest club.

At that moment the circle of onlookers opened up to make way for Yug-the-Strong, Chief of the tribe, and Yeg-the-Soothsayer, who had come down from the caves to investigate the commotion. Yeg had been a great warrior in his youth and was reputed to have once felled an ox single-handed by talking at it nonstop until it collapsed in the mud from nervous exhaustion; hence Yeg's nickname of 'Oxmire.' For the benefit of the two elders Ag repeated what had been said and Ug confirmed it. Yeg's face darkened as he listened.

"It's not safe," he pronounced when Ag had finished. The tone was final.

"So we learn how to make it safe," Og insisted.

"That's ridiculous," Yeg declared flatly. "If it got loose it would wipe out the whole valley. The kids would fall into it. On top of that, the fallout would foul up the river. Anyhow, you'd need half the tribe to be carrying wood up all the time, and we need the resources for other things. It's a dumb idea whatever way you look at it."

"You've got no business screwing around with it," Yug said, to add his official endorsement.

But Og was persistent and the arguing continued for the next hour. Eventually Yeg had had enough. He climbed onto a rock and raised an arm for silence.

"How this could be made safe and why we should bother anyway is still unclear," he told them. "Everything about it is unclear. Anyone who still wants to mess around with unclear energy has to be soft in the head." He turned a steely gaze toward Og. "The penalty for that is banishment from the tribe . . . forever. The law makes no exceptions." Yug and Ag nodded their mute agreement, while a rising murmur of voices from the tribe signaled assent to the decision.

"Throw the bum out!"

"I don't want no crazy people collecting free rides outa my taxes."

"Let the Saps down the end of the valley take care of him. They're all crazy anyway."

Og lodged a plea with the appeal-court in the form of Ag, who passed it on to Yug.

"Beat it," was Yug's verdict.

An hour later Og had drawn his termination pay in the form of two days supply of raw steak and dried fish, and was all packed up and ready to go.

"You'll be sorry," he called over his shoulder at the sullen group who had gathered to see him on his way down the trail. "It won't do you any good to come chasing after me and telling me you've changed your minds when winter comes. The price to you will have gone out of sight."

"Asshole!" Ug shouted back. "I told you you'd blow it."

Over the months that followed, Og traveled the length and breadth of the valley trying to interest the other tribes in his discovery. The *Australopithecines* were too busy training kangaroos to retrieve boomerangs as a result of not having got their design calculations quite right yet. The tribe of *Homo erectus* (famous for their virility) were preoccupied with other matters and didn't listen seriously, while *A. robustus* declared that they had no intention of becoming *A. combustus* by being ignited and becoming extinguished at the same time. And so Og found himself at last in the remote far reaches of the valley where dwelt the *H. saps*, who were known for their strange ways and whom the other tribes tended to leave to their own devices.

The first Sap that Og found was sitting under a tree,

staring thoughtfully at a thin slice of wood sawn from the end of a log that was lying nearby.

"What's that?" Og asked without preamble. The Sap looked up, still wearing a distant expression on his face.

"Haven't thought of a name for it yet," he confessed.

"What is it supposed to do?"

"Not sure of that either. I just had a hunch that it could come in useful . . . maybe for throwing at hyenas." The Sap returned his gaze to the disk of wood and rolled it absently backward and forward in the dust a couple of times. Then he pushed it away and looked up at Og once more. "Anyhow, you're not from this end of the valley. What are you doing on our patch?" Og unslung an armful of sticks from his pack for the umpteenth time and squatted down next to the Sap.

"Man, have I got a deal for you," he said. "You wait till you see this."

They spent the rest of the afternoon wheeling and dealing and ended up agreeing to joint-management of both patents. The Sap had got a good deal, so it followed that Og must have got a wheel—which was what they therefore decided to call it. The chief of the Saps agreed that Og's trick with the sticks constituted a reasonable share-transfer price, and Og was duly installed as a full member of the tribe. He was content to spend the remainder of his days among the Saps and never again ventured from their end of the valley.

The winter turned out to be a long one—over twenty-five thousand years, in fact. When it at last ended and the ice sheets disappeared, only the Saps were left. One day Grog and Throg were exploring far from home near a place where the Neanderthals had once lived, when they came across a large rock standing beside a stream and bearing a row of crudely carved signs.

"What are they?" Grog asked as Throg peered curiously at the signs.

"They're Neanderthal," Throg said.

"Must be old. What do they say?"

Throg frowned with concentration as he ran a finger haltingly along the row.

"They're like the signs you find all over this part of the

valley," he announced at last. "They all say the same thing: OG, COME HOME. NAME YOUR PRICE."

Grog scratched his head and puzzled over the revelation for a while. "So what the hell was that supposed to mean?" he mused faintly.

"Search me. Must have had something to do with the guys who used to live in the caves behind that terrace up there. Only bears up there now though." Throg shrugged. "It might have had something to do with beans. They were always counting beans, but they were still lousy traders."

"Weirdos, huh? It could have meant anything then."

"Guess so. Anyhow, let's get moving."

They hoisted their spears back onto their shoulders and resumed picking their way through the rocks to follow the side of the stream onward and downward toward the river that glinted through the distant haze.

KNOW NUKES

Before the 1940s, the future confronting the human race was bleak. With the global population increasing and becoming ever more dependent on energy-dense technologies to sustain its food supplies and rising living standards, there seemed no escape from the catastrophe that would come eventually when the coal and the oil ran out. But few worried unduly. It was only after an escape from the nightmare presented itself—suddenly and unexpectedly, with the harnessing of nuclear power and the prospect of unlimited energy—that people began to worry. People can be very strange.

My own position on this subject is that nuclear power is cheaper, cleaner, and safer than any other source of energy that the human race has so far come up with. To see why, let's set to rest some of the myths that it has become fashionable to repeat, and consider the facts.

The first fact is that there cannot be an absolutely safe energy source. By definition, "energy" is the capacity to do physical work. Whether the results are considered beneficial or otherwise involves only a value judgment, hence, no energy technology can be risk-free. Attempting to judge the acceptability of any particular risk in isolation is meaningless.

Society must weigh it against the benefits obtained in return, and compare the result with those obtained with the alternatives.

Despite the hysterical media reactions to Three Mile Island and Chernobyl, nuclear power remains the least threatening to human life of all the major energy technologies. The energy yields of processes involving the atomic nucleus are orders of magnitude greater than anything attainable from rearrangements of the outer electron shells of atoms, which is the basis of all conventional chemical combustion. This means that nuclear fuels are enormously more concentrated, and far smaller quantities are needed. Over five thousand times as much coal, for example, has to be mined, transported, and processed as uranium to deliver the same amount of energy— two hundred trains per year, each consisting of over a hundred cars, for each one-thousand-megawatt plant, compared to a single carload of uranium oxide—which entails an enormous supporting network of heavy industries with all their attendant risks and hazards. Two to three hundred fatal accidents happen annually among U.S. coal miners alone, but like automobile accidents they occur in one's and two's spread through the year in different places, and remain largely invisible. Airplane crashes kill far fewer people than automobiles do, but when they happen they are sensationalized. In the Western world, nuclear power generation has never killed anybody.

Chernobyl didn't say anything new about nuclear engineering. A plant that is ineptly designed and recklessly operated can be dangerous, as is equally true of bridges, dams, high-rise buildings, or any other kind of heavy engineering. It did say something about a political and economic system run by an incompetent bureaucracy, in which the wishes and safety of the people don't figure into policy-making. It's difficult to see how the same kind of thing could occur in Western light-water reactors as some critics claim. The accident at Chernobyl was due to the graphite core of the reactor catching fire after the cooling system failed. Western models don't possess a graphite core—in fact such a basis for design was expressly rejected by the U.S. in 1950, precisely because of this risk. Furthermore, the cooling water in Western systems is *also* the "moderator," needed to keep the chain reaction going. Hence, if the coolant flow fails for any reason, the reaction automatically stops, leaving only the residual fission products in the fuel as sources of heat to be disposed of, which represents typically about 5 percent of the reactor's normal output. But with the design used at Chernobyl, where the graphite is the moderator, operation continues at full power if the cooling water fails. The two designs are about as comparable to each other as the *Hindenburg* and the Goodyear blimp. Saying that we should shut down our industry because of what happened at Chernobyl makes as much sense as calling for the dismantling of the U.S. farming system because the Soviets have made a mess of theirs.

The facts of Three Mile Island were that no one was killed, no one was hurt, and no member of the public was ever in the slightest danger. TMI did not bring us to the brink of a major catastrophe. Some bizarre circumstances occurred and there were operator errors in responding to them, which led to loss of coolant and damage to the core that included melting of some fuel. However, the safety systems responded in the way they were supposed to by shutting the system down. The outer layers of containment were never challenged, let alone breached, putting the conditions well within the worst-case design accident that the plant had been built to withstand. For some time there was speculation that an accumulation of hydrogen gas might explode. But this would have been simply a chemical detonation, certainly nothing of a thermonuclear nature as was suggested by the headline H-BLAST IMMINENT that appeared on at least one newspaper. It was established later that the hydrogen couldn't in fact have exploded since there was no oxygen present; but even if it had, the shock would have been comparable to that imparted by a handheld sledgehammer—hardly enough to damage a reactor-vessel with steel walls twelve inches thick. The engine block of a car absorbs more stress thousands of times per minute. And even if the vessel had cracked, any radioactive material released would still have had to get through a four-foot concrete shield and a steel containment shell outside that to reach the environment. Yes, some radioactive gas did fill the containment building and was subsequently vented to the outside. But the dire warnings of the tens of thousands of cancer deaths that we heard would follow as a consequence are ridiculous. The maximum increase in radiation dose that would have been experienced by somebody immediately above the plant was measured by EPA, HEW, and NRC as eight millirems at most in the course of several days; a routine dental X ray delivers twenty-five millirems in seconds. When a dam bursts, a drilling platform collapses, or a gas storage tank explodes, you don't get three days for the luxury of holding press conferences or to talk about evacuating. To me that makes nuclear—properly respected and implemented—a very benign and forgiving technology.

More people seem to be realizing at last that a nuclear power plant can't explode like an atom bomb. The mechanism that enables a bomb to detonate has to be built with extreme precision to work at all, and a power plant contains nothing comparable. And besides that, the uranium used in each is quite different. Natural uranium contains about 0.7 percent of the fissionable 235 isotope, which is enriched to more than 90 percent for bomb-grade material. For the slow release of energy required in power reactors, by contrast, the fuel is enriched only to 3.5 percent. It's simply not an explosive. A power plant is about as close to a bomb as a barrel of damp sawdust without a detonator.

So, what about a meltdown? Even if TMI wasn't one, couldn't next time be? Yes, it could. The chance has been estimated—using the same methods that have worked well in other areas of engineering, where there have been sufficient actual events to verify the procedures—to be about the same as the chance of a major city being hit by a meteorite one mile across. And even if it were to happen, the result wouldn't automatically be the major catastrophe that many people think. Computer simulations suggest that if the fuel did melt its way out of the reactor vessel, it would sputter about and solidify around the massive supporting structure rather than continue reacting and burrow its way down through the floor. For over twenty years the British have been testing an experimental reactor in an artificial cave in Scotland and subjecting it to every conceivable failure of the coolant and safety systems. In the end they switched everything off and sat back to see what happened. There was no meltdown, nothing very dramatic. The core quietly cooled itself down, and that was that.

But *what if* the computer simulations turn out to be flawed, and *what if* the the British experience was a fluke?

Then mightn't the core turn into a molten mass and go down through the floor? Yes, it might. And then what would happen? Nothing much. We'd have a lot of mess down a hole in the ground, which is probably the best place for it. But *what if* there was a water table near the surface? In that case we'd create a lot of radioactive steam, which would blow back up the hole into the containment building, which again would be the best place for it. But *what if* some kind of geological or structural failure caused it to come up outside the containment building?

Now we are beginning to see the kinds of improbability chains that have to be constructed to produce disaster scenarios for scaring the public with. Remembering the odds against any major core disintegration in the first place, then *if, on top of that,* there was a water table below the plant, and *if* the steam burst through the ground outside the building . . . it would most likely expand high into the sky and dissipate. But beyond that, *if* there happened to be an atmospheric thermal inversion to hold the cloud down near the ground, and *if* there was a wind blowing toward an urban area, and *if* the wind happened to be just strong enough to move the cloud without disrupting the inversion layer, then yes, you could end up killing a lot of people. The statistical predictions worked out at about 400 fatalities per meltdown—perhaps not as bad as you'd guess. And that's if we're talking about deaths that couldn't be attributed to the accident as such, but would materialize only as slight increases in the cancer rate in a large population, over many years, i.e., increasing an individual's risk from something like 20.5 percent to 21 percent. Since air pollution from coal burning is estimated to cause 10,000 deaths per year in the U.S., for nuclear power to be as dangerous would require a meltdown somewhere or other every two weeks.

But if we are talking about directly detectable deaths—from acute radiation sickness within a couple of months—it would take 500 meltdowns to kill one hundred people. On this basis, even having twenty-five meltdowns every year for 10,000 years would cause fewer deaths than automobiles do annually.

Very well, that puts major accidents more in perspective. But what about the hazards associated with normal operation?

What about the thing that has become a new fad phobia word: *radiation*?

Yes, it's true that even an unmelted-down nuke in proper working order releases some radiation into the environment. In the units used to measure radiation dosage, a person sitting on the boundary fence of a large plant for a year would soak up about a tenth of a millirem above what he'd get from the natural background anyway. An average year's TV-watching incurs ten times as much as this, and a coast-to-coast jet flight—because of the increased intensity of cosmic rays at altitude—fifty times as much in five or six hours.

In fact there's hardly anything in the environment that doesn't emit some radiation. The rocks under our feet, the air we breathe, everything we eat and drink, and even our body tissues all contain traces of radioactive elements, the dose from all of which adds up to several thousand times anything contributed by the nuclear industry. The emission from the granite that Grand Central Station is built from, for example, exceeds the permissible NRC limit for industry. Grand Central Station wouldn't get a license as a nuclear plant.

This is in no way meant to suggest that massive doses of radiation aren't dangerous. Napalm bombs and blast furnaces aren't very healthy, either, but it doesn't follow that heat in any amount is therefore harmful—you wouldn't last long at a temperature of absolute zero. The science of toxicology has long recognized the phenomenon of "hormesis"—in which substances that are lethal in high doses turn out to be actually beneficial in small doses, by stimulating the body's defense and repair mechanisms (all medicines become toxic at high enough doses). In his book *Hormesis With Ionizing Radiation*, Professor T.D. Luckey of the University of Missouri, an internationally recognized expert on the subject, lists twelve hundred references to experimental evidence accumulated on organisms of every description, supporting the contention that the effect is true of radiation as well.

Nevertheless, we're constantly hearing that any level of radiation is harmful, however small. A simple prediction from this hypothesis is that cancer rates in areas with higher backgrounds ought to be greater. But the fact is they're not. Colorado, for example, with double the average radiation, due mainly to altitude but also because of its soil composition, has a cancer rate only 68 percent the national average. The correlation remains negative (i.e., the higher the radiation background, the lower the cancer rate) across the country as a whole—with a spectacular −39 percent correlation coefficient. (Judging from their previous statistical manipulations, antinuclear groups wouldn't hesitate to use such a correlation to "prove" that radiation *prevents* cancer.)

And then, of course, there's the waste. Well, after the foregoing heresies about accidents and radiation, would it come as a complete surprise if I suggest that the *ease* of getting rid of the waste is one of nuclear power's major advantages? This is another consequence of its being so much more concentrated than conventional sources: because the amount of fuel required to release the same amount of energy is so much smaller, so is the amount of waste produced. And the waste that is produced isn't as hazardous as most people imagine. It's considerably less dangerous, in fact, than many other substances that are handled routinely in far greater quantities with far less care, which we accept as a matter of course.

Over 90 percent of the spent fuel that comes out of a power reactor can be reprocessed into new fuel and put back in (saving in a plant's typical forty-year lifetime the equivalent of four billion dollars worth of oil). Burning it up in this way is the most sensible thing to do with it, and the industry was designed on the assumption that this would be the case. What's left after reprocessing constitutes the "high-level" waste that needs to be disposed of. A large, one-thousand-megawatt power plant produces about one cubic yard of it—small enough to fit under a dining room table—in the course of a year's operation. A coal plant of equal capacity produced ten *tons* of waste per *minute*. (Most of the fuss we read about in the newspapers fails to distinguish between this and low-level waste, consisting of things like used gloves, boots, and tools, which present a negligible hazard.) A facility to reprocess spent fuel in the U.S. was commenced as a joint project by government and industry at Barnwell, South Carolina. But in early 1977 the Carter administration halted further work on Barnwell, essentially for political reasons, and at the same time cut the utilities off from the military reprocessing that had been handling domestic wastes safely for twenty years. Thus 100 percent of what comes out of reactors is having to be treated as if it were high-level waste, to be stored in ways that were never intended, and this is what gets all the publicity—a needlessly manufactured political problem, not a technical one. (The rest of the world is continuing to reprocess its spent fuel, regardless.)

We often hear about the "unsolved" problem of the wastes remaining radioactive for tens of thousands of years. Yes, it's true that high-level wastes contain fission products that have long half-lives—and then, so does garden soil. But these don't constitute a problem; they just provide big numbers to frighten people with. For obviously, if the energy release is spread over so long a time, the intensity of it can't be very great. Rusting iron has a long half-life; gunpowder has a short one. The main danger is from the *short*-lived isotopes, such as iodine 131 with a half-life of eight days. To allow these to burn up, the spent fuel is put into cooling ponds at the reactor site for six months prior to being shipped away for reprocessing.

What then? Well, the current proposal is to reduce the waste to a powder, fuse it into a high-stability glass, seal the glass in steel cannisters, and bury the cannisters in a concrete repository two thousand feet underground. And let's make no bones about the fact that we're talking about a significant concentration of gamma radiation that would have to be confined and handled with great care. If all the electricity generated in the U.S. were produced by nuclear power, the amount of high-level waste produced each year would be enough to kill ten billion people. Sounds scary, doesn't it? But we also produce enough barium to kill one hundred billion people, enough ammonia and hydrogen cyanide to kill six trillion, enough phosgene to kill twenty trillion, and enough chlorine to kill four hundred trillion. There's no doubt enough gasoline around, too, to kill us all several times over, and enough pills and drugs in family medicine closets. But we don't worry unduly, because there's no way in which the population will be evenly exposed to any of those substances—everyone isn't suddenly going to sit down and start eating them. And this is far more true of nuclear wastes, sealed deep underground.

Every foot of shielding rock reduces gamma radiation by

a factor of ten, which means that there's no hazard to anyone above ground from the waste that remains buried. What hazard there is comes from the risk of some of the waste finding its way inside somebody. To do this, it would have to escape from the repository and be ingested or inhaled. And let's not forget that the toxicity of nuclear wastes decays with time. After ten years of burial nuclear waste would be about as toxic as barium if it were ingested; if it were inhaled, it would be a tenth as toxic as ammonia, and a thousandth as toxic as chlorine. After a hundred years these figures fall to one ten-thousandth, one hundred-thousandth, and one ten-millionth respectively. Nature's biological waste-disposal program dumps a thousand million tons of ammonia into the atmosphere every year, and we use chlorine liberally to clean our bathtubs and swimming pools.

In a year a one-thousand-megawatt coal-fired plant produces 1.5 million tons of ash—thirty thousand truck loads—that contains large amounts of known carcinogens and toxins, and can be highly acidic or alkaline depending on the sulfur content of the coal burned. Getting rid of it is a stupendous task—a *real* waste-disposal problem—and it ends up being dumped in shallow landfills that are easily leached out by groundwater, or simply being piled up as mountains on any convenient site. And that's only the solid waste. In addition there is the waste that's disposed straight up the smokestack, which includes six hundred pounds of carbon dioxide and ten pounds of sulfur dioxide every *second*, and the same quantity of nitrogen oxides as 200,000 automobiles. Various studies have concluded that this is enough to cause twenty-five premature deaths and 60,000 cases of respiratory disease annually—*per plant!*

A one-thousand-megawatt nuke, by contrast, produces nothing in addition to its cubic yard of high-level waste, because there isn't any chemical combustion—no ash, no gases, no smokestack. Because of the compactness of nuclear processes, nuclear power constitutes the first major technology in history in which it has actually been possible to contain all the wastes produced and isolate them from the environment. The radioactive elements that exist naturally in rocks find their way into water supplies and foodstuffs far more easily than anything from inside the repository ever could. Uranium left to itself releases more radiation into the environment then if it were mined, fissioned inside reactors, and the wastes sealed up deep underground. Thus nuclear energy could be looked upon as a way of cleansing the environment of a lot of potentially harmful radiation, concentrating it in places where it can't harm anyone, and getting some useful work out of it in the process.

Professor Bernard L. Cohen of the University of Pittsburgh has produced a book, *Before It's Too Late,* which covers all aspects of nuclear-related risks in a very comprehensive, yet understandable manner, and compares them to other kinds of risk that we encounter daily. It turns out that if the U.S. were to go to all-nuclear electricity, the total increase in added health risk—covering everything from uranium mining to final disposal of the wastes—would be equivalent to raising the speed limit by six thousandths of one mile per hour. The risks eliminated would, of course, be far greater.

There have been a lot of suggestions that the spread of nuclear power will make available the resources and materials for politically unstable nations or terrorists to make bombs. The fact is, however, that to whatever degree such possibilities might exist in today's world, domestic nuclear power is irrelevant. Any group that has the determination and funds to make a bomb can do so, and whether or not they have access to civilian generating-technology has nothing to do with it. Expertise is available and can be bought for a price, and with laser separation techniques the materials to produce bomb-grade enriched U-235 exist in the rocks everywhere. There are at least half a dozen ways of producing weapons material that are cheaper, simpler, faster, and less hazardous than going through the enormous complications of trying to make it from new or spent power-plant fuel, which is totally unsuitable. Slowing the introduction of nuclear power among Third World nations does nothing to reduce potential weapons threats. It does, however, retard their economic development and perpetuate the differences in health and living standards which create the tensions that make such threats more likely. (It also delays the appearance of another ten Japans on the planet. Just a thought.)

As alternatives, fossil fuels and natural gas are more expensive—when prices aren't distorted by politics—and inferior in terms of health and safety. With solar, the big drawback that advocates overlook is its extreme diluteness. To get an idea of how dilute it is, consider a lump of coal needed to make one kilowatt-hour of electricity, which would weigh about a pound, and ask how long would sunlight have to shine on that piece of coal to deposit the same amount of energy. Well, its shadow—which represents the sunlight intercepted—would have an area of about fifteen square inches. In Arizona, the sun would have to shine on that area for one thousand hours to deliver one kilowatt-hour of energy, which at twelve hours of sunshine per day is almost three months. For the average location in the U.S., it would be twice that. But if we wanted to get one kilowatt-hour of electricity out of that sunbeam, then, at the 10 percent conversion efficiency typically attainable today, it would take *five years*—to get the same useful energy that a small piece of coal will yield in minutes! That's how concentrated the energy is in coal, and how dilute it is in sunshine.

The sun's shining for tens or hundreds of years on forests represents an enormous concentration of energy in time, all done by nature for free. And subsequent compaction by geological processes to form coal or oil adds another dimension of concentration in space, which man carries a stage farther by the activities of wood-gathering, mining, and transportation. Hydroelectric power is another example of extreme concentration. Solar energy evaporates billions of tons of water from the oceans, which then fall over huge areas of land and drain through natural systems of streams and rivers to strategic points suitable for dams. Again, most of the work, involving enormous concentrations both in time and space, and stupendous amounts of energy (one hurricane releases as much as one thousand hydrogen bombs) is done by nature for free.

I doubt if the people who talk glibly about attempting to match such feats artificially comprehend the scale of the engineering they're proposing. (It's ironic, too, that these tend to be the same people who spread alarm about irresponsible technologies and the risks of their growing beyond control. The engineers and scientists involved in the energy business understand how puny our human efforts really are, and appreciate all the help they can get.) For a one-thousand-megawatt solar-electric conversion plant, for example—the same size as I used to illustrate nuclear—we're talking about covering fifty to a hundred square miles with 35,000 tons of aluminum, two million tons of concrete, 7,500 tons of copper, 600,000 tons of steel, 75,000 tons of glass, and 1,500 tons of other metals such as chromium and titanium—one thousand times the materials needed to construct a comparable size nuclear plant. These materials are not cheap, and real estate isn't free. Neither is the labor to keep miles of collector area clean. Moreover, these materials are all products of heavy, energy-hungry industries—to the degree that many studies have concluded that building solar plants would produce a net energy loss—and produce large amounts of waste, roughly 10 percent of which is highly toxic. So much for "free" and "clean" solar power.

When a power engineer talks about a one-thousand-megawatt plant, he means one that can deliver a thousand megawatts on demand, anytime, day or night. A nuclear plant can do this; so can a conventional fossil-fuel plant. But a solar plant can only operate when the sun is shining, which straightaway gives it a maximum availability of 50 percent—low enough for a regular plant to be considered prohibitively uneconomical. And then cloudy weather would reduce it below that optimum (I live in northern California, and counted over ten weeks of continual rain one winter). Hence, a solar plant would require some kind of energy storage system, such as pumping water up to a high reservoir, which would be allowed to flow back down to drive turbine generators in the nonproductive periods. At present there is no really satisfactory way of storing large amounts of electrical energy. Futhermore, if we use the industry's standard criterion, a practicable system would need to be capable of recharging at five times the plant's nominal rating. This means that for a "one-thousand-megawatt" solar plant to mean the same as it means for other kinds of plants, it would actually have to have a peak generating capacity of six thousand megawatts, adding vastly more to cost, complexity, and adverse environmental effects.

Decentralizing by putting solar panels on everybody's roofs wouldn't reduce the cost or the amount of materials used, either, but simply spread them out more thinly. In fact, it would require more, for the same reason that McDonald's uses less oil to cook two tons of french fries than eight thousand housewives who fry half a pound each. The storage problem wouldn't go away, either, but would become each household's own responsibility. In a battery just big enough to start a car, gases can accumulate that one spark can cause to explode, sometimes with lethal consequences, as some unfortunates have discovered when using jumper leads carelessly. Imagine the hazard that a basement full of batteries the size of grand pianos would present, which a genuinely all-solar home would need to get it through a bad spell in, say, Minnesota in January. Who would do the maintenance and keep the acid levels topped up? And then there would be the problem of keeping the panels free from snow and wet leaves—not in the summer months, but when the roofs are slippery and frozen. Even today, the second biggest cause of accidental deaths in the country, after automobiles, is falls. If we build all those houses with skating rinks on the roofs and bombs in the basements, we'd better build a lot more hospitals and emergency rooms, too, while we're at it.

I'm certainly in favor of developing outer space, but for the right reasons. The idea of solar-power satellites has never struck me as one of them. The intensity of solar radiation outside the atmosphere is about six times greater than on the ground, which isn't a lot, really. I don't see how it could justify the huge cost of putting all that technology in orbit (ten thousand shuttle launches to build a satellite capable of powering New York City, by one estimate I've seen—and that excludes the ground equipment) to reconcentrate energy diluted by ninety-three million miles worth of the inverse square law, when we can produce it at the sun's original density right here.

Now, all this isn't to say that solar doesn't have its uses. It does, and it can be beneficial in remote places far from a power grid. And if somebody who happens to live in the right kind of place finds it a worthwhile way to shave a few dollars from his utility bill, there's nothing wrong with that. But it would be a mistake to imagine that the problem is simply a domestic one of keeping the dining room at 75°F and warming the bath water. The real issue is of running the aluminum smelters, steel mills, fertilizer plants, factories, and transportation systems that keep a modern, industrial society functioning. Solar will never make a significant contribution here (which is why people who don't *want* a modern, industrial society are so much in favor of it, and would like everything else to be forcibly shut down). This is where nuclear energy really emerges in a class of its own—not just as the best way of meeting energy needs today, but as the pointer toward doing all kinds of things in much better ways tomorrow.

Some people argue that we don't need nuclear power because we already have other ways to generate electricity. This is rather like somebody in an earlier century telling Faraday that we didn't need electricity because we already had other ways to heat water. But what made electricity so important, of course, was its ability to do things that were totally unprecedented—things unachievable to any degree by existing technologies. Our entire science of electrical engineering and electronics is the result. A similar relationship holds with the ability to manipulate nuclear processes. Our present use of nuclear energy—as a replacement for conventional heat sources to generate electricity by steam turbines—represents merely a tiny first step into a whole new, qualitatively different realm of capability.

From unaided muscle power through to rocket engines and generating plants, the evolution of civilization has reflected the harnessing of progressively more concentrated energy sources. The true significance of nuclear technology in the twentieth century is that it points to the next step in the process, opening up the prospect of entirely new processing methods that will obsolete most of today's cumbersome and polluting industries, much in the same way that the introduction of electricity revolutionized the coal-based methods of the nineteenth century. For example, at the hundred-million-degree temperatures of a nuclear plasma, all atoms are stripped of their electrons and become raw, highly charged nuclei, which means they can be manipulated simply and cheaply by magnetic fields. This gives us a method for economically extracting the trace elements that exist in all forms of rock, desert sand, seawater, and construction debris, without requiring geologically concentrated ores to make it worthwhile and hence replacing all of our existing primary metals industries. Also, we have a total recycling method for all forms of waste.

Or consider the chemicals industry. The conventional way of combining reactants into new products is to brew them together in big vats, usually under heat to supply the reaction energy. Heat energy, however, is broadband—it exists over a wide range of wavelengths. This means that energy is available at favorable wavelengths for many different reactions among the molecules involved, and therefore a variety of compounds will be formed. The typical result of this is that only a fraction of the reactants actually go to form the product that was desired, which raises its cost, and the marketing department tries to find profitable applications for the sludge left over. But in laboratories, lasers are now being used to drive chemical reactions with narrowband energy, at just the absorption wavelength of the molecule required. The result is that all of the reactants involved form useful products, and processes that conventionally need hours, days, or even weeks now take place in milliseconds. Recombining reactants from a tuned plasma state offers the same possibilities on an industrial scale.

Cheap, high-temperature process heat opens the way to new sources of raw materials, and a means of desalinating seawater inexpensively to irrigate enormous areas of currently useless land. Furthermore, at nuclear plasma temperatures seawater cracks thermally into its constituent atoms, providing a potentially unlimited supply of hydrogen as a base for a whole range of synthetic liquid fuels to replace gasoline. And finally, there's the prospect of putting a permanent end to all materials-shortage problems by transmuting elements on a bulk scale. All atoms can be broken down into protons, and the protons built up again into whatever we want—a whole new science of structure-building that stands to nuclei as chemistry today stands to molecules. Eventually, we'll make our materials the way nature does in the stars, with unlimited energy as a by-product. And when we've developed such technologies here on Earth we can ship them up into orbit and to the Moon, and that's how we'll build our colonies and starships.

And here, I think, we at last touch upon what the current controversy is really all about. The opposition movement doesn't reflect so much an attitude against nuclear power per se, as against the whole notion of continuing worldwide industrial growth and technological progress, and against the energy sources, economic principles, and political institutions that make those things possible. It represents an essentially Malthusian ideology that sees a planet with finite resources straining to support an exponentially increasing population until either nature imposes limits through its traditional agencies of famine, disease, and war, or we impose artificial ones by curtailing growth, and accept simpler lifestyles. Anything else will simply produce more people than we can support comfortably, and hasten the day when everything runs out.

Beneath the camouflage, this really aims at preserving the privileges enjoyed by the world's "haves." In any period of history, a society's total wealth—its economy—depends on the level of technology available to support it. No previous economy has ever been able to support more than a privileged minority at reasonable standards of comfort and affluence: either a few privileged families, later an entire class, and in recent times a minority of privileged nations. When a privileged group entrenches itself, two things tend to happen: one, a rationale is constructed, based on religion or some other belief system, to justify the existing social order and induce the masses to accept their inferior lot, e.g., by promising that they'll get theirs in some hereafter; and two, good reasons are found why the progress that has enabled the privileged to get where they are has gone far enough and should be halted right now, before any more from lower down the pyramid move up to crowd the limited space at the top. Today we see it as Malthusianism: "finite resources" are the reason why everyone can't be rich, and the inevitability of "limits to growth" means that global industrialization will have to plateau out at its present level. Imposed worldwide, such an ideology would deny hundreds of millions of human beings any chance to enjoy decent standards of health, education, and comfort, or the opportunity to live rewarding, productive lives. Instead they would be forcibly kept at a subsistence level of existence . . . or worse. It is estimated that holding back the introduction of nuclear technologies to the Third World has already caused more deaths than the Nazis were responsible for during their entire regime—including all the casualties of World War II. Malthus would say it's just as well, since those people would have lived miserable lives anyway—and besides, we don't have the resources to change anything, which in any case are getting smaller. I say we do have the resources, and they're getting bigger.

To apply the observed population dynamics of animal species to human societies is to deny the qualities that set us apart. Unlike animals, who simply consume resources and react to circumstances with fixed behavior patterns, human beings are capable of creating new resources and adapting their behavior to the new conditions that they bring about. In primitive, labor-intensive, rural societies, with no life insurance, social security, retirement pensions, or machines to do the work, having big families to ensure that at least one or two of the children survive to adulthood to provide for one's old age makes sound economic sense. When long-established customs like this persist for a while alongside industrialization and rising living standards, of course the population is going to increase. It happened in Europe in the eighteenth century, in America in the nineteenth, and now it's happening in the developing nations of the Third World. It's a sign that things are getting better, not worse. Since World War II, improved health and diet have caused a significant increase in the average height of Japanese children. But obviously it would be ridiculous to infer from this by simple extrapolation that a hundred years from now they'll be as tall as skyscrapers. The average height is adjusting to a new equilibrium with changed conditions. It's the same with populations. Our experiences with such advanced societies as those of North America and Western Europe show that when human populations reach sufficiently high levels of well-being and security, attitudes, values, and lifestyles change, and they become self-limiting in numbers in ways that Malthus never dreamed of.

Periodically, the process of evolution passes through abrupt phase changes comparable to the ones in physics that govern the transitions between solid, liquid, and gas, in which completely new laws come into play and the old limits cease to mean anything. A qualitatively distinct realm opens up, with new resources available suddenly, which are not simple extrapolations of what went before. Usually this results when a revolutionary ability of some kind—a new technology—emerges. Thus, the earliest self-replicating molecules depended on the supply of abiotically produced organic compounds washed down off the land into a few favored environments, and we can imagine some primordial, microscopic Malthus concluding gloomily that life would forever be restricted to thin strips of coastal shallows and tidal pools. But that doomsday prophesy collapsed when the blue-green algae invented the chlorophyll molecule and set up the photosynthesis industry, opening up the entire surface of the oceans as a planet-wide biomass factory. Sexual reproduction and DNA, the patenting of hemoglobin and harnessing of oxygen as a higher-power energy source, all represented breakthroughs into new realms of capability, and eventually the development of the first functioning spacesuit in the form of the amphibian egg paved the way for migration into and colonizing of a completely new, initially hostile environment.

What these examples illustrate is that *new technologies create new resources*—and always on a scale dwarfing everything that went before. Human civilization is a continuation of the same evolutionary process, operating at the level of applied intelligence. And the same principle applies, in which new technologies create new resources—for a resource is not a resource and can create no wealth until the knowledge and the means exist for using it. The harnessing of steam, the application of electricity, and the exploitation of oil all opened up eras of wealth creation that were as qualitatively distinct from each other as they were from the economies based on wind, water, and muscle power of the Middle Ages. By the yardsticks that matter, the average Englishman of today enjoys a better standard of living than Queen Victoria did, and most Americans are millionaires by the measures of a century ago. And all the world's peoples want to be living that way a century from now. They could be, too. But when the demand is translated into energy needs—no less than providing a globally stabilized population of, say, ten billion, with energy per person at a rate probably greater than that of the U.S. today— the amount needed is utterly beyond any approaches that are merely variations of what we have. Only a breakthrough into the next realm of energy control could do it. The nuclear-based technologies that we are just glimpsing, with yields and densities orders of magnitude greater than anything attainable from conventional sources, represent such a break-through. The so-called alternatives do not.

The tiny pockets of energy that happen to be, fortu-itously, trapped around the surface of this planet are merely our starting capital for launching the business. As with any business, it would be silly to suppose that we have to exist on our starting capital forever. The capital must be invested to create the earnings that will enable the business to grow and pay its way as its bills get bigger. Just as the wealth of today's Western world is the payoff from yesterday's invest-ments in coal and steam, so a portion of the return must be invested to provide the global payoff that will be tomorrow's nuclear economy—an economy capable for the first time ever of enabling every child born on the planet to grow up with the expectation of a healthy body and an educated mind, and with the freedom to pursue the opportunity to become the most that he or she is capable of.

So, can we make nuclear energy work, safely, cleanly, and efficiently? Sure we can. When we take a long, hard look at the alternatives, we see that we have to. Fortunately for all of us, the Neanderthals who discovered fire saw things the same way.

ALL IN A NAME

There really is no excuse for some of the nonsense dispensed to the public by the mass media on subjects such as nuclear power. Oscar Wilde once said that, its failings notwithstanding, there is much to be said in favor of journalism in that "by giving us the opinion of the uneducated, it keeps us in touch with the ignorance of the community."

Perhaps we would have avoided today's (temporary) hysteria over nuclear power if we had stuck to the precedent that we set when we named the first of the artificial transuranic elements "plutonium." Instead of being carried away with highfalutin names like "californium," "berkelium," and "mendelevium" for the ones that came after, we should have continued in the way we'd begun and called them "mickey-mouseium," "donald-duckium," and so on. I mean, with that kind of nomenclature, who couldn't have loved nuclear power?

Does this mean that the Chernobyl reactor was fueled with goofium?

DOWN TO EARTH

It has always been taught that Sir Isaac Newton was born in the same year that Galileo died, 1642. However, certain documents and diaries recently unearthed in Pisa have revealed not only that the two scientists were contemporaries, but that they actually met. This occurred during a summer vacation that Newton spent touring Italy. The find also shows how Newton's universal law of gravitation was derived from Galileo's studies of falling bodies, and explains the legend of the apple. As far as can be reconstructed, it all went something like this.

Scene

A warm sunny day in Pisa. The Leaning Tower stands midstage, surrounded by the town plaza. The door at the base faces the audience. As the CURTAIN *rises, Galileo, dressed in the traditional manner of the medieval Italian professional class, is sitting in the top gallery of the tower, eating his lunch. Beside him on the balustrade is a flagon of Chianti. On his other side is a wooden lunch box and next to it, a bag of apples. Near him on the top story of the tower, is a pile of bricks and rubble left by construction workers. The moon is visible in the sky near the top of the tower. Galileo selects one of the apples, but as he is about to take a bite, he stops and examines it.*

GALILEO Oh-oh. Eesa not so good, this one. (*He pulls a face and tosses the apple nonchalantly over his shoulder, but in the same movement inadvertently knocks the lunch box off the balustrade so that both objects fall together out of sight to the rear. A moment later an indignant shout comes from backstage.*)

NEWTON Gadzooks!

GALILEO (*turning and peering down*) Santa Maria! Was accidente. Scusate!

Newton enters from behind the tower. He is wearing an English gentleman's outfit of blue velvet coat with lace ruffs, white breeches, and silk stockings, and he is carrying a cane. He appears, smoothing a dent from his three-cornered hat.

NEWTON (*muttering*) That travel agent shall hear of this. 'Tis not safe to walk abroad by day in these parts. (*He puts his hat back on his head, looks up, and shouts toward the top of the tower.*) And what, sir, is the meaning of this outrage? Thou art a menace to decent, God-fearing citizens. What hast thou to say for thyself?

GALILEO (*shouting back*) I already said, was accidente. Ees not expected for people to be out there in midday sun. You Engleesh?

NEWTON I do have that distinct honor.

GALILEO You okay?

NEWTON It's hardly any thanks to you if I am. Had the luncheon box not fallen a matter of mere seconds after the apple was despatched—as was evidently the case—me brains would have been done in as well as me feather. A negligence suit would have been incontestable, and I can assure you that the sum involved would not have been a trifling one.

GALILEO *(curiously)* Why you so sure that box falla after apple, eh?

NEWTON A matter of observation and simple logic, my good man. Both objects arrived at the same instant. It is common knowledge, is it not, that in falling, a heavier body will acquire a greater velocity than a lighter one. The box was clearly heavier than the apple. Therefore one is obliged to conclude that it commenced its descent later.

GALILEO Well, ees not so, see. Both falla from 'ere at same time. I am up 'ere. I see.

NEWTON *(sighs)* That's quite absurd. I have no doubt whatsoever that the two trajectories terminated simultaneously, which contradicts your assertion. Obviously your recollection has been distorted by preconceived notions or a subjective error.

GALILEO Ees not so, Engleesh. I know what I see. Maybe itsa your observations that not so wonderful.

NEWTON *(to himself)* Hrrmph! What an extraordinary suggestion. *(He resumes shouting.)* Very well. We'll see about that. Kindly repeat the experiment, and this time watch closely.

GALILEO No, you watch. *(He takes another apple and picks a brick from the pile of rubble, then leans out over the parapet.)* You ready?

NEWTON *(backing to a safe distance)* Proceed.

Galileo releases the brick and the apple together. They fall and land at the same time. Newton stares in amazement.)

NEWTON 'Pon me soul, the fellow's right! This is indeed a more intriguing business than I had given mind to pondering before. *(He looks up.)* Perforce I must retract my words. It seems I owe you an apology, sir.

GALILEO Grazie.

NEWTON Do it again.

GALILEO Certamente.

Galileo continues dropping pairs of apples and bricks from the top of the tower. While this is going on, various people enter from left and right. Some exit again, shaking their heads, while others stay to watch. Eventually the stage around the foot of the tower is littered with apples and bricks, and a crowd of curious bystanders has gathered behind Newton. Oblivious to them, Newton looks up once more, and as he does so, he sees the moon above the tower. He straightens up slowly, staring at it.

GALILEO Whatsa matter now down there?

NEWTON (*after a pause*) I have a conundrum to exercise your wits, sir. Consider as an hypothesis that the tower were constructed as high as the moon itself. That condition satisfied, and given that the apple and brick were released without imparted momentum, would they plunge to the ground in the manner we have been observing, or would they remain suspended as does the moon? If the former, then why, pray, does the moon itself fail to obey that same compulsion? And if the latter, what form of agency would preserve them in seeming in defiance of the nature of all objects to fall to the earth? Well, sir, answer me that.

GALILEO You losta me somewhere. Say again.

NEWTON (*muttering*) Oh, God help us. (*In a louder voice*) Would they stay up? If so, why? If not, what keeps the moon up?

Galileo looks up at the sky and scratches his head. After a moment or two he looks down again.

GALILEO I gotta one for you. Ask question other way round. Moon goes around Earth like stone on string, yes? So, where ees string? Why Moon not go off on straight line?—not, why doesn't eet fall down?

NEWTON (*to himself*) Egad, a conundrum for a conundrum. Would not the apple and the brick participate also in the tendency to be propelled tangentially? Methinks we have the elements of a contradiction.

GALILEO One force up, one force down. Both forces same, so notheeng moves—just like moon. Ees okay, no?

NEWTON (*thinks, then shakes his head and shouts back*) The outward force on the apple and the brick would differ by virtue of their different masses. How, then, assuming equality of angular velocity, could equilibrium be preserved for both?

GALILEO Ees okay eef downward forces different too. Brick ees 'eavy, apple not so 'eavy.

NEWTON Hmm, were that true, then the masses would tend to cancel. All objects would describe similar trajectories . . . Aha! And that would imply that all bodies would experience equal acceleration towards the ground.

GALILEO Which ees what I 'ave been saying. Everytheeng 'its ground at same time. Makesa no difference. What you theenk we just been looking at?

Newton stands thinking to himself. For the first time, the sound of the wind becomes audible in the background.

NEWTON This could be a matter of some considerable import unless I'm not mistaken. Does there exist, I wonder, some method of formulation whereby these astounding truths might be reduced to some lawful mathematick? (*He calls up again toward the top of the tower.*) I say, how view you the possibility that these principles might be committed to some system of orderly symbolic brevity? (*aside*) I'm dammed if I can understand anything written in this wretched olde worlde English meself.

GALILEO Ees getting windy up 'ere. What you say?

NEWTON (*cupping a hand to his mouth*) I said, perhaps we should essay the construction of a precise formulation of these discoveries. Might I suggest that we repair forthwith to an alehouse—provided such establishments be not unknown in these latitudes—in search of more congenial surroundings, suitably conducive to discussion. What sayest thou to that?

GALILEO (*as the sound of the wind rises*) Eh?

NEWTON Oh damnation! (*He draws a deep breath and cups both hands to his mouth.*) How can we put this into numbers? Are there any pubs near here? . . . Pubs— vino, or whatever? . . . Sit down and talk.

GALILEO (*nodding vigorously*) Ah, si. (*He gestures toward the far side of the plaza*) There am one or two over de square. One meenute. I come down. (*He disappears from sight.*)

Newton stands frowning to himself while he waits.

NEWTON What did that fellow say? It sounded like m-one m-two over d squared . . . (*He gazes down at the objects strewn around the foot of the tower and rolls one of the apples absently with his foot. Suddenly he gasps.*) Good grief, that's it! Why, the man must truly be a genius!

Galileo appears from the tower door. He points offstage and begins walking to the right. Newton remains transfixed. After a few paces Galileo stops and looks back.

GALILEO Why you standa like that, Engleesh? I thought you wanna talk somewhere.

NEWTON (*disbelievingly*) My dear fellow . . . An insight of sheer brilliance! I am overcome with respect, and I must confess, not a little humbled.

GALILEO What you talkeeng about?

NEWTON You mean . . . (*His expression changes at once.*) What exactly did you say up there?

GALILEO I said there are a couple of pubs over de square. Ees what you ask, no? (*He waits impatiently as Newton produces a notebook and begins scribbling furiously.*) What you doeeing now?

NEWTON (*breezily*) Oh, merely a few purchases that I was reminded of, which I would not wish to escape my mind. (*He stuffs the notebook back in his pocket, straightens his hat, and takes a tighter grip on his cane.*) There, that should suffice. Now, where were we? Ah yes, to a tavern. Very good. Lead on, my dear fellow. Lead on.

Black-out. They exit right.

CURTAIN

MERRY GRAVMAS

It is a fact that Sir Isaac Newton was born on December 25 (in 1642). I mentioned this one evening when Jackie and I were with a group of friends in a Sonora bar. After some debate, we decided that the date is too much to be a coincidence: Providence is trying to tell us something.

We finally agreed that the time has come for a change. We're all part of Western scientific civilization, after all, and things have been dominated for too long by traditions rooted in ancient Palestinian mysticism. In future, therefore, we have decided that as far as we are concerned, the customary holiday season celebrates the birthday of the intellectual founder of mathematical, analytical method. Further, to commemorate the formulation of his famous universal law, the name of the feast shall be changed from "Christmas" to "Gravitational mass," or, more simply, "Gravmas."

Who knows?—the whole thing could spread like wild-fire. Two thousand years from now, it might form the basis for the philosophy and worldview of a whole, new global culture, which by that time may revolve around a dominant race of supertech, spacegoing Chinese. . . .

*   *   *

"Is that you, Li?" Cheng Xiang called, looking up from the notescreen propped against his knee. He had been amusing himself with a few tensor integrals to clear his mind before taking his morning coffee.

The sounds of movement came again from upstairs. Moments later, his ten-year-old son appeared, floating down the staircase on an anti-g disk. "Good morning, father."

"Merry Gravmas."

"And to you." Li hopped off the disk and stood admiring the decorations that the family robot had put up overnight. There were paper chains hanging in hyperbolic catenary curves and sinusoids, Gaussian distribution bells, and pendulums wreathed in logarithmic spirals. In the corner opposite the total-sensory cassette player, there stood a miniature apple tree with binary stars on top, a heap of gaily wrapped gifts around its base, and its branches adorned with colored masses of various shapes, a string of pulsing plasma glows, and striped candies shaped like integral signs. "It looks nice," Li said, eyeing the presents. "I wonder what Santa Roid has brought this year."

"You'll have to wait until your brother and sister get here before you can open anything," Xiang told him. "What are they doing?"

"Yu is sending off a last-minute Gravmas present to a schoolfriend over the matter transmitter to Jupiter. Yixuan is helping Mother program the autochef to cook the turkey."

"Why does everyone in this family always have to leave everything until the last minute?" Xiang grumbled, setting down the screen and getting up. "Anyone would think it wasn't obvious that the ease of getting things done varies inversely as the square of procrastination."

Li walked over to the window and gazed out at Peking's soaring panorama of towers, bridges, terraces, and arches, extending away all around, above, and for hundreds of meters below. "How did Gravmas start?" he asked his father.

"Hmph!" Xiang snorted as he moved to stand alongside the boy. "Now isn't that typical of young people today. Too wrapped up in relativistic quantum chromodynamics and multidimensional function spaces to know anything about where it came from or what it means. It's this newfangled liberal education that's to blame. They don't teach natural philoso-phy any more, the way we had to learn it.''

"Well, that kind of thing does seem a bit quaint these days," Li said. "I suppose it's okay for little old ladies and people who—"

"They don't even recite the laws of motion in school every morning. Standards aren't what they used to be. It'll mean the end of civilization, you mark my words."

"You were going to tell me about Gravmas . . ."

"Oh, yes. Well, I presume you've heard of Newton?"

"Of course. A newton is the force which, acting on a mass of one kilogram, produces an acceleration of one meter per second per second."

"Not *a* newton. *The* Newton. You didn't know that Newton was somebody's name?"

"You mean it was a person?"

Xiang sighed. "My word. You see—you don't know anything. Yes, Newton was the messiah who lived two thou-sand years ago, who came to save us all from irrationality. Today is his birthday."

Li looked impressed. "Say, what do you know! Where did this happen?"

"In a quasi-stable, in a little town called Cambridge, which was somewhere in Britain."

"That's in Europe, isn't it?" Li said.

"Oh, so you do know something."

"My friend Shao was in Europe last year," Li went on distantly. "His parents took him on a trip there to see the ruins. He said it was very dirty everywhere, with the streets full of beggars. And you can't drink the water. It sounds like a strange place for a civilization like ours to have started from."

"Strange things happen. . . ." Xiang thought for a while. "Actually, according to legend, it didn't really start there."

"What?"

"Gravmas."

"How do you mean?"

"Supposedly it was already a holiday that some ancient Western barbarian culture celebrated before then, and we stole it. It was easier to let people carry on with the customs they'd grown used to, you see. . . . At least, that's how the story goes.''

"I wonder what the barbarian culture was like," Li mused.

"Nobody's quite sure," Xiang said. "But from the fragments that have been put together, it seems to have had something to do with worshiping crosses and fishes, eating holly, and building pyramids. It was all such a long time ago now that—"

"Look!" Li interrupted, pointing excitedly. Outside the window, a levitation platform was rising into view, bearing several dozen happy-looking, colorfully dressed people with musical instruments. The strains of amplified voices floated in from outside. "Carol singers!" Li exclaimed.

Xiang smiled and spoke a command for the household communications controller to relay his voice to the outside. "Good morning!" it boomed from above the window as the platform came level.

The people on board saw the figures in the window and waved. "Merry Gravmas," a voice replied.

"Merry Gravmas to you," Xiang returned.

"May the Force be proportional to your acceleration."

"Are you going to sing us a carol?" Xiang inquired.

"But of course. Do you have a request?"

"No, I'll leave it to you."

"Very well."

There was an introductory bar, and then,

> *"We three laws of orbiting are,*
> *Ruling trajectories local and far.*
> *Collisions billiard,*
> *Particles myriad,*
> *Planet and moon and star.*
> *O-ooo . . ."*

KNOWLEDGE IS A
MIND-ALTERING DRUG

I sometimes suspect that one of the reason writers write is that it gives them an excuse to do the research. In an age when people are constantly being urged to be goal-oriented and efficiency-conscious, and get sent by their firms to seminars to learn how to manage their time, it's easy to develop a guilt complex over reading anything other than a company procedure manual. But I find the most enjoyable reading is that which is purely for fun or out of curiosity—with no conceivable relevance to making money, furthering one's career, or with any other such redeeming quality whatsoever. One solution to any residual guilt from company indoctrination is to be a writer. Then it becomes possible to relax and enjoy whatever one pleases, rationalizing it by the thought that "Who knows? I might need it for a book one day."

I remember once, when I was in my teens, a friend accused me of never being bored by anything—which can be an unforgivable aberration among teenagers. I had never thought about that, but it seemed worth investigating. I resolved, therefore, that to test the allegation, I would force myself to read for one hour on the dullest subject I could think of. I couldn't think of anything that sounded more dull than Greek architecture, and so, when I was next in the public library, I took down a couple of formidable-looking tomes on the subject and steeled myself. It turned out to be fascinating, and I ended up staying until closing time.

It's easy to get carried away, sometimes. *Voyage From Yesteryear* featured a huge, fusion-powered spacecraft, with a population of tens of thousands, that traveled to Alpha Centauri, the nearest star to us. The entire structure rotated to simulate gravity, and at one point I was writing a part of the story that included a conversation between a boy who was born during the voyage, with no experience of planetary gravity, and his father, who grew up on Earth. To the boy it was self-evident that a thrown baseball moves in a straight line, and the hand of the catcher is carried in a curve by the spin of the ship to intercept it; but the notion of something going up, reversing, and coming down again made no intuitive sense at all. Then, having written that much, I found it difficult to convince myself that a baseball trajectory as seen by somebody on the inside of a spinning structure *would* look like the curve of one thrown up from the ground on Earth. I spend a whole week deriving from first principles a set of equations to transform curves from fixed to rotating coordinates and drawing graphs of the results—the simulation of "real" gravity turned out to be surprisingly close. Then, of course, I had to write the procedure into computer programs "in case I need to do it again some day" (I never have). That took another week. And after all that, when I finally edited the draft, I deleted the paragraphs in which the conversation took place, because by that time it didn't seem so important.

The Proteus Operation required a lot of research into modern history and World War II, the beginnings of nuclear physics and the Manhattan Project, and on the biographies of the several real-life people who appeared in the story. There was a six-month gap between my writing the prologue and Chapter One—a result of getting carried away again.

When I was writing *Inherit the Stars* back in England, I received a lot of help with background material from my customers. One of them was a physicist at Sheffield University, called Dr. Grenville Turner, who used one of our computers to analyze moonrock samples from the Apollo missions.

On one occasion, while we were eating lunch on the campus lawns, I mentioned the idea of having the moon captured by the earth, as is described in the book. Gren though for a while as he munched a sandwich, and then said suddenly, "You're dead! It won't work."

"Why not?" I asked him.

"Stromatolites."

"Never heard of them."

Stromatolites turned out to be a kind of fossil coral found in Australia that preserves records of the tides from hundreds of millions of years ago. Stromatolites show that lunar tides have existed since the beginnings of Earth's history, and therefore the moon couldn't have arrived comparatively recently in the way the book said. I eventually managed to fudge that around in such a way that it actually became supporting evidence for the capture theory, but the reason I mention it here is that it led me off into a new line of research on the ancient Earth and the processes that have shaped it into what it is today. I believe that much of this kind of thing is taught in schools these days, but it was all new and fascinating to me, because, as you may recall, the curriculum that I took hadn't been updated since the days of King James the whichever. Some other readers may not have met this in school, either. So, for them—or maybe anyone interested in finding out if they can be bored, if it sounds like that kind of subject; but they may get a surprise—here is a distillation from the notes I compiled. They're not doing anyone much good in the bottom of my filing cabinet.

EARTH MODELS—ON
A PLATE

What do the coastlines of South America and Africa, an Australian aborigine's fireplace, and earthquakes have to do with the world's oldest magnetic tape recorder?

The answer to this question provides a good example of how science works, following up every clue, fitting together scraps of seemingly unrelated information, and sometimes turning conventional wisdoms around completely in order to arrive at the right question. It also provides a fascinating insight into some of the processes that have shaped the world on which we live.

The story begins back in the days when it first became possible to construct accurate maps. People began noticing the similarity in shape between the coastlines of South America and Africa, and couldn't avoid the feeling that the pieces "ought," somehow, to fit together. The first recorded thought of this kind was voiced by the English philosopher and scientist, Francis Bacon, in 1620. This soon led the more curious among mankind—which of course includes just about every scientist—to ask, "Were South America and Africa ever joined together?" and, "If they were, why aren't they now?"

A clear answer to the first question required a precise definition, expressible in numbers in the way scientists like, of just what, "joined together" means. The problem is that the coastlines that happen to exist today aren't really the thing to go by. As a glance at any physical map will show, coastlines are fairly arbitrary and can change beyond recognition with even minor variations in sea level. If all the ice in the Earth's polar caps and glaciers were to melt, sea level would rise by about two hundred feet, and the large areas that we find plastered with fossil remains of shallow-water animals and plants on what today is dry land testify that this has indeed happened on numerous occasions. Conversely, estimates of the amount of ice that must have existed during the recent Pleistocene ice age suggest that sea level then must have been seven hundred feet lower than today. Hence, we need a more meaningful boundary than contemporary coastlincs to define the continents.

For the most part, continents are surprisingly flat on top—which is why small changes in sea level can make such big differences to coastlines—and slope gently out into the oceans to the edge of the continental shelf, which off New York, for example, lies about five hundred feet deep and one hundred miles into the Atlantic. Beyond the shelf, the seabed falls steeply and levels out again at an average depth of ten thousand feet to become the floor of the deep-ocean basins. Somewhere down this "continental slope," therefore, lies the "true" edge of what constitutes a continent.

A number of best-fit-by-eye attempts were made to match South America and Africa at various depths, and although yielding similar results, they all rested ultimately on the somewhat vague assertion that "it looks about right," which lacks testable precision and is the kind of thing guaranteed to make scientists uncomfortable. So, in 1955, Sir Edwin Bullard, professor of geophysics at the University of Cambridge, and a research student called Everett, developed a computer program that would calculate a best fit as the solution that gave the minimum area of gaps and overlaps between two corresponding contours anywhere down the continental slopes. The fit that finally met this criterion occurred at the five-hundred fathom (three-thousand-foot) contour, at which depth the average misfit was between fifty and sixty miles. Three small overlap areas occurred: one where the northeast corner of Brazil intruded upon the projecting area of the river Niger, and two submerged areas that lay farther south. All in all, the result was considered excellent. To achieve this fit, South America needed to be rotated through an angle of 57 degrees about the point on the earth's surface at latitude 40 degrees north, longitude 30.6 degrees west, which is in the Atlantic, close to the western Azores. Try it on a map and see.

What this says is that at this depth the continents match in a way that seems too close to be explained away by coincidence. The operative word here, however, is "seems"—coincidences do happen. To elevate the idea above pure speculation, we need some corroborating evidence. The problem is similar to that of deciding if the two doors of a closet have been cut from the same piece of timber, in which case the obvious thing to look at first is the grain pattern across the join. It's important, of course, to distinguish between similarities that mean something and others that don't, such as scratches made after the doors were hung in place. In the case of continents, an example of the latter would be the evidence of extensive rain forests which geologists a few million years from now will observe in the basins of the Amazon and the Congo. Obviously they would be wrong if they inferred from this that the two places had been joined in the twentieth century—the match would be simply the result of similar environments working on similar raw materials.

The true "grain" of continents consists of the mountain belts and old, deep-lying rock strata. When these significant geological formations were distinguished and compared for age and structural characteristics, they showed an extraordinarily good correspondence across the best-fit join selected by the computer analysis. Furthermore, nothing comparable to them appears in the structure of the ocean floor separating the two regions today. Now if somebody observed that the two closet doors matched but the fixed upright strip between them was different, he would conclude that the doors had been cut from the same piece of wood at some time, and the upright inserted between them afterward—it's the simplest explanation that fits the facts. The same conclusion followed, too, for the continents. Data on the ages of the relevant rock formations indicated that the join had persisted until at least five hundred million years ago. All this was not especially new. As long ago as 1912, the German meteorologist Alfred Wegener based his then revolutionary proposal of continental drift on exactly this kind of information, and his work was subsequently expanded by many investigators.

So, we have five hundred million years as an upper limit for the date of separation. How about a lower limit? It turned out that the areas of overlap in the best-fit solution enable a date to be fixed for this, too. Any parts of the continents that overlap must have formed after there was a gap for them to form in. One of these regions was the Niger Delta. The sediments that make up this formation are all younger than fifty million years and extend well over a hundred miles into the Gulf of Guinea. This says that the separation must have been at least this much by that time. To narrow these limits down further, we need to introduce glaciation and ice sheets into our story.

Between 350 and 250 million years ago, the continents of the southern hemisphere were covered extensively by ice. Rocks can be carried over enormous distances by moving ice, and are dumped wherever they happen to have got to when the ice melts—for example, Norwegian rocks carried by the glaciers of the most recent ice age are quite common in parts of Britain. Huge glacial deposits exist today all over eastern Brazil, which appear to have resulted not from the melting of glaciers localized in valleys, but of vast sheets of ice. In some places these deposits are more than two thousand feet thick—about ten times the depth of the deposits left by the recent ice age in Europe. The thrust patterns in the wrinkles and folds of the underlying rock indicate that the ice moved from southeast to northwest, i.e., from somewhere in the direction of the Atlantic. Well, where did all that material come from?

Let's be scientific and consider the alternatives before jumping to conclusions. Is it possible, for instance, that a large landmass once existed between today's coast and the continental shelf, which was shoveled up by the ice and carried inland? Not really. All the studies that have been made of glaciation indicate that ice sheets don't work that way. They scratch and polish existing terrain, and carry away the looser debris, but they don't grind whole slabs of continent down to nothing. And besides, although one hundred million years sounds a long time, it isn't anywhere near long enough for that kind of major surgery. Very well, could there have been another continent offshore in what today is the South Atlantic—an "Australantis?" No. This conjecture runs into trouble, too, for despite romantic legends to the contrary, continents don't sink beneath the sea. Oceanic crust—the material that forms the floors of the ocean basins—is entirely different from continental crust. The floor of the South Altantic is perfectly normal, which means that any continent that once existed there would somehow have had to transform itself from twenty-five-mile-thick continental crust into five miles of oceanic crust plus twenty miles of upper mantle (the deeper layer that lies beneath the crust all over the earth), or else have disappeared without trace.

So let's take the simple way out again, and go back to our original idea. If Africa was joined to Brazil at one time, we have a ready-made source for all those Brazilian glacial deposits. What's more, investigations in western Africa revealed widespread evidence of glacial erosion in an east-west direction—i.e., out into the Atlantic—but very little in the way of subsequent deposits left by melting. And as a clincher, the Brazilian deposits include many erratic blocks of such rock as quartzite, dolomite, and chert, which resemble none of the structures that make up Brazil, but which are common in southwest Africa. Quantitative analysis of the glacial evidence brings the upper limit for the date of separation down from five hundred million years to two hundred million. We still have fifty million years as the lower limit.

During the period that lasted from 135 million to 100 million years ago (Lower Cretaceous), the strips which today form the South American and African coastal regions both consisted of chains of sedimentary basins—low-lying flooded areas where successive layers of rocks were laid down, the types differing as depth and other environmental factors changed. The sequences of the sediments found on both sides of today's ocean are similar, and bear no resemblance to the basin floor between the continental slopes. And this, of course, is just what would be predicted if both sequences were in fact formed as parts of the same process at a time when the intervening basin didn't exist. The case seems to be getting stronger. For a better idea of what kind of process this was, we need to turn to biology.

Fossil remains of fish and other organisms preserved in these sediments, particularly the lower layers, include many freshwater species that could never have survived in seawater. This implies that at up to about the same time on both edges of what is today the Atlantic, the water that was laying down the sediments was not ocean. Then, above the freshwater deposits, we find layers of minerals and salts of the kinds left by evaporating seawater, dating from between 110 million and 100 million years ago and again corresponding on both sides. But above the salts the two sequences begin to diverge; and the more recent they get, the more pronounced the differences become.

This is all consistent with the suggestion of the two continents fracturing from each other at about this time and moving apart. The rift valley opening up between them would give us the chain of low-lying basins, with freshwater runoff from the surrounding highlands accounting for the earlier sedimentation and fossil record. The sea's eventual penetration of the rift explains the salt deposits, and the progressively diverging layers above the salts testify to gradually differing sequences of events taking place in what were becoming gradually different places.

Thus, the conclusion seems pretty inescapable that not only do continents break up and move, but their voyages can take them vast distances. In fact, the courses they have followed can be charted with surprising accuracy, which brings us to the next set of clues in our scientific detective story. They concern mysteries that other researchers were finding in the natural magnetism of rocks.

The Earth possesses a magnetic field, which behaves as if there were an enormous bar magnet buried beneath the surface, roughly aligned with the rotational axis. From demonstrations at school with iron filings on a sheet of paper, most people are familiar with the "lines of force" that are said to surround a magnet. A typical line of force from the imaginary terrestrial magnet would emerge from its "north" pole, located not far from the geographic pole, curve up out of the atmosphere like an ICBM to flatten out near the equator, and plunge back down again to reenter the surface and terminate at the magnetic south pole. Now, anybody on the Earth's surface who decides to measure the characteristics of the force lines in his vicinity (our ever-curious scientist, for example) will discover two things: first, they always point the same way, north-south; and second, they intersect the Earth's surface at an angle that tilts up or down depending which side of the equator he's on, and which gets larger as he moves farther away from it—hence the ''dip'' of a compass needle. Thus a compass will tell him not only which direction is north, but also how far north or south of the equator he happens to be. (It won't tell him anything about how far east or west of anywhere he is; to know that, he must first get curious about clocks.)

Many rocks contain grains of substances that are naturally magnetic. When these rocks form, either by cooling from volcanic lavas or by settling as sediments, these grains tend to align with the Earth's field. Hence their tiny individual fields all line up the same way and reinforce, giving the rock as a whole a weak but distinct ''fossil magnetism.'' Measurement of this can determine how far north or south of the equator a rock sample was when it formed, and which way it was lying at the time, while the time itself can be fixed by atomic dating. The mystery was that the early results of such experiments seemed to indicate that the Earth's magnetic poles had wandered all over the planet—in fact the poles do move to some degree, but the amounts suggested by the new figures were unheard of. Things got worse when comparisons of results seemed to indicate that the poles must have been in different places at the same time!

Then a group of British investigators looked at the problem the other way round: the same results would have been produced if the poles stayed where they were, but the rocks moved around while they were being formed. Interpreting data from their own country in this fashion, they postulated that in the last two hundred million years, Britain has rotated clockwise through thirty degrees and at the same time traveled a considerable distance northward—which tied in well with depictions of a subtropical prehistoric Britain that had emerged from other work. Other scientists found that a similar interpretation could explain data collected in Australia, and before long everyone was doing it.

South America and Africa turned out to have followed a zigzag course which 350 million years ago would have put the South Pole somewhere inside South Africa. This, of course, explains the huge ice sheets that we met earlier. The line splits at around 100 million years ago to mark the point at which the two continents went separate ways, and provides an independent corroboration of the date arrived at previously from other evidence. The continuing movement northward into warmer climatic zones also explains how the older glacial features of Africa come to lie today beneath layers of coarse rock formed from windblown desert sands.

Applying the same process to the other continents leads to the conclusion that they all originated from the breakup of a single supercontinent, which geologists have christened "Pangea." In Pangea, the east coast of North America fitted against North Africa; Greenland and Newfoundland closed up and fitted with Europe; and Australia, Antarctica, and India were bunched together along the eastern side of Africa. The group of southern continents was separated from Asia by a V-shaped ocean called the Tethys, whose apex lay in the region of the present eastern Mediterranean. The Tethys was squeezed out of existence when India, Arabia, and part of the Middle East hinged northward like a scissor blade and drove underneath Asia to lift up the Tibetan Plateau (although some people think the Black Sea could be a remnant of it). The dinosaurs could have marched along an ancient chain of mountains from Poland and Germany, into the Ardennes of northern France, through Cornwall, Brittany, and Ireland, and down the Appalachians without getting a foot wet. These mountains were formed during an even earlier sequence of events that resulted in the coming together of Pangea itself from previously existing continents.

So, what does the aborigine's fireplace have to do with all this?

When certain kinds of rock are heated to the right temperature, they will, upon cooling again, take on a weak magnetism aligned with the Earth's field, just like naturally forming rocks. In 1969 a team of geologists and archaeologists from the Australian National University were collecting samples of the hearthstones of ancient aborigine cooking fires. The problem with one particular set of samples, taken from the shore of a dried-up lake called Lake Mungo, was that the direction of magnetization was the wrong way round: what should have been north was south, and vice versa.

The phenomenon of reversed rock magnetism was not in itself new—in fact, the observation that naturally formed rocks were frequently found to be magnetized the wrong way round was one of the things that had aroused interest in rock magnetism in the first place. Attempts to devise various mechanisms of self-reversal to account for this all came to nothing, which led to general acceptance of the only alternative explanation available: that the Earth's field itself must have reversed. The picture finally put together from the data indicated that the Earth's field has been reversing itself at irregular intervals and for erratic periods for as far back as reliable measurements can be made—about ten million years—and there's no reason to suppose that the same thing wasn't going on before that. Some "flips" lasted for only a few thousand years, while others persisted for over half a million; on average, the Earth's field seems to have spent about half its time being "right" and the other half "wrong"—which agrees with the observed fact that about half the rock samples studied have reversed magnetism. The significance of the Lake Mungo results was that they show the reversals to have continued into modern times: the samples date from about thirty thousand years ago, which to geologists is only yesterday.

So what?

Well, it leads up to the answer to the second question we started out with which was: If the continents were joined together once, why aren't they now? In other words, What makes them move apart? To link this back to rock magnetism, we have to move our investigation off the continents and down into the deep-ocean basins.

Nineteenth century sailors were well aware of the Mid-Atlantic Ridge, a submerged mountain chain, miles high, that runs all the way down the middle of the North and South Atlantic, from far above Iceland (Iceland is a part of it that protrudes above the surface) to the Antarctic. Later surveys revealed that this formation is just part of a network of ocean ridges that encircle the globe and run through every ocean—although not always down the middle. They can be seen clearly on any world map that shows submarine contours.

In 1960, Professor Harry Hess of Princeton University developed the idea that these ridges were the crests of upflowing currents of fluid rock rising and solidifying from deep below the crust. Material from the underlying mantle was flowing upward to form the ridges, and then spreading out sideways, cooling and sinking as it became more dense, to form newly created ocean floors—visualize two Niagaras face to face and flowing backward. Hess came up with a figure of several centimeters a year for the rate at which the ocean floors are spreading away from the ridges. This doesn't sound much, but it turns out to be sufficient for all of today's ocean floor to have been created within the last 200 million years, which is less than 5 percent of geological time. This accounted well for other facts that had been coming to light about ocean beds, and which up until then no one had been able to explain. For one thing, the sediment layers on the ocean floors were far thinner than they should have been if the sediments had been accumulating throughout Earth's history. And for another, no sample of sediment from the seabeds had ever been recovered that was older than 100 million years. Both these results accorded well with the idea of seafloor spreading . . . but it was all very new, and many scientists felt uneasy about it. Something more conclusive was needed.

It came from other scientists who were sailing research ships around the oceans while the debate was in progress, measuring the magnetic fields above seabeds. The results they were getting were peculiar. They discovered distinct zones of strong and weak fields all over the oceans, and the change from one kind to another could occur over a few miles. Furthermore, the zones were not scattered randomly, but formed well-defined stripes, hundreds of miles long, of alternating field strength. In 1963, two researchers at Cambridge University, Fred Vine and Drummond Matthews, connected them with Hess's ideas and published a short paper that was to mark the beginning of a new era in the Earth sciences.

The Vine-Matthews theory pointed out that if the ocean floors were indeed spreading sideways from the ridges and solidifying from a molten state, the kind of magnetic variations observed would be just what should be expected from the periodic reversals of the Earth's field. A strip of material emerging along the crestline of a ridge at a time when the

Earth's field was in the same direction as it is today would be magnetized in the "right" direction. At some later time, this strip will have been pushed a distance away from the ridge—although still lying roughly parallel to it—by newer material appearing behind. If the Earth's field had reversed during this interval, the material currently forming along the crest would be magnetized in the opposite direction. Eventually a whole series of strips would appear, alternately magnetized to either add to or subtract from the Earth's field, depending on its direction at a given time, and this would result in precisely the kind of pattern found by the survey ships. The pattern would, in effect, constitute a series of time markers written magnetically onto the ocean floors, becoming progressively older with increasing distance from the ridge crests.

If this theory is correct, the sequence of field reversals read from the ocean-floor stripes should tally with that deduced from continental rocks. Subsequent comparisons confirmed this to be the case. Also, the patterns of stripes on opposite sides of the ridges are found to be symmetrical about the crestlines, as would be expected from outward spreading in both directions—in the Atlantic, for example, the pattern east of the ridge runs north-south and is a mirror image of the pattern west of it. And finally, rock and fossil samples brought up from the ocean beds by drilling ships tell a continuous story of the ages of the Earth, just like the exposed strata of a cliff face, such as the Grand Canyon; the difference, however, is that the record on the seabed reads sideways, with the youngest rocks lying closest to the ridges and the oldest thousands of miles away—again, just as the theory predicts.

So there you have it—the world's oldest magnetic tape recorder. Admittedly its specification might look a little odd to anybody familiar with conventional computer magtapes. A regular magtape, for example, moves at a speed of 45 inches per second against this one's 0.000000037 inches per second (3 centimeters per year), writes at a data density of 1,600 bits per inch, compared to 0.0000032 (1 bit every five miles), and writes at a speed of 7,200 bits per second, versus 0.00000000000013 (1 bit per 250,000 years). That's really pretty bad as performance standards go, and I can't see IBM selling very many. On the other hand, though, we shouldn't forget its high reliability (at least 200 million years without a breakdown, and almost certainly a lot longer), superb rugged construction (unaffected by burial beneath a few miles of seawater and several billion tons of mud), and state-of-the-art technology (obsoletes all earlier models). Any offers?

This all seems to add up to a fairly satisfying answer to the questions we began with. But as tends to be the case in science, one question answered raises others that weren't there to begin with. Specifically, in this instance, now that we've established the continual creation of new crust at the ocean ridges, we find ourselves forced to ask what happens to it afterward. If it remains in existence indefinitely, the Earth would have to be getting bigger to make room for it. But there are many reasons for believing that the Earth isn't expanding. Therefore the appearance of new crust at the ridges must be balanced by the disappearance of old crust somewhere else. Where, then, and how, is the old crust disappearing? The answers this time lie in the realm of earthquakes and volcanoes.

Earthquake and volcanic activity is mainly confined to a network of narrow belts encompassing the globe—the familiar ones that run across dry land, plus the ocean ridges, whose activity qualifies as volcanic. These belts divide the surface of the earth into about a dozen irregularly shaped "plates," ranging in size from the Pacific Plate, almost as large as the ocean, down to the Turkish Plate, not much bigger than Florida, which fit together like an enormous piece of spherical crazy paving. The new science of "plate tectonics" (from a Greek word meaning builder) sees changes in the Earth's surface features as the results of continuous plate movements. The plates are about forty miles thick and carry the continents with them like lumps of solidified low-density slag that have floated to the top of the denser material beneath. Wegener's original concept of continental drift is not really accurate in this light; it is the plates that "drift," and the plate margins that separate them bear no resemblance to the outlines of continents.

The two plates that meet along a plate margin can be moving in any of three ways: away from each other, sideways past each other, or toward each other. Gaps between plates don't happen; when plates move apart, new material from the mantle below flows upward to form new crust which welds itself onto the trailing edges—this is the process taking place at the ocean ridges. These are called "constructive" margins. Margins that consist of plates slipping past each other are called "transform faults" and account for many of the world's earthquake belts. The pressure across a transform fault is enormous and causes the plates to weld at the edges, with the result that they become progressively more deformed as the rest of each plate moves on regardless. Eventually something has to give. When the stress exceeds the strength of the rock, the weld fractures and the sides of the fault spring past each other in opposite directions to catch up with their respective plates. The movement may be only a few feet, but it can represent the explosive release in a matter of minutes of stress energy that has been building up for centuries—often, of course, with devastating results. Once the stress has been relieved, the pressure creates a new weld and starts the cycle over again. The San Andreas Fault through San Francisco is a margin of this type—between the Pacific Plate, which is moving northwest, and the American Plate, which isn't.

The third type of margin occurs where two plates are moving toward each other, and again something has to give. What happens in this situation is that one plate is deflected downward beneath the other and plunges back into the molten material of the mantle whence it came. That's *how* old crust is destroyed.

The deepest parts of the oceans are the long, narrow "trenches," which can extend down to thirty-thousand feet. The trenches mark the margins between colliding plates and result from the bending downward of the surface of one plate as it is forced beneath the other. Examples are the Japan Trench and Marianas Trench in the western Pacific, the Tonga Trench north of New Zealand, the Peru-Chile Trench off the west coast of South America, and the Puerto Rico Trench east of the Caribbean. That's *where* old crust is being destroyed. These are called "destructive" margins.

As a map will show, these deep-ocean trenches always lie alongside chains of islands. The islands are formed from the accumulated sediments on the upper surface of the descending plate, which are scraped off as it slides beneath the overriding plate. The friction between the two plates generates sufficient heat to melt the rocks involved in the process, and much of this molten material finds its way back to the surface, making them volcanic island chains. And finally, the plate movements do not occur smoothly, but as alternations of sticking and slipping as was the case with transform faults; hence, we end up with earthquake-prone volcanic island chains. In fact it was analysis of earthquake shockwaves and of the heat-flow patterns obtained in the ocean trench regions that enabled this process to be understood to the point that clear profiles can be reconstructed of descending cold slabs of oceanic crust material which today are melting back into the mantle hundreds of miles beneath the surface.

Sometimes two plates meet head-on that happen to be carrying continents on their backs. As we have already seen, continental crust is too light to sink down into the mantle with the descending plate. Instead, it remains on the surface and collides with the other continent to build mountains. Mountains form in long, thin chains because plates collide along long, thin margins. So when India drove underneath Tibet, the continental crust being carried from both directions piled up to form the Himalayas. Africa's voyage northward drove Italy into Europe like a battering ram to create the Alps, and shocks radiated outward from the impact point to produce effects visible far away today—for example, the shallow folds that form the "Downs" of southern England. Hence, contrary to some ideas that were in vogue early in the century, it doesn't look as if our planet is destined to be eroded down into an enormous billiard ball. New mountains are being built as quickly as the old ones are being worn away, and they'll continue to be built for as long as the energy source that drives the plates lasts out.

So, what does drive the plates?

This brings us right up to date and into the area of much of the research going on today. Hess's original proposal was that the upflowing material at the ridges pushes the plates apart, but later findings have made this improbable, or at least, insufficient in itself. A more recent idea is that deep-seated convection flows in the mantle give rise to horizontal currents beneath the crust that drag the plates with them. Another theory attributes the movements to the release of gravitational energy as the plates slide downward along the gradients between the ridges and the trenches. No conclusive choice seems to warrant being singled out at present, but the causes are undoubtedly complex and could turn out to involve all three of these mechanisms and maybe more, perhaps operating in varying degrees in different places.

All in all, we've come quite a way from looking at a map of the world and wondering why a couple of coastlines should look vaguely similar, and in the process a fascinating story has unfolded. Who knows what other stories might emerge from the seemingly insignificant things that other scientific detectives are getting curious about today? . . .

Did you know that some points in the sky emit X-ray pulses that flash on and off thirty times a second? . . .

GENERATION GAP

"Could be them eyes,
Or maybe that smile,
But you've got the style
That drives me just wild.
Yeaaaah! Owwww!
Ooh-wah, ooh-wah, ooh-wah, ooh-wah . . ."

Arnie Brewster hummed along with the week's number-one hit blaring from the car's hexaphonic speakers, and shouted the *"Yeaaah! Owwww!"* out loud as he left the San Francisco Bay Bridge freeway at the Berkeley exit. The lines of the black, maroon-trim, General Motors Leopard were low, sleek, and curvy—contrived by its designers to convey subliminal suggestions of phallic imagery and sexual potency. The dummy air-intakes and racing exhausts carried connotations of power and strength, laced with a hint of danger; the imitation wood-grain interior paneling, and leather-scented upholstery spoke of sophistication and taste; and the dash-mounted driving compass, padded steering wheel, and authentic-looking manual gearshift projected the qualities of competence, confidence, and rugged masculinity that the General Motor's marketing psychologists had identified in the self-images of 72.3 percent of the males, aged twenty-five to forty, in the educational, occupational, and income groups at which the Leopard had been targeted.

Actually, the engine concealed inside the shell was a low-cost, four-cylinder model imported from Taiwan, and the mounting frame a modified chassis originally developed for a brand of golf cart. But Arnie Brewster was oblivious to anything like that as he came out of the exit curve at thirty-five miles per hour to the accompaniment of synthesized wind-noise and tire squeals injected into the sound system. He pictured himself as Stephan Blane, the suave undercover CIA agent of the series *Department Five*, with a tense but trusting blonde flinching beside him as he raced to elude a hail of bullets from the blue Ford following behind.

In fact, Arnie thought that in looks and mannerisms he did resemble Stephen Blane. He wondered secretly if other people saw the same similarities. To help them make the connection, he sometimes practiced nodding to himself in the slow, narrow-eyed way that Blane did when pondering a problem, or raising his chin defiantly with one eyebrow lifted, which always struck him as roguish and cavalier.

As the car's computer quietly overrode the gas pedal to keep him safely back from the truck in front, he wondered if Mr. Myelow's secretary, Patty, was listening to the same channel on her way home, and if she was, whether the tune was conjuring up a Blane-image of him in her mind also. He had no doubt she was one of the young swingers that the documentaries talked about, and he was sure, too, that she found him interesting—the way she pretended to ignore him was a sure giveaway. Perhaps she harbored a secret fascination for mature, self-assured men. The thought was tempting. . . . But as Dr. Korban, the senior psychiatrist in *The Mind Menders* had said in the episode about the ex-paratrooper who went berserk with a flamethrower and cremated everybody in the office because of their attitudes toward his affair with the computer operator, mature, serious-minded men keep their business and their private lives separate. Oh, the sacrifices that the wise and noble chose so selflessly to bear!

He arrived home in Berkeley and parked in the driveway, looking up automatically as he climbed out to see if there were any UFOs hovering overhead. There weren't. So, slinging his two-hundred-dollar ski jacket—an essential part of the rugged and carefree, open-air man's wardrobe—over his shoulder and hooking a thumb casually in his belt, he sauntered up to the door, at the same time stealing a nonchalant glance across the street to see if Laura Thompson was watching through her drapes—cars were frequently parked outside the Thompsons' until the early hours, and there had been a program not long ago about spouse-swapping in suburbia. She wasn't.

The sound of the TV greeted him when he entered the house. Light was showing from the living room. As he hung his jacket in the hallway, he noticed in the mirror that he had missed shaving that morning. With his partly unbuttoned shirt and fleece-lined leather vest, the shadowy chin and cheeks gave him a lean, work-hardened look that enhanced his features, he thought. It reminded him of the part that Vincent Calom had played in the movie *Big Man's Country*—the scene where he returned home to his firelit cabin after a day of timber felling to find his devoted wife ladling stew from an iron pot, while their son hung his rifle over the fireplace after keeping watch over the homestead for the day. Arnie leaned closer to the mirror and narrowed his eyes to make them look hard and steely. Then, drawing himself up tall and savoring the feeling of hard-won pride that came with being Man, the Provider, the Protector, he turned and strode into the living room.

Beth was sprawled in the recliner before the six-foot wallscreen, dressed in red-white candy-stripe glitter pants and a yellow, cutaway tunic top as worn by female engineering officers in *Galactic Command*. She had made her hair orange with green stripes, put on dark purple lipstick and eyeshadow, and was eating onion dip and crackers. Arnie waited expectantly. Beth took no notice. After a few seconds he said, "Hey, it's me, like, I'm home, you know . . ."

"Shhh! Joseph Donnelly has found out about Sylvia and Hank. He's gone out and bought a gun. I gotta see what happens." Beth scooped up some more dip and glanced at him. "Why don't you go get a shave? Stan and Ella are coming over, remember? You look like an ad for a hangover cure or something."

Arnie snorted and walked out again. There was no other sign of life. No doubt Kenny was shut up in his room, wasting his time as always with the garbage that kids filled their heads with these days. Mumbling irritably to himself, he stomped away to the kitchen to light a joint and pour himself a beer.

In the commercial showing on the screen an hour later, the couple who had arrived for dinner were average, healthily image-conscious people, he in a satin-edged coat, and wearing an iridescent wig of optical fibers, she in a *Psi-Lady* meditation suit, with a combination purse and video-game cartridge carrier. Ella and Stan were watching from the couch. "Wasn't she in some kind of murder movie or something . . . after she got divorced from Tony Sentini?" Ella murmured, munching absently and keeping her eyes on the screen.

"Yeah—*Terror in the City*," Beth said, still in the recliner. "She plays a clairvoyant who can replay murders in her head. She puts the detective straight after he's run out of clues."

"Johnathan Field," Arnie added.

"Huh?" Stan said.

"Johnathan Field. He's the detective on the case. That's how she proves she can do it. Everyone thinks she's a fake, see."

"Oh."

On the screen, the two guests were sipping before-dinner cocktails. Suddenly the woman nudged her husband and pointed to a faint finger-smudge on her glass. "*Body-grease!*" she whispered behind her hand. The husband put down his own glass hurriedly, glancing from side to side and looking apprehensively at the cutlery. Moments later the scene ended with a shot of the couple departing early on a pretext, and then the embarrassed host consoling his distraught wife.

"Donna Janson is psychic," Beth commented.

"Huh?" Stan said.

"Donna Janson—she's psychic . . . in real life. She can really do it."

"Oh."

"She was in that movie a couple of weeks back," Ella said. "The one where the brain surgeon was supposed to put a computer chip in the general's head, but the nurse switched the gurneys on the way to the operating theater, so they did it to the Russian spymaster instead."

On the screen, the hostess's wise and knowing mother was educating her daughter in the use of "Bodyguard." After spraying fingertips and palms, they embarked on a tour of the house together, rapturously drenching drawer handles, doorknobs, lightswitches, toilet seats, phone buttons, and anything else carrying the risk of indirect contact with another human being. The ad ended with the husband and wife again, this time waving good-bye to their guests after a brilliantly successful dinner party, and then flinging their arms ecstatically round each other—presumably after taking suitable precautions by copious application of Bodyguard.

"She predicted that earthquake last year," Beth said. "Where was it, India? Indianesia? Indi-something, anyhow. Her manager said so, too, so it's true."

"Donna Janson wasn't in that movie," Stan told Ella. "She was in the one where the doctor put his wife's lover's brain inside the gorilla after they had the car smash. That's what you're thinking of."

"Was it? . . . Maybe it was." Ella shrugged. "So what's the difference? They were both brain surgeons, weren't they?"

"I'm just tellin' ya, that's all."

"Yeah, well, I didn't ask, did I? Why are you always picking on me?"

"I'm not picking. I just—"

"Did I ever tell you I was psychic?" Beth said. "That time after the dog got hit by the truck, I knew it was gonna happen. I always said it was gonna happen one day. And when the phone rang yesterday, didn't I say, I bet that's my sister, Arnie? And wasn't it my sister?"

"Hell, you knew she was going to call because of the tickets," Arnie said.

"YOU ARE!" Ella shouted suddenly as Wally Klein began introducing the news. She shook her head, flinging her hair from side to side, and gnawed at her knuckle. "You're always picking on me, Stan. Why do you do this to me? You try to humiliate me and I don't know why. What did I ever do to get treated this way? I don't deserve it. You think you can do better for yourself? Okay, then go do it, but don't come crawling back to me when she's spent all your money. I've had it, see!"

Stan's mouth was frozen half open in the act of biting at a pickle. He stared at Ella in astonishment. "Shit, all I said was—"

"Don't you lay a finger on her in this house," Beth warned him sharply. She sat up and put an arm around Ella's shoulder. "There, Ella, it's okay."

"JESUS CHRIST!" Stan roared, leaping to his feet. He rushed across the room, banged his forehead against the side of the lounge doorway, and stood there, pounding a fist against the paneling. "You know you mustn't do that, Ella," he muttered. "I have this anger, see . . . and you gotta help me keep control of it. It's from when I was in the Army. . . . Combat sickness—know what I'm trying to say?"

"You never went outside New Jersey and Arkansas the whole time you were in the Army," Ella told him.

"GODDAMIT, WHY DO YOU HAVE TO CONTRADICT EVERYTHING I SAY?" Stan shouted, spinning round. "That's what you think, huh? Well maybe there were a lotta things I did in the Army that I never told you about, okay?"

Arnie gave a slow, narrow-eyed nod. "Look, why don't we all calm down and discuss this like sane, civilized people?" he suggested, rising to his feet.

"I AM BEING SANE AND CIVILIZED!" Stan bawled. "It's her. She's got paranoid delusions or whatever you call them things. It's those pills. Ella, didn't I tell you not to mix 'em with the yellow ones?"

"SHUDDUP, ASSHOLE! WHAT DO YOU KNOW ABOUT ANYTHING?" Ella screamed.

"CUT IT OUT!" Beth shouted above both of them. Silence descended abruptly.

"Ahem," a new voice said. All faces turned toward the hall doorway. Arnie groaned beneath his breath and covered his eyes with a hand.

It was Kenny, and as usual he was looking outrageous. It was embarrassing. He was wearing one of the tweedy jackets, with buttons and lapels, that were part of the latest teenage cult craze. He had pants with ridiculous creases that made them stick out from his legs, a pointed strip of colored material tied around his neck, and his head was shorn almost bald, with the little hair he had left brushed flat and parted; his face was like a ghost's, without a trace of cosmetic, and his shoes were rubbed shiny like a pair of bathroom faucets.

"I didn't mean to interrupt, but I'm just on my way out," Kenny said. "I didn't realize we had company. Mr. and Mrs. Williams, hello."

"I ain't having you coming in here and talking to our friends like that," Arnie growled. "You know what I mean—with all that talk you pick up outside. They're Stan and Ella, see. They got names."

Kenny grinned good-naturedly. "Oh sure, I forgot. Sorry, Dad."

"How many times do I have to tell ya?" Arnie demanded. "I'm Arnie, see. And that's Beth. Get that? We got names, too. Anyone'd think we're things or something. It's some kinda psychological problem with you. A deliberate, symbolic rejection. I know about things like that, see."

"I'm sorry. I'll try and remember how you feel," Kenny promised.

"And don't keep apologizing all the time," Arnie told him. "You're telling me it doesn't matter, right? What's wrong with you kids? It's insulting to talk to people like that, without no feelings—like they don't matter. People who are worth something are worth expressing feelings at, ain't they? Well, what's the matter with us? Aren't we worth the effort of yelling and screaming at?"

"Sure you are . . . er, Arnie. But it's just that—"

"THEN START YELLING AND SCREAMING AT ME FOR CHRISSAKES!" Arnie exploded. Kenny started to say something, then stopped, hesitated, and finally shook his head. Arnie flopped down into an armchair.

Ella stared silently at the floor. Then Beth said to Kenny, "It just ain't right, the way you kids behave—turning your backs on the world and trying to run away from it. I mean, where's it supposed to get you in the end? Okay, so you're only fifteen, but you have to grow up some time. What about all the time you'll have wasted, huh?"

Stan unglued his forehead from the side of the lounge

doorway and turned. "Your ma's right, kid," he said. "I don't know where you kids think you're heading either, but let me give you some advice, and I've been around: Get wised up. You've gotta get in touch with the real world and start acting like real people."

Kenny stared for a second, then shook his head incredulously and gestured at the wallscreen. *"That* has got something to do with the real world? You can't be serious! When did you last look out of a window?"

"What do you know about anything?" Beth challenged, turning in the recliner. "You're always shut up back there with your nose inside a book."

"Books?" Stan looked nonplussed. "He reads books?"

"Hundred of 'em," Arnie said. He tossed out a hand wearily. "They're all round his room, stacked on the shelves . . . everywhere."

"We read a book just a couple of months ago, Stan, don't you remember?" Ella murmured distantly.

"Sure, why not?" Kenny said. "All the kids collect books. You can find them in yard sales and flea markets. And a couple of stores that specialize in them have opened up in the city. They're not that expensive, either."

"Why would anyone bother?" Beth asked. "They can get all they want on TV."

"The pictures are better," Kenny said. Beth stared at him uncomprehendingly. "You go at your own speed, pause whenever you want to think about something, and you can go back over it if you need to."

"But you have to spell out all them words," Beth objected.

"Well, yes, there is that," Kenny agreed. "But it gets easier after a while, with practice."

"It was about astrology and birth signs," Ella said, looking at Stan. "How tuning in to stars and planets and stuff can keep you healthy and make lots of money. You went out and bought that set of charts, and the personalized horoscope computer that cost eighty-five dollars."

"Yeah, Kenny's got lots of books like that, too," Beth said.

"That's astronomy," Kenny told her. "It's not the same thing."

"Does it keep you healthy and make you rich, too?" Arnie asked.

"Not directly, unless you happen to be a professional astronomer or science writer," Kenny replied. "But then I doubt if superstitions based on simplistic notions of cause-and-effect are likely to do much for you, either—except make you eighty-five dollars poorer, maybe."

"It's the same as them 'mathematics' that you and that Marvin Stewart kid are always scribbling on pieces of paper," Arnie grumbled. "What do you think they'll ever do for you?"

"Paper?" Stan repeated, blinking his eyes. "You mean with pens? They write things on pieces of paper with pens?"

Ella stared in disbelief. "You mean without any button-pad, even? No screen?"

"They've even got a game they play without a screen," Beth told them. "Chess, or something, they call it. They push pieces of wood around on a board."

Stan gave Kenny a worried look. "You mean that's it? They just move pieces of wood around on a board? Nothing else happens?"

"It doesn't even have batteries," Beth moaned miserably.

"That's what you get for your trouble, Stan," Arnie said in a hopeless voice. "You do your best, and all you get is rejection. No gratitude, no appreciation. And on top of that they have to be reasonable with you all the time, and discuss everything . . . and talk in that low-key kind of way that drives you crazy—as if you're not worth arguing with." He shook his head. "They don't try to solve their problems, Stan. They think about them."

"That's bad," Stan said. "You mean just sitting there, staring at nothing—not doing anything about anything?"

"Right." Beth waved vaguely at the screen, which was showing baton-swinging police clashing with demonstrators in a street riot somewhere in South America. "It ain't as if they don't ever get to see the proper way to handle life . . . I mean, everyone has problems, right? But people need to do something positive about them—like they throw something, scream, smash things, go out and have a breakdown and beat up on somebody, or whatever. . . . But kids these days don't do things like that any more. All they do is sit and talk, and then say the problem's gone away, or maybe it ain't so bad or something. They won't face up to anything.''

"Hyperpassivity,'' Ella pronounced. "That's what Dr. Friedmann said was wrong with Alice's daughter in *Bayview Apartments*. Too much thinking is the first sign of losing touch with reality. It's a big problem everywhere with kids. There are some pills that will get him back up to a normal level of hype.''

"Thanks, but I'm sure I can manage fine without,'' Kenny said hastily.

"Don't keep thanking people,'' Arnie complained. "It ain't good manners. It sounds like people are doing you favors or something . . . as if they're nobodies trying to get liked.''

"Well that god-awful music you play in there won't get you anyplace,'' Beth said to Kenny. She turned toward Ella and Stan. "You know the kind of stuff I mean—no beat or feel to it at all, just noise.''

"The kids across the street from us are always playing it out the window,'' Stan said, nodding. "It's primitive, not even electronic. I went over there one night and set fire to their rose bushes.''

"What's that place you were talking about the other week?'' Arnie asked Kenny. "Beat Heaven or something? I mean, what's it all about, huh? Where in hell is Beat Heaven supposed to be?''

"Beethoven,'' Kenny said with a sigh.

"Same difference. So where in hell is that?''

"Is that where they wear all the freaky clothes, Kenny?'' Ella asked, giggling and waving her hand at his general appearance.

"They don't say anything, kid,'' Stan told him. "Are you ashamed to be yourself? Is that what it is, huh?'' He gestured down at his own crotch-hugging white pants with scarlet side-stripes, tucked into calf-length astronavigator boots, officer's belt with Alpha Centauri Squadron buckle, and navy, white-trimmed blouse, complete with Strikefleet shoulder patch. "See. You should try to find yourself, and then tell the world who you are—like a starship admiral, for instance. It's easy once you find yourself and make the effort to fit in.''

"But I never lost myself," Kenny said. "And I'm not a starship admiral."

"You have to be something sooner or later," Ella insisted. "You can't spend your whole life staring at books and listening to crazy music. You have to get involved eventually. It ain't all gonna change to suit you."

There was a short pause. Then Beth lowered her eyes and said dismally, in the voice of someone finally revealing a long-concealed secret of congenital madness in the family, "He says he wants to be some kind of scientist." She looked at Arnie. "What was it, a fizzy-something?"

"Physicist," Kenny supplied. Arnie looked away to hide his shame.

"But that kind of thing is for nobodies, like schoolteachers, technical waddyacallits, or people who make things," Ella protested. "Why would anyone wanna do something like that?"

Arnie showed his empty palms. "That's the way they are, Ella. They *want* to work, and learn things. They say it shouldn't be the government's job to keep them. Something to do with 'ethics' and that kind of crap. . . . I don't know."

Kenny looked around and shook his head. For the first time his expression betrayed rising exasperation. He pointed at the screen. "Look . . . that idiot behind the desk is telling you how the U.S. is more respected in the world today because of the way we've strengthened our strategic forces, right? But they only voted the appropriation a year ago. They haven't actually spent any money yet. They're still only talking about what to spend it on. And even if they had spent it, it couldn't have made any difference on that kind of time scale. It would be ten years at least before any new weapons ordered through last year's budgets could be produced and deployed. But they're talking as if it had all already happened, and taking the credit for it.

"Can't you see what's happening? Things in the real world don't happen fast enough to be entertaining any more. So the media have created a make-believe world that runs at several times the speed of real time, with a crisis every half hour and always an instant solution.

"It's the same with all the other 'crises' that they invent and then say they've solved. How could a crime wave of 'epidemic proportions' that nobody had heard of before suddenly materialize in two months, just before Ed Callones ran for governor—and with a program already worked out to fight it? . . . And then have been 'successfully eliminated' in just as short a time after he was elected? It couldn't have. Things don't change that quickly. The 'economic recoveries' that somebody or other is always supposed to be masterminding every six months are from slumps that never happened. The 'environmental catastrophes' that are always supposed to be imminent never materialize. And yet people everywhere believe it all and carry on paying. . . .''

Kenny looked from one to another of the four faces staring blankly back at him. He exhaled a long sigh. "It doesn't matter. . . . I guess I got carried away a little. I was going out anyhow. I'll just be on my way. You folks have a good evening.'' With that he turned away quickly and left, closing the door behind him.

An uncomfortable silence persisted for a while. Finally Stan said, "Gee, I didn't realize you guys had it so bad. . . . I guess he'll probably grow out of it, huh?''

"What was he talking about?'' Ella asked, still dazed after Kenny's outburst.

Arnie was still looking down at the floor. Beth came over and leaned her head against his shoulder. "Oh Arnie,'' she sobbed. "We tried, didn't we? Where did we go wrong?''

Outside, Kenny pulled his parka on over his jacket and walked around to the back of the house to pick up the backpack, suitcase full of selected books, and crammed briefcase that he had dumped from his bedroom window. He carried his things to the end of the street and waited in the shadows of the shrubbery by the corner streetlight. After about ten minutes, Marv Stewart's battered '95 Chevy van appeared. Marv was at the wheel, with Bev Johnson and Harry wedged in next to him up front. Kenny slid open the side door and hoisted his bags inside. Then he climbed in to join the crush of young people jammed in the back amidst coats, rucksacks, suitcases, sleeping bags, and bundles of books. "Okay, Kenny?'' Marv called from the front as the van pulled away. "Any problems?''

"No,'' Kenny answered. He felt drained, now that the

worst was over and he was committed. "It went okay. Did everyone else make it?"

"All here," Tom Pearce's voice said from somewhere in the shadows nearby. "You're the last."

Kenny gradually made out the forms as his eyes adjusted to the darkness. Tom, who could read IBM microcode and wanted to get into AI research, was propped just behind him, next to Nancy, who had painted the murals in Giuseppe's restaurant in Oakland. Sheila Riordan, who understood tensor calculus and wrote plays, was behind them, with Kev, the chess expert, and Charlie Cameron, who was into number theory and could recite pi to fifty places. . . . And yes, the others were all there, too, farther back. Kenny leaned back and made himself comfortable between his backpack and a pile of blankets. "So what's the schedule?" he called out to Marv.

"Down the Interstate and on through L.A., bound for Phoenix. We'll probably stop for breakfast somewhere near the Arizona border."

"When do you think we'll make Boston?" Kenny asked.

"Aw . . . should be sometime around Tuesday, I figure."

"Uh-huh."

Kenny settled back into the shadows and closed his eyes to rest. He wondered if it really was the way people said. Boston—home of the revolution of the New Wave generation, who were sweeping away the rejected, outmoded values of an era that was ending, and replacing them with new ways born of the rebelliousness of youth.

It was said that there were bookstores on every block there, galleries exhibiting paintings and sculptures, theaters, science labs, and symphony orchestras playing to packed halls. The University had allegedly closed down its faculties of paranormal phenomena and antitechnology to make room for arts, sciences, engineering, and business, and there were free public lectures on everything from differential geometry and molecular evolution to space engineering and nuclear physics. People ate real steaks with wine in restaurants with candlelit tables; portrait painters worked at easels set up on the sidewalks; and string quartets played in the streets.

It had been a tough decision in some ways; but sooner or later people had to take responsibility for their own lives,

Kenny thought to himself—even if it did cause some upsets and misunderstandings in the short term. His folks would miss the money he'd been getting from working illegally at the computer store on Saturdays to supplement their phoney welfare checks, but they'd manage okay in the end. He was satisfied in his own mind that he had met his responsibilities to the best of his ability; he owed them no more. Eventually, the time came when you had to think of yourself. He'd explained it all as best he could in the letter that he'd left in his room. They'd come to understand in the end, he was sure . . . even though it might take them a while.

RULES WITHIN RULES

Patrick and Michael Flynn were twin brothers, the sons of a family doctor who practiced in a sleepy Irish village called Ballaghkelly. The village was little more than a crossroad buried in a huddle of houses and outlying farms, and boasted one church, a school, a few tiny stores, a newsagent's that was also the post office, and three pubs. Little ever happened to change the routine of a typical day in Ballaghkelly. At six o'clock every morning, Willie Maherty's one-horse dray would clatter off on its round of the farms to collect the churns from the previous day's milkings before the day warmed. Twice in the day and once in the evening—exactly when was always a standby topic of conversation if the weather looked settled— the bus from Kilkenny would arrive and depart again. And after nightfall, the farmers would begin gathering in O'Toole's, Mulligan's, and O'Shaughnessy's to nod and murmur over their pints of porter while they reiterated worldly wisdoms that had been handed down from father and grandfather for generations. Life had always been that way, and nobody—in the unlikely event of such a thought entering his head—could have conceived of its being any other.

Patrick was a voracious reader and did brilliantly in

school. Kevin Halloran, the schoolmaster, became convinced that the boy was a prodigy and persuaded him to try for a scholarship to study mathematics at the university in Dublin. Patrick was accepted, gained a degree with honors after some years, and then departed to pursue postdoctoral studies in America, which was somewhere across the sea, in the opposite direction from England—whichever way that was. Michael, too, was studious, but his vocation lay in a different direction. He left home to train at the Catholic seminary in Waterford, and shortly after Patrick left for America, Michael was installed as the new parish priest in a town not far from Limerick.

Although the brothers corresponded, they did not meet again for several years. Then Patrick wrote from America to say that he had been offered a research fellowship at Cambridge, England, and that before taking up his new position he would come back to Ballaghkelly on a short holiday, which he referred to in his letter as a "vacation." Michael, too, obtained leave of absence and came home for the big family reunion. There was a fine party at the Flynns', as good as any wedding or funeral wake that even the oldest in Ballaghkelly could remember, and in the course of the evening it seemed that every pair of feet from twenty miles around had passed over the threshold, bearing some well-wisher to join the family in a glass of stout and perhaps sample one—or two, or maybe a few—of the choice blends of whiskey brought in for the occasion. At last, after it was all over, and their father had tottered unsteadily but contentedly away to his bed, with their mother closing the door after him and warning them sternly not to touch any of the mess until morning, Patrick and Michael found themselves alone with their glasses, staring at the logs crackling in the large brick fireplace in which, as boys, they had watched faces and dragons together, many years ago.

"Ah, 'tis a wonderful place ye've been tellin' me about, Patrick," Michael said distantly. "With them Americans drivin' their motorcars along roads as wide as ten boreens, and flyin' around in the sky as naturally as the likes of us would take the bus into Kilkenny. . . . And walkin' around on the moon itself, if you're not after pullin' me leg."

Patrick took a sip from his glass. "And that isn't the half

of it, Michael. There's the size of the place . . . Do you know, the nearest part of the U.S.A. is two hundred times farther away from here than Dublin, yet it's still nearer to us than it is to the other side. Can you imagine that?''

Michael tried to visualize what it meant, but in the end shook his head with a sigh and sank back in his chair. "Anyhow, about yourself, Patrick," he said. "Ye told us enough about America in the letters ye wrote. But there was never a time when ye said anythin' about what ye were doin' in that university.'' His brow creased uneasily. "Ye wouldn't have gone and got yourself mixed up with the makin's o' these bombs and things, now, would ye, Patrick? 'Tis the devil himself's work ye'd be doin'.''

Patrick gave a short laugh. "You don't have to worry yourself about anything like that, Michael. There are some areas of research that aren't connected with the weapons program, you know.'' Michael looked relieved. Patrick went on, "In fact I'm not involved with any aspect of applied research at all. My work is all to do with pure mathematics—in fact, an area called number theory, if you'd really like to know.'' Modesty had prevented him from saying much about this in his letters. Now, however, with the euphoria of being home again—and perhaps also from the effects of the party and the drink—he was unable to keep just a hint of a swagger out of his voice.

Michael seemed not to notice. "Ah, so that's what it's called, is it?'' he replied, nodding slowly. "And what would ye be doin' with the numbers? Is it some kind o' computin' with them electronic machines?''

"We use computers a lot, but that isn't really what it's all about,'' Patrick said. "Number theory is simply the study of the properties of the whole numbers themselves, and of the rules for manipulating them.''

"And that could keep an honest man busy for a lifetime?'' Michael sounded dubious.

Patrick laughed again. "A lot more than that, Michael, believe me. People have been developing it for centuries, and they've still only scratched the surface. My work only touches upon one little piece of it.''

"Is that a fact, now?''

"It has to do with the implications of something known

as Gödel's Incompleteness Theorem. It, er . . . it deals with the inherent limitations of any formal system of rules, no matter how complex.''

"Ah.'' Michael gazed silently into the fire for a few seconds. "Gödel, you say, eh?''

"Kurt Gödel . . . an Austrian mathematician. He formulated the theory in 1931. What it says is that all consistent axiomatic systems of number theory include undecidable propositions.'' Patrick paused for a second. "Well, actually the original was expressed in more technical terms, and it was in German, of course . . . but that's about what it boils down to.''

Michael squinted and rubbed his nose with the crook of a finger. "Well, it might as well be in German still, for all the sense I can make of it,'' he confessed. "It's havin' a bit o' fun at your brother's expense, ye are, if I'm not mistaken. Now could ye imagine me in the pulpit on a Sunday, railin' me congregation with that kind o' talk? Why, wouldn't Mother McCreavy from the village be down to the post office at the crack o' dawn the next mornin', writin' letters to the Holy Father himself? Away with ye now, Patrick. If what ye just told me can't be said in God's own English, then it's likely as not that it's without any meanin' at all. I'm thinkin'.''

Patrick grinned apologetically. "I guess I just couldn't resist it.'' He refilled their glasses from the bottle standing between them. "It concerns the systems of rules that govern mathematical proofs. What it says is that no set of rules can ever be complete enough in itself to enable every true statement to be proved. There will always be at least one statement that can only be proved by bringing in another rule from outside the system. And if you add that rule to make a new, bigger system, then the new system will contain at least one statement that would require yet another rule to prove it, and so on. There's no end to the process. However big you make the system, it can never be complete enough to prove all true statements. That's why it's called the Incompleteness Theorem.''

A silence fell while Michael tasted his drink and sat back to reflect on this. Eventually he said, "You'd think, now, wouldn't you, that rules and such would be somethin' a priest would know all about, for isn't every day of his life just a matter of passing on a few simple rules of livin'? But I'm blessed if I can tell the head from the tail o' what you're tellin' me now, Patrick—blessed if I can at all.''

"Actually, that's not a bad analogy," Patrick said. Michael looked puzzled. Patrick sat forward and spread his hands to explain. "People, nations, society in general . . . they all have systems of rules—laws—that govern the ways they behave. Now this comparison is only a loose one, you understand, but it gives an idea—no system of social rules is ever complete, is it? For who writes the laws that govern the lawmakers? You see my point—such laws would have to be written from outside the system. But then the same question would still apply: Who would write the laws to govern whoever wrote *those* laws? You could go on as long as you like, but you could never completely solve the problem.''

Michael considered the proposition for a while. " 'Tis a sad picture of the human race that you're paintin','' he commented at last. "Ye make it sound as if everybody in the world is unable to live a decent life without rules to stop them from robbin' each other and cuttin' each other's throats.''

Patrick sighed. "True, but what can you do? That's the way the world is out there. They're all in a rat race, scrambling and trampling over each other to get a bigger piece of the cake. And when a bunch of them get into a position where they can write their own rules, it brings out the worst. Sooner or later they have to be regulated somehow, but that never solves the problem. All it does is shift it another level higher up.''

"How would ye be meanin'?'' Michael asked.

"Oh, the legal system over there in America is a good example," Patrick replied. "The lawyers make money by complicating the problems that they're supposed to be solving, which suits them fine, but doesn't suit the clients. They can get away with it because the rules let them, and they write the rules. It's the same with price-fixing cartels in business, or the lobbying that corporations can do to get tariff laws and other restrictions passed to get an edge over their competitors. And it's the wealthy who get to influence how loopholes are written into the tax code. You see—whenever a group can write its own rules, it writes them in its own favor. Everyone else loses.''

Michael shook his head sadly. "That's a terrible thing

. . . that with all these machines and all, and them fellas walkin' around on the moon, they'd still be havin' this kind o' trouble with each other. Ye'd think, now, that with all their talk about puttin' the Russians in their place, the government would have somethin' to say about these carryin's on. Have they no care at all for the people that's payin' the money for the motorcars for them to go paradin' themselves around in with all their grand speeches and smilin' faces?''

''That's my whole point, Michael,'' Patrick agreed, nodding. ''You're right—in theory the government ought to be able to prevent things like that through the power of law. But in practice it doesn't work out, because the government in turn isn't subject to any law but its own, and the same thing happens. The federal bureaucracy is out of control. A bureaucrat's status and income are geared to the size of the department he runs and the number of people in it. Therefore they all want their departments and budgets to grow bigger. To justify that, they have to have problems that are getting bigger instead of being solved, and the legislation that emerges makes everything worse, not better. Take the welfare system as an example—it costs more than anything else in the government budget. If everybody in the country became self-sufficient, the agencies would be out of business. So laws get passed which guarantee that there'll always be a bottom layer of dependents who'll never be able to climb out of the trap—such as minimum wages that make them unemployable, or housing standards that drive prices above anything they can afford. And then, of course, we've got the defense industry and the military—they don't *want* any relaxation of tensions with the Soviets. And the banking system that finances the government also owns the contractors that the government spends the loans with—so they're making money with both hands by billing the taxpayer for lending their own money to themselves. It's a good deal—you sell a few billion dollars worth of sophisticated weaponry, put it down holes in the ground for ten years and wait for it to become obsolete, then scrap it all and start over again. And while the banks are owed money, they write the rules.''

Michael stroked his chin thoughtfully as he stared into the fireplace. ''And there's honest people toilin' away the lives that God meant them to enjoy, just to pay for it all, eh?

And to think, with all them machines and the clever fellas in the universities, couldn't they all be livin' like kings?''

"I guess so." Patrick sighed. "But they won't. Too many people would have to come down a peg or two, and they're the ones who write the rules. Oh, I suppose you could think in terms of a world government or something one day, but the same would happen eventually because there wouldn't be any rules to control *them*.''

"Maybe they should try lookin' in that number theory that ye were tellin' me about," Michael suggested. "Wasn't it all to do with writin' rules within rules, and isn't that what we're talkin' about now?''

Patrick frowned. "Number theory doesn't apply here," he said. He kept his voice even to avoid sounding as if he were talking down to his brother. "The analogy was only a loose one. Gödel's theorem merely deals with sets of formal symbolic axioms. It doesn't have anything to say about social rules and how people should behave toward one another. You're reading too much into it.''

"I have to disagree with ye, Patrick," Michael said. "It has everything to say—about some very good social rules that were written down a long time ago now, and very concisely.''

Patrick stared across with a puzzled frown. "I'm not with you, Michael," he said. "What do you imagine Gödel's theorem says that has anything to do with people?''

"*Tch, tch.*" Michael shook his head reproachfully. There was a faint smile on his face, and his eyes twinkled in the glow from the fire. " 'Tis a shame ye've never seen it, Patrick," he replied. "It's been all these years now, and ye mean to tell me that ye've never noticed what the first three letters of Gödel are?''

THE ABSOLUTELY
FOOLPROOF ALIBI

The phone on Professor Osbert Osternak's desk rang. "Excuse me," the snowy-haired chief scientist of the Erwin Schrödinger Memorial Research Institute said to the younger man sitting across from him. "Yes? . . . This is Professor Osternak, yes. Who is this, please? . . . Oh?" The old man's eyebrows shot upward almost to his hairline. "Oh really? That is most interesting." He settled back in his chair and sent an apologetic shrug across the desk. It seemed that this was going to take a while. "Yes, that is true, quite true. . . . Yes. That is so. But how do you— . . . . Of course. Amazing! And so it happens. . . . So, what can I do for you? . . ."

Dr. Rudi Gorfmann, Osternak's deputy, wearing a black bow tie and dress shirt beneath his white lab coat, sighed impatiently. The old fool would be prattling on for half the evening now, and Gorfmann wanted to be on his way to Innsbruck for the Celebrity Club's charity fund-raising banquet. He stood up and turned to face away across the office. With its antiquated wooden bookshelves and paneling—even a chalkboard!—it was as much of an anachronism as the mind it belonged to. Gorfmann paced across to the window of the Gothic "Keep," which on its rocky eminence formed an incongruous focal point for the Institute's modern laboratory blocks and reactor housings, and stared out at the peaks of the Bavarian Alps, frosty against the darkening sky. His reflection stared back from the glass: a clean-shaven face, neatly groomed blond hair, gold-rimmed spectacles. Meanwhile, Osternak's voice babbled on behind. "This is unbelievable. When does he intend to do this? . . . Ach, so . . . Can we get together and talk about this? . . ."

Old scientists should be forcibly retired at forty, Gorfmann fumed to himself. Newton, Einstein, anyone of brilliance . . . none had done anything useful beyond their twenties. All they had achieved after that was to place the seal of unchallengeable authority on ideas that had become outmoded, making further progress impossible until they died off and made room for new blood with new vigor. If it weren't for such tyranny of age and tradition, Columbus would have landed on the moon, Watt would have harnessed fusion energy, and the Wright brothers would have built the first starship. And Rudi Gorfmann would have . . . He realized that Osternak had stopped talking on the telephone, and turned back to face the desk.

"I'm sorry," Osternak said, gesturing for Gorfmann to be seated again. "But it was rather important. I know you have a dinner to get to. Now, where were we?"

Gorfmann remained standing. "I protest at this policy of indecisiveness and timidity that you are imposing on the Institute," he repeated.

"But I'm not imposing anything, Rudi. The directors are in full agreement that—"

"On scientific issues they follow your lead, which makes it the same thing. My question is, are we scientists, dedicated to discovery in a spirit of boldness, with confidence in our own judgment . . . or old women cowed by superstitions and frightened of anything we don't understand?" Gorfmann jabbed a finger in the direction of the window. "Outside, in that building down there, is what's probably the most significant breakthrough in the entire history of physics, maybe in entire history, period—a tested, proven, up-and-running transfer gate. We are talking about a working *time machine!* . . . The implications are staggering. Everything we thought we knew about logic and causality will have to be revised. The very fundamentals of physics—space, time, energy, matter, charge—all take on new meanings. Unimaginable technologies will grow from it. . . ."

"Rudi," the professor interrupted patiently. "I am aware of all this."

"What I'm saying is that it is *ours*!" Gorfmann said, punching a fist into his other palm. "Us—the scientists here at the Institute. It was our work that made this a reality. The rewards and the recognition that it deserves belong to us."

Osternak nodded. "And I'm sure that in time you will receive them."

Gorfmann snorted derisively. "When, with the snail's pace of the way things are moving? Fifty years from now? A century? What use is that to me? I am young, and I still have a life ahead of me that I mean to enjoy. I want the rewards and everything that goes with them, *now*. But all we get is restrictions, restrictions, this ridiculous blackout on publicity, and tests, tests, and more tests." He waved a hand in Osternak's direction. "Look, I'm sorry if this success has come a little late in life for you—there is nothing I can do about that. But it doesn't have to be that way for me. I say we should go public now. I would like to make the first official announcement during my speech tonight."

Osternak shook his head. "It is too early for anything like that. You said yourself a moment ago that the implications are staggering. It is precisely for that reason that we cannot risk the turmoil that this kind of news would unleash, until we understand all of the ramifications fully." The professor waved at the equations strung across the blackboard on the wall. "We still don't understand the effects on mass-energy conservation, or the intricacies of sequential nested loops. From the animal experiments it appears that two passes through the chamber in too short a time can severely disrupt the central nervous system. We have no idea why. I understand your feelings, but with things like that unresolved, our byword for the foreseeable future can only be caution."

"Caution, caution, all I ever hear is 'caution'!" Gorfmann exploded. He turned his hands upward appealingly. "It wasn't caution that—"

"I'm sorry, Rudi, but I must insist." For the first time there was an edge of sharpness to Osternak's voice. "The

consequences of inviting pestering and interference from outside would be catastrophic at this stage of the project. That
position is final. I want your solemn word not to utter one
word about it, either tonight or on any future occasion,
without express official direction. Is that understood?''

Gorfmann marched across to the door and grasped the
handle without saying anything.

''Rudi,'' the professor called as he opened the door.
Gorfmann turned and looked back. ''Your assurance, please.''
Osternak's tone left no room for debating.

Gorfmann bit his lip in suppressed frustration. It was
either that, he could see, or he'd be out of a job before he got
out of the building. And that would mean an end to any
chance of benefiting from his involvement with the project—
ever. Not to mention the impossibility of getting hired by any
other of Osternak's cronies in the business, and a complete
ban on publication. . . . It was true: The old fart could ruin
him. He glared balefully through his spectacles and nodded
his head once, stiffly. ''Very well. But I protest.'' With that
he turned about and marched out of the office.

''Have a good evening, Rudi,'' the professor's voice
called after him.

As he came out, he noticed a cloth lying on the floor on
the opposite side of the corridor, outside the cleaners' closet
next to Professor Prandtl's office. Such sloppiness offended
him, and at another time he might have tossed it back inside.
But at this particular instant he was too annoyed to bother and
walked away, making a mental note to have a word with the
cleaners about it tomorrow.

Feeling debonair and resplendent in his black tie and
evening dress, Rudi Gorfmann walked up to the spotlit po-
dium and smiled to acknowledge the applause following the
toastmaster's introduction. ''Thank you, ladies and gentle-
men.'' He paused and looked around the tables of white
shirtfronts and glittering hands and throats. ''I have something confidential to announce concerning our work at the
Erwin Schrödinger Memorial Research Institute.'' He looked
from side to side ominously. An expectant silence fell. ''Up
there, in our castle-laboratory in the mountains, we are not
really making a Frankenstein monster. But the image is one

of the conditions that we have to meet under the terms of our contract. You see, we are funded by the proceeds from the will of an eccentric German billionaire who had a fixation about bats and cats.'' Appreciative laughter came from around the room. ''But seriously, thank you again for asking me to come and say a few words tonight. It is probably not often that a professional scientist gets an opportunity to speak on these occasions. Therefore I will make the most of that opportunity by saying a few words about science. . . .''

At his table afterward, he was the center of attention. ''I thought that what you said about quantum mechanics was fascinating, Dr. Gorfmann,'' the platinum blonde sitting on one side of him said. ''I believe that quantum mechanics might be the explanation for telepathy and ESP. What do you think?''

''First one must be certain there is something that needs explaining,'' Gorfmann replied profoundly.

''Oh, it's been authenticated, no doubt about it,'' a tall, thin-haired man opposite declared airily. ''In fact I have irrefutable experience of it myself.''

''I am sure some people would consider it irrefutable.''

''But we have a lot of science in the world already, and a lot of people still aren't happy,'' a bejeweled, middle-aged woman said from farther along. ''It can't guarantee happiness, and that's what counts.''

''What can?'' Gorfmann asked. ''That's not what science ever set out to accomplish. Its purpose is discovery, no more.''

''But people don't look at it that way,'' the bejeweled woman's husband said, as if that meant something.

''What I mean is, those people who spend lots of money on gadgets because they expect wonderful things, and then find out that they're just as miserable.''

''More so. They're broke,'' a sandy-haired man said. The others smiled.

''Then perhaps they should re-examine their expectations,'' Gorfmann suggested.

Buffoons, all of them, he thought inwardly. Functionally incompetent, overindulged children. If intellectual defectives like these could brainwash a society of drones into lavishing them with accolades and riches, what would those of genuine ability accomplish if they put their minds to it? It was the likes of Osternak, with their pathetic notions of modesty and professional ethics, who kept the glamour out of science and deglorified it, consigning themselves to second-class roles in the world when they could have been running it. Things would change when Gorfmann got where he was aiming.

"What do you think is the best way of teaching children to be rational and logical?" the brunette who was with the sandy-haired man asked.

"You can't. They already are. But you can unteach them."

The head waiter came to the far end of the top table, which was where Gorfmann was sitting, and asked the club secretary something. The secretary indicated Gorfmann with a motion of his hand, and the head waiter approached. Gorfmann looked up inquiringly.

"Dr. Gorfmann?"

"Yes."

"I'm sorry to interrupt, but there is a telephone call for you. You may take it at the table if you wish."

"Oh?" Gorfmann looked surprised. He wasn't aware of anything urgent. "Very well. Yes, thank you. I'll take it here."

The head waiter nodded in the direction of one of the doorways, and another waiter who had been waiting there came forward carrying a cordless phone on a tray. He deposited the tray beside Gorfmann's plate and retired to a discreet distance. The other guests diverted their attention to leave Gorfmann a measure of privacy.

"Hello? This is Rudi Gorfmann speaking."

"Just checking," a man's voice replied. There was a hint of a chuckle in it, as if the speaker was feeling pleased with himself and couldn't quite contain it.

"Who is this, please?"

"It doesn't matter. Let's just say that, as I know you'll be pleased to learn, you're even cleverer than you think."

"Look, I don't—" There was a click, and then a buzz came on the line. Gorfmann put the phone down and sat back in his chair, baffled. The waiter, who had been hovering, came forward. Gorfmann nodded, and the waiter took the tray away.

The platinum blonde next to him glanced around and saw that the others were still talking among themselves. She laid a hand lightly on his arm and leaned closer to whisper. "Some friends of mine will be getting together later at the Claremont. Do you know it?"

"The ski lodge, higher up in the pass, above the Institute? Yes, it's very nice up there."

"It will be just a few late-night drinks, and maybe a small party. If you've no other plans, perhaps you'd like to join us?" The blonde held his eyes pointedly. "It can be a very friendly atmosphere."

Gorfmann considered the proposition. He had left his car at the Institute and driven down to Innsbruck with Dr. Hoetzer, since they had some technical things to discuss. So Hoetzer would have to drop him off at the Institute, but it was on the way to the Claremont, anyhow. "Thank you," he said. "No, I have nothing else planned. Shall I meet you up there later?"

"I'll be waiting," the blonde said alluringly. "My name is Lisa." Gorfmann smiled at her conspiratorially.

He sat back in his chair to sip his wine and surveyed the room with a satisfied eye. Yes, indeed, it was going to be a good life, he decided . . . once he had found a way to get around that doddering fossil, Osternak.

"I tried talking to Osternak about it tonight before we left," Gorfmann said, gesticulating in Hoetzer's wagon as they drove back from Innsbruck. "I wanted to say something at the banquet, in fact. But he wouldn't listen. I think he's getting past this kind of work. Perhaps we should start organizing ourselves to do something about it." He eyed Hoetzer surreptitiously as he spoke, gauging his reaction.

"Well, let's see what happens at the policy meeting next week," Hoetzer replied tactfully. They came out of the last of the bends on the steep climb from the Weiderwasser bridge and saw the lights of the Institute's main gate ahead. "Where's your car parked, Rudi?" Hoetzer asked, happy to change the subject.

"In front, outside the Keep," Gorfmann replied.

The general parking area for staff was inside the main gate, adjoining the maze of alleys and irregular-shaped yards between the various buildings, known collectively as the "compound." At the front of the Keep, however, there was an enclosed gravel forecourt with a small parking area reserved for senior personnel, which opened onto the road via a separate gate.

"I wonder, could you do me a small favor?" Hoetzer asked.

"What's that?"

"I need to pick up a generator set that I'm borrowing. It's just behind the gate from the compound into the center parking area. I could use some help lifting it into the wagon."

Gorfmann pulled a face in the darkness. He wanted to go home, change into more casual wear, and then be on his way up to the Claremont to meet Lisa as quickly as possible. But there was no way out of it. "Of course," he said, forcing a genial tone.

"Thank you so much."

"Not at all."

They turned into the main gateway, and Hoetzer stopped to let the security guard know what they were doing—the guard seemed aware of the arrangement already. Then they drove across to the other side of the almost empty parking area, and Hoetzer reversed into a slot in front of the compound gate. "Hardly the best dress for this kind of thing," Hoetzer said cheerfully as he climbed out.

"No," Gorfmann agreed. He took off his topcoat, folded it, and put it on the seat before joining Hoetzer on the other side of the gate. The generator was mounted on a steel-frame base with a lifting bar at each end. Gorfmann looked it over and undid his tie before tackling it. They manhandled the generator through the gate and across the few meters to the wagon. "The guard seemed to know about this already," Gorfmann remarked as Hoetzer opened the rear door.

"Oh yes. I cleared it with security this afternoon. I just didn't want to drive all the way down to Innsbruck and back up again with the weight."

"Very sensible."

They heaved the generator up onto the tailboard, and the wagon sank on its suspension as it took the load. Hoetzer slammed the door shut and dusted his hands together in a manner indicative of a job well done. "Thanks so much," he said again.

"Don't mention it. Look, I'll tell you what." Gorfmann gestured in the direction of the compound gate. "Why don't I just go through the Keep? It'll be quicker than driving around, and you won't have to stop."

"It wouldn't be any trouble. . . ."

"No, the walk would be quicker."

"Well, if you're sure."

"Yes. I'll see you tomorrow."

"Okay, then. Good night, Rudi."

"Good night. Thank you for the ride."

Gorfmann walked back through the gate and began cross-ing the compound through the jumble of shadows cast by the surrounding structures and laboratory buildings. As he forgot about Osternak and Hoetzer and generators, and his mind turned to thoughts of the promise that lay ahead with Lisa, his pace quickened, and he began whistling to himself.

"Hey, Rudi," Hoetzer's voice called from behind him. Gorfmann stopped and looked back. Hoetzer was standing just inside the gate, holding something up. "You forgot your coat."

"Oh, silly of me," Gorfmann called back. He turned and retraced his steps.

"That won't do. You're turning into an absentminded professor already," Hoetzer said, handing it over.

"I hope not. We've got one too many of those already."

"Now, now, Rudi."

"Thank you. Good night again."

"Good night."

Slipping his coat on as he walked, Gorfmann crossed the compound again and entered the rear door of the Keep, which to his mild surprise he found unlocked—but that happened sometimes. He walked along the darkened passageway that led to the front lobby and went out through the main entrance to the executive forecourt, feeling in his pocket for his keys. But at the bottom of the shallow steps outside the door, he stopped dead in sudden bewilderment. His car was not there.

Fuming, he paced from one end of the forecourt to the other, thinking that someone might have moved it for some reason, but the reaction was a mechanical one—it was obvi-ous just by looking that there was nowhere else the car could have been. Finally, accepting the inevitable, he stormed back into the lobby, slamming the door behind. "What in hell's going on?" he muttered to himself as he crossed back to the passageway leading to the rear door. "Oh God, this is too much. Not at a time like this, of all nights!"

He went back through the compound, across the staff parking area, and reported the loss to the security officer on duty at the main gate. Then he signed for one of the Institute's pool cars and used that to go home and change into casual wear before carrying on up to the Claremont. By the time he got there, he was beginning to get over his misfortune. It was quite late next morning when he left again, and he went straight to the Institute. By then he was feeling still irritable at the inconvenience, but much better.

In the transfer-chamber control room, Gorfmann typed the parameters for the test run into the supervisory console, verified the readback on the display screen, and confirmed the command. "Envelope profile verified and locked," he reported to Kurt and Hilda at the other stations. "How are we doing on the interface?"

Hilda consulted another panel. "Override is released," she said.

"Probe vector, Kurt?"

"They're still adjusting the resonators."

"Estimate another ten minutes to phase three," Gorfmann said into a microphone on his console.

"Check," a voice replied from a grille by the screen.

A phone rang at the back of the room. Moments later, Josef called from the desk by the door, "Reception calling for you, Dr. Gorfmann."

"Put it through." Gorfmann picked up the handset from the hook on one side of the console. "Hello, Gorfmann here."

"Main Gate Reception. There is an Inspector Wenkle from the police department here, asking to see you."

Gorfmann frowned, surprised. He had only reported a stolen car—hardly earth-shattering enough to warrant a personal visit, he would have thought. He sighed at the fastidiousness of plodding officialdom. "Very well. Show him into the visitor room there, would you. I'll be over in a few minutes."

"Very good."

Gorfmann turned toward Kurt, who was entering numbers from a list into a keyboard. "Take over here, please, Kurt. I have to go and see someone at the main gate. And remember what I told you about the synchronizing calibration. It is most important for it to be accurate."

"Sure."

"Is it about your car?" Hilda asked.

"Probably, but that is a personal matter. You have your work to worry about. Kindly attend to it." Gorfmann hung his lab coat by the door at the back of the room and left.

Kurt and Hilda made faces and exchanged shrugs. "Snotty today, even for him," Kurt observed.

"Well, he has just lost a brand-new car," Hilda said.

"What did he need a car like that for anyway?" Kurt asked. "Planning on moving to Hollywood or somewhere, is he?"

"Oh, he's a big celebrity now, didn't you know?" Josef said from the back. "Science guru of the trendy set. Big hit at the dinner in town last night."

"I wonder if we could transfer him back to another century," Kurt mused distantly. "How about the Dark Ages? I figure they could have used some help then."

"Perhaps somebody already did," Josef said. "That could be what turned them off science for a thousand years."

Gorfmann entered the visitor room and closed the door behind him. A man wearing a tan raincoat and Tyrolean hat, and holding a thin leather document case under one arm, turned away from examining the exhibits in the display case on the far wall. He was of medium height and build, with a swarthy face, big nose, and thick black mustache. He nodded his head to indicate the caption FUSION PHYSICS over a section of the display. "It says there that if all the energy you could get from the fusion fuel in the oceans is represented by the distance across the Atlantic, then on the same scale Arabia's oil reserves measure six thousandths of an inch," he said.

"That sounds about right," Gorfmann agreed.

"Amazing, isn't it? And yet you still read things that say we're about to run out of it."

"You shouldn't believe everything you read."

"Is that the kind of work you do here?"

"Some sections of the Institute are involved in related areas. I myself am concerned with more fundamental aspects of physics. Inspector, look, I am extremely busy. We are about to begin an experimental run. Could we get to the point, please?"

"Of course." Wenkle's manner became more brisk. He removed his hat and sat down near the end of the table, which took up most of the room, motioning with a hand for Gorfmann to take the head chair, across the corner. Gorfmann did so. Wenkle put the document case down next to his hat and took out a manila folder, from which he produced several forms clipped together, and some handwritten notes.

"I take it this is to do with my car," Gorfmann said after Wenkle had perused the papers in silence for a few seconds.

"Er, yes . . . Dr. Gorfmann."

"Well, have you found it?"

Wenkle studied his notes for a moment longer. "First, could we go over some of the information you gave when you reported the loss? The vehicle was left on these premises, is that correct?"

"Yes, but is this really necessary? You have just said that I've already given you this information."

"We do like to double-check our facts, if you wouldn't mind, sir. It will only take a few minutes."

"Very well. Let's get on with it."

"Now, let's see, you left the car here at the Institute, and went down into Innsbruck yesterday evening. How did you get there?"

"I drove down with a colleague—Dr. Hoetzer, from the plasma laboratory. We had some technical matters to discuss. It seemed opportune to use the time."

"I see. And at what time did you leave?"

"At six o'clock."

"Approximately."

"No. Precisely."

"Ah . . . I noticed when I arrived that staff parking seems to be inside this gate. Is that where you left your car?"

"No. There is also a small parking area for senior personnel at the front of the Keep, where the offices are. It has its own driveway, leading directly out to the road.''

"So the thief wouldn't have had to go past the security post here at the main gate?''

"That is correct.''

"What was the purpose of your trip?''

"I was a speaker at a fund-raising banquet given by the Celebrity Club at the Hotel Ibis. Is that sufficient?''

"More than adequate.'' Wenkle added some comments to his notes and turned the page. "And you left the hotel in Innsbruck with Dr. Hoetzer at? . . .''

"Oh, I'd say about ten.''

"Precisely?'' Wenkle's tongue poked at his cheek for the merest fraction of a second.

Sniff. "Approximately.''

"And what time did you arrive back here?''

"Let me see. . . . We left the ballroom at around ten, a few minutes to collect coats and get Hoetzer's wagon from the garage . . . Oh, it must have been around ten-thirty, ten forty-five at the outside. I found that my car was gone, and I reported it. Now, if you're completely satisfied, Inspector . . .'' Gorfmann half rose, bracing his hands on the edge of the table to indicate that he was ready to leave.

Wenkle, however, shifted another form to the top of the papers in front of him and studied it, giving no sign that he was finished. Gorfmann held his pose for a few more seconds, then conceded with a sigh and sat down again. Finally Wenkle said, "Yes, we do have some information, Dr. Gorfmann. Your car was found this morning, at the bottom of a two-hundred-meter cliff less than a kilometer away, on the steep stretch of road between here, and the Weiderwasser bridge. From the impact point where it struck the rocks, it was evidently traveling at considerable speed, and the skid marks where it went off the road indicate that it was out of control.''

Gorfmann looked stunned. "My God! . . . Is it badly damaged? It was almost new.''

"Completely burned out, I'm afraid. I assume your insurance will take care of that.''

"And that driver? Was he? . . .''

"Oh, no doubt killed instantly. The body was burned to

a cinder. We're having to run checks on dental and medical records to try and identify him.''

"I see. . . . That's terrible. . . . Have you been able to determine when this occurred, Inspector?''

"Not really. As I said, the car was found early this morning. But from the amount of burning and the degree to which it had cooled, the accident itself must have happened many hours earlier. It could have been at any time during the night or the previous evening. The car was in a gorge, invisible from the road. We were alerted only when somebody reported the broken fence and headlamp glass, after daybreak this morning.''

Gorfman licked his lips as the full awareness sank in. "Well, if there's anything else I can tell you . . .''

"Just one thing. Out of curiosity, do you have your car keys with you now?''

"Yes.''

"May I see them, please?''

Gorfmann reached into his trouser pocket and drew out a leather-tagged key ring containing as assortment of keys. "That one, and that one," he said, separating out two of them.

"Thank you. Er, do you have another set, by any chance?''

"I do, as a matter of fact. I keep them in the desk in my office, here at the Institute.''

"When was the last time you saw them?''

"Oh . . .'' Gorfmann made a vague motion in the air that could have meant anything. "I don't know. You don't really notice after a while, if you know what I mean. They've been there since I bought the car.''

"Have you been to your office this morning?

"Well, no actually. . . . I, er, I was somewhat later getting back down from the Claremont than I intended, and since we were due to conduct some rather important tests, I went directly to the lab. I was there until you arrived.''

"And you haven't heard of anything unusual being reported from there today—somebody breaking in, for instance?''

"Breaking in?'' Gorfmann looked surprised. "No, nothing like that at all. Why?''

In reply, Wenkle reached inside his document case

again and drew out a plain white envelope. From it he took a key ring with just two keys on it, smoke-blackened and dulled. It also had a medallion attached, bearing a distinctive red motif and encased in a plastic coating that had been partially melted. "Are these the keys from your desk, Dr. Gorfmann?" he inquired.

Gorfmann stared in astonishment. "Why, yes. . . . Yes, they are."

"Can you explain how they came to be in the thief's possession?"

Gorfmann blinked rapidly behind his gold-rimmed spectacles. "No, Inspector, I can't," he replied, for once completely bemused. "I have no explanation to offer at all."

One side of the road had been closed off for a short distance by temporary barriers, reducing the traffic to a single lane. A few cars waited at one end while a policeman wearing a Day-Glo orange overjacket directed traffic through in the other direction. Rudi Gorfmann looked on glumly from a rocky projection above the gorge, while from behind the barriers a tow truck from Innsbruck winched what was left of his car slowly up the precipice. Inspector Wenkle and several other officers, along with two men from the insurance company, were watching from in front of some cars parked in a line along the verge. A cold breeze was coming down from the mountains, and Gorfmann drew the collar of his fur-lined parka closer around his neck and face.

At least, whoever had taken it hadn't had long to derive much pleasure from the act, he reflected with a twinge of satisfaction. Serve him right. Too much riffraff on the loose altogether, these days—with no sense of decency or respect for other people's rights or property. No discipline in the schools, that was what it was. Too many do-gooders hamstringing the police.

After Wenkle's visit to the Institute the previous day to inform him about the accident, he remembered recalling that Osternak hadn't been seen by anyone that morning, which was unusual because the professor went by strict habits. For a while, Gorfmann had wondered secretly if maybe—just maybe, for some reason—it might have been Osternak who had gone over in the car. Perhaps he had lost his keys, or forgotten where he'd parked his own car or something, and in some kind of emergency borrowed Gorfmann's—he knew that Gorfmann kept a spare set of keys in his desk. Unlikely, admittedly . . . but not impossible. But then Osternak had reappeared later in the afternoon and shattered that fond hope. Now Gorfmann would have to go through the chore of choosing, buying, and getting them to fix all the problems and squeaks in another piece of moron-engineered incompetence that passed as a new car.

But it was a thought. . . . Maybe he could doctor the brakes of Osternak's car one of these dark, slippery nights. . . . Tricky, though. Gorfmann's position at the Institute would make him an immediate suspect. It wouldn't do to simply leave a trap like that, which he could have set as easily as anyone else. It would have to be done in such a way that he'd have an absolutely foolproof alibi.

"It feels as if winter's on its way," a voice said. Inspector Wenkle had walked over and was standing next to him.

"Yes, quite a nip in the wind. Have you made any progress in identifying the culprit?"

"Not yet, but it's still early. There's information to come in from a lot of places. From the X rays, it seems that he had a surgical pin in his knee—you know the kind of thing I mean?"

"Yes indeed. In fact I have one myself. It was from a climbing accident, many years ago."

"They're quite common. . . . Oh, and there was another thing. I talked to Dr. Hoetzer. Apparently he almost had an accident himself last night, immediately after dropping you off. He tells me that as he was driving out of the main gate, a car came out of the gateway higher up at the Keep, swerving all over the road at considerable speed, and almost collided with him head-on. It seems probable that it was your car, Dr. Gorfmann."

"Good heavens! Then I must have just missed him by minutes."

"So it would appear. But it does fix the time of the theft at around ten-thirty. If anything else turns up, of course I'll let you know."

"Thank you. I would appreciate it."

"Well, I must be getting back. Good day, then."

"Good day, Inspector."

The solution occurred to him a half hour later, as he was leaving the site in his pool car after the wreck had been hauled away. Of course! With a time machine at his disposal, he had the means for constructing the *perfect* alibi! Literally perfect. For what better way could there be of establishing that he had been in another place at the time a murder was committed, than actually *being* there? He could arrange for there to be two of him! Let even the best Wenkle in the world find a hole in that if he could. Gorfmann was so pleased with the inspiration that he laughed and chuckled out loud to himself all the way back to the Institute.

For the alibi to be effective, Osternak would have to be done away with in a manner that required the killer to actually be there, physically, at the time. That way, the incontestable demonstration that he, Gorfmann—i.e. his other self—had been somewhere else would prove his innocence beyond question. And the perfect occasion had been just two nights before, when he knew, moreover, that Osternak had been working late, alone, in his dingy office up in the Keep. He also knew that Osternak, being Swiss, kept a revolver in the middle drawer of his desk. As the police would reconstruct it, the professor would have disturbed an intruder who had discovered the gun, and in the ensuing confrontation been shot with his own weapon. The time would be known precisely, and Gorfmann would have been miles away, in full view of hundreds of people. It was perfect. There would then be one other key participant to be taken care of to avoid possible complications, of course, but recent events had even provided a means of accomplishing that.

By the evening of that same day, he had completed his plans. He waited until it was late at night, when the Institute was still. Then, wearing loose black clothing, his face darkened by streaks of greasepaint, and carrying a bag with a day's supply of food and a flask of hot coffee, a kit of tools, and a formal evening suit with dress shirt, he materialized stealthily from the shrubbery by the executive parking area and let himself into the Keep. He crossed the lobby and went along the darkened passageway to the rear door that opened out into the compound, and from there, keeping to the shadows, made his way over to the dome containing the time-transfer gate. Inside the control room, he activated the supervisory console, and working quickly, primed the system for a simple transfer back to the early morning hours of the the day before last—he couldn't risk arriving later, when people might be around. That meant he would have to find somewhere to lay up through the day, but that wouldn't be difficult.

He set the initialization routine on automatic with a delay of thirty seconds, then hurried through to the transfer room itself, climbed inside the safelike, metal-walled chamber, and closed the door. A few seconds later his head seemed to explode in a riot of colors, and he felt as if his body was fizzing from head to toe, like a can of shaken-up soda. Then the sensation passed, leaving only a tingling in his fingers and a mild feeling of nausea, which quickly passed. He opened the door carefully. All outside was dark and still. He went through to the control room and the console display verified that the time and date were as he had intended. Satisfied, he crossed back to the Keep and made his way up to one of the attic rooms, hardly ever visited, which was used to store old office machinery, archived documents, and some pieces of surplus furniture that even included a comfortable four-seat couch. Yes, he would be fine here for a day, he decided, looking around. He'd even brought himself a couple of books to read. And the wait would be well worth it.

It was early evening when Gorfmann emerged and crept down to the floor on which Osternak's office was situated. Policemen were always making such a big thing about how thorough they were. The way to prevail against them was to be even more thorough. And how could such pedestrian, one-dimensional minds stand a chance against thoroughness combined with scientific training?

The corridor ran from front to back of the building, between doors leading to stairways at both ends. He waited behind the door to the rear until he saw his earlier self come in at the other end from the front stairs and go into Osternak's office. After a few minutes' wait, he tiptoed along to Professor Prandtl's office, which would suit his purpose nicely—it was opposite Osternak's, and Prandtl was away on a lecture visit to the U.S. until the following week. He turned the handle gently, eased the door open, and slipped inside . . . and instantly recoiled back out again. There was somebody in there—lying on the sofa beneath Prandtl's window, wrapped in blankets and seemingly asleep. Gorfmann didn't know what to make of it. Somebody with domestic troubles staying away from the house, perhaps? But he didn't have time to wonder, for he was out in the open in the corridor, and anyone could appear at any moment. He looked around for an alternative, spotted the cleaners' closet next to Prandtl's office, and quickly hid himself inside. It would give him just as good a view of Osternak's door, anyway.

The secret was to be thorough and check everything. He waited, watching, through the crack from the closet. The first thing was to be absolutely certain that the time sequence he was on was as he remembered.

And then the handle of Osternak's door rattled and turned a fraction. Gorfmann brought his eye close to the crack to observe. Osternak's door had opened partly, and through it he could see the version of himself that he had been two days ago, standing with one hand on the door handle and looking back into the room. "Your assurance, please," Osternak's voice demanded sharply from inside the office. And then Gorfmann's eye drifted downward, and he saw to his consternation that a cleaning cloth was lying on the floor, right outside the closet. He must have dislodged it from one of the hooks inside the door in his hurry to hide himself. Instinctively, he crouched down, pushed the door open a fraction, and started to reach out.

His other self nodded his head stiffly. "Very well. But I protest." It was no good. There wasn't time. Gorfmann pulled the door to again and watched, petrified, through the crack as his other self came angrily out of Osternak's office.

"Have a good evening, Rudi," Osternak's voice called out.

His other self closed the door, glanced down at the cloth, hesitated for a split second, then snorted and walked away. Gorfmann straightened himself up slowly, shaking with relief and silent laughter. Of *course* . . . it *had* to work out that way. It had already happened!

His speech at the banquet had ended at about ten minutes

after eight. It was now almost six o'clock. He emerged from the closet and went along to the accounts office, which overlooked the front parking area, and just to be doubly certain, watched himself depart at six exactly with Hoetzer in Hoetzer's wagon. Then he went up two floors and along to Hoetzer's office, where he switched on the large graphics printer that Hoetzer used for generating enlarged particle-trajectory diagrams from detector photographs, and set it to high-resolution mode. If left in that condition all night, the circuits would overheat and burn out. He didn't want to damage the machine, but a couple of hours would give it time to warm up nicely. Happy that all was going according to plan, he went back up to his hideout to wait. The secret was to be thorough, thorough . . .

He emerged two hours later at eight-fifteen, wearing thin cotton gloves now, and went down to the pay phone located in an alcove off the front lobby—that way there wouldn't be any record of the call on the Institute's telephone account.

"Thank you for calling. This is the Hotel Ibis, Innsbruck."

"Hello. I believe you have a banquet there tonight, being given by the Celebrity Club?"

"Yes, sir, we do."

"I need to speak with one of the guests, please. It is most urgent."

"One moment." Gorfmann thought he heard somebody come in through the back door from the compound. He leaned out from the alcove and peered along the darkened passage leading to the rear of the building . . . but there was no one. He remembered the figure on the couch in Prandtl's office and prayed that something wasn't about to go wrong now, through factors he couldn't possibly have anticipated. That would have been too unjust. But there seemed to be something strange afoot in the place. . . . Then the operator at the Ibis came back on the line. "The guests are all eating at the moment, sir."

"I'm sorry, but it is important," Another pause.

"Whom did you wish to speak to, sir?"

"I wish to speak to somebody there called Gorfmann. A Dr. Rudi Gorfmann."

"Who is calling?"

"Just put me through, please."

"One moment. I'm transferring you to a table phone."

"Thank you." Jubilation surged through him. It was all working!

Then a voice on the line said, "Hello? This is Rudi Gorfmann speaking."

He didn't believe it himself. "Just checking," he said, smothering the impulse to laugh.

"Who is this, please?"

"It doesn't matter. Let's just say that, as I know you'll be pleased to learn, you're even cleverer than you think."

"Look, I don't—" He hung up.

The next thing to do was get Osternak out of his office for a few minutes to allow himself to slip in. That was why he had switched on the printer a couple of hours previously. He inserted more coins and punched in the number of the direct line to Osternak's office. Through the deserted building from the floor above, he caught the muted sound of a telephone ringing. Then a voice in the receiver said, "Hello?"

"Professor Osternak?" Gorfmann said, roughening his voice.

"Yes."

"Sorry to trouble you, Professor, but this is Security at the main gate."

"Yes?"

We've just had a call here from Dr. Hoetzer, in Innsbruck."

"Oh?"

"He says that he was in a hurry to leave this evening, and that he left a piece of equipment switched on in his office—a graphics printer, I think he said."

"Oh dear. That could be unfortunate."

"So I understand. But apparently a certain procedure has to be followed to turn it off. I offered to take the directions down over the phone, but Dr. Hoetzer was short of time. He said you were up there tonight, and your office is only two levels down from his."

"Oh, I see. You'd like me to go up and turn it off for him."

"If it wouldn't be too much trouble, Professor."

"Oh, good heavens, no. No trouble at all. I'll attend to it right away."

"Thank you very much."

"Not at all. Good night."

"Good night, Professor." Gorfmann replaced the phone. "Heh, heh, heh. And good-bye, Professor," he murmured in his natural voice. Since Hoetzer's room was at the far end of the building, Osternak would use the rear stairs. Gorfmann moved swiftly across the lobby and went up the front staircase by the elevators. He halted at the double doors into the corridor leading to Osternak's office and peeped through in time to see Osternak's door open and the professor emerge and disappear through the doors at the far end. Gorfmann waited until the far doors had swung shut then walked quickly to the open door of Osternak's office. Inside, he went straight to the desk and rummaged through the drawers. The gun was there. He checked the chambers. It was loaded. That was the final thing that might have gone wrong. He went through the drawers, rifling them and scattering the contents the way an intruder would, swept the papers off a side table, tossing down a few books from the shelves for good measure. Then he turned over a chair and a small table to give the appearance of a struggle, and threw down a candlestick, a figurine, and the clock from the mantleshelf over the fireplace, making sure that the clock was broken and showed the correct time. Finally he turned off the desk lamp, loosened the bulb in the ceiling light until it went out, turned it off at the switch by the door, and stood back in the shadows to wait.

He heard the door from the rear stairs open and Osternak's footsteps approaching less than a minute later. The professor appeared in the doorway, hesitated when he saw the darkness inside, then advanced a pace into the room and flipped the wall switch. Nothing happened. Then he did exactly what Gorfmann had anticipated: He came on into the room to try the desk lamp.

There would be no melodramatics or gloating speeches, Gorfmann had decided. Besides being rather distasteful, they provided an additional opportunity for things to go wrong. It would happen just as if he were a real intruder. When Osternak was halfway across the room, Gorfmann stepped forward to be sure of his aim and fired twice at the heart. Osternak cried out in shock and reeled away, clapping a hand to his chest, crashed into a chair, and fell over it in a heap. Gorfmann moved forward cautiously and waited, but the form lay motionless, picked out in the light from the doorway. Gorfmann reached up and tightened the ceiling-lamp bulb. The light came on to reveal the professor staring upward with glazed eyes, with a mess of blood covering his hand and chest, and spreading onto the carpet. Gorfmann grimaced to himself and walked over to turn the light off again at the wall switch. From the doorway he surveyed the scene for anything he might have overlooked. Finding nothing, he pocketed the gun—an intruder would hardly have left it; it would be found later in a place where it would seem to have been thrown away—and went back up to his hideout room for the tools that he'd brought. Now it was time for the really diabolical part of the whole thing.

For the remaining problem now, of course, was that there were two of him in existence—a situation that would cause impossible complications and which obviously couldn't be permitted to last. And since the mind of his alter ego could be guaranteed to work in the same way as his own—it was the same mind, after all—it wouldn't take long for the alter ego to figure out what was going on—again an intolerable state of affairs. Therefore the alter ego would have to go. The world was only big enough for one Rudi Gorfmann, anyway.

However, the beautiful thing about it all was that chance had already provided him the means. Wenkle had pinpointed the theft of his car as having occurred no earlier than ten-thirty. It was not yet eight forty-five. Hence he had over an hour and a half to do a sabotage job on his car, parked out front in the executive parking area. Then he would wait for the thief to appear, and force the events that followed into a different sequence. For if he prevented the theft from occurring, then obviously the car would still be there when his other self returned from Innsbruck. The accident would still happen, but with the subtle difference that the body recovered would be his unwanted other, unsuspecting self's, not the thief's. That meant, of course, that he would be on a new timeline and things would proceed from there on in a different way—but that would be no different from playing life by ear in the normal way that people did every day. In other words, he could handle it. The important thing was that Osternak would have been killed after surprising an intruder, who stole Gorfmann's car and in his panic to get away went over the cliff. An unidentifiable body would be recovered from the wreck, and a very alive Gorfmann—himself—would reappear to deplore the tragedy. Brilliant!

He worked deftly and surely, fixing the primary braking system in such a way that it would feel normal the first couple of times the pedal was depressed, and then fail catastrophically. And just to be sure there would be no chance of recovery, he disabled the emergency brake. He finished well before ten, and feeling pleased with himself, cleared away his tools and settled down to wait well back in the shadows of the shrubbery for the thief. After Hoetzer dropped him off upon their return from Innsbruck, he had come through the Keep and out the front door. The thief might come from that direction, or from another.

And then a light came on in one of the windows one level up, overlooking the forecourt—in the accounts office, Gorfmann ascertained from its position relative to the front door. A face appeared inside, pressing forward to peer down and shielding its eyes from the reflected light off the glass. Gorfmann remained motionless, deep under the shadow of the shrubbery. What was somebody doing in the accounts office at this hour? The face withdrew, and a moment later the light went out again. Was this something else to do with the figure on the sofa in Prandtl's office? Something strange was going on. Less than a minute later the performance repeated: the light in the accounts office came on once more, the same figure came to the window and peered down, went away, and the light went out again. Perhaps somebody on the staff was using the premises for nocturnal romantic trysts, and getting some sleep in Prandtl's office in anticipation of an active night. How disgraceful. Gorfmann would have something to say about that if he found out who it was. At least it might explain the presence of the thief, he reflected. But the thing to remember for now was the need to be careful with others around.

And then he heard footsteps approaching in haste, not from anywhere near the front door, but on the gravel path coming around the corner of the building from the side door by the library. Moments later, a figure came running around the corner, clad in a light-colored sweater. Gorfmann waited until he was certain that the figure was indeed heading for the car, then stepped out into view—but without getting too close for comfort—and called out sharply, "Who are you? What do you want?"

The figure stopped abruptly, recoiled, and fled back around the building. Gorfmann blinked behind his spectacles in the darkness, his hand feeling suddenly very slippery around the gun he'd been holding in his pocket as a precaution. Exit one thief. Was it really as easy as that?

And then he heard more footsteps coming across the lobby inside the main door and barely had time to duck back under the shrubbery before the door opened and a different figure appeared, this time wearing a topcoat over evening dress, its tie loosened as he had loosened his before helping Hoetzer with the generator. It was his alter ego. There could be no mistake about it. Fascinated, he watched himself climb into the car and start the engine. The lights came on, and the car backed out, changed into forward gear, and disappeared along the driveway and out onto the road. Then he heard it accelerating away downhill in the direction of the Weiderwasser bridge.

So, it was done. The timeline had been changed. A strange feeling of elation and sudden weariness came over him as he moved forward into the light from above the entrance and stood for a while, savoring the fresh night air and looking up at the stars. At the same time, he experienced an inner wonder at this new, awesome power that he had glimpsed, there for those with the nerve to grasp it. Yes, it was going to be a very new world, indeed.

Now it was time to become the Gorfmann who would go back to the main gate and report the stolen car. But that Gorfmann was supposed to have just come back from a banquet. He went in through the main door, and a patch of brake fluid on one of his shoes caused him to slip on the tiled floor of the vestibule. He cursed reflexively as he almost lost his balance and then went through to the men's washroom a short distance along the passage leading to the backdoor to clean up. A few minutes later he emerged, carrying the soiled coveralls, and moving cautiously since he was still mindful that there were others in the building, made his way back up to the attic to put on the evening dress that he had brought with him for the purpose. As he straightened his tie and pulled on his topcoat, he grinned at himself in the mirror in fond anticipation of replaying the same night with Lisa all over again. Time machines could be worth millions! The last thing he had to do was clean up the attic room to remove all traces of his occupancy, bundle up the gun and the other things he had used, and on the way downstairs, lock them away in his own office until he had a chance to dispose of them properly.

On his way down, he almost ran into Osternak.

Neither the professor nor his clothes had a mark on them.

Gorfmann stopped dead and stood, paralyzed. His eyes widened behind his spectacles. His head shook from side to side in a barely discernible motion of protest. "It can't be," he whispered.

The professor stared back at him, seeming equally bemused for a second or two, but then his features relaxed, almost as if he thought something was funny. "Oh, but it can," he said.

"How is this possible?"

"I don't understand it. You don't understand it. That's what I've been trying to tell you, Rudi, but you wouldn't listen. Do what you will. You can't win."

Something snapped inside Gorfmann's mind then. An insane look came into his eyes, and he shook his head again, violently this time. "Oh, but I can." Gorfmann produced the gun from inside the bundle he was holding. "So, I can't win, eh? We'll see about that." He motioned for Osternak to walk ahead of him, down the stairs. "And don't try anything clever, you old goat. I didn't hesitate to shoot you before, and I won't again."

"There's nothing you can—"

"Save your breath."

They reached the ground floor and went out the back of the Keep into the compound. Gorfmann was breathing rapidly and heavily, his eyes darting fearfully this way and that. The older man moved warily, avoiding provocation. They entered the transfer dome and went into the control room, where Gorfmann activated the supervisory console and began flipping switches with one hand, all the time keeping the gun in the other trained on Osternak.

"What do you think you are doing?" Osternak asked.

Gorfmann's voice was by now little more than a hiss through his teeth. "As you say, I don't know what went wrong. But we are going to do it again, and this time I will get it right." He motioned toward the door through to the transfer chamber. "In there."

"Rudi, for heaven's sake, listen to me. You don't—"

"Shut up."

"A second pass through the process will—"

"Move, or I'll shoot you now and take you through dead. It's all the same to me."

Osternak stepped into the chamber. Gorfmann squeezed in with him, keeping the muzzle of the gun jammed against the professor's ribs. He closed the door. Moments later, Osternak felt a brief dizziness as the transfer proceeded, nothing more. But Gorfmann screamed suddenly, sounding hideous in the confined space, and the gun clattered to the floor as he clutched his hands to the sides of his head. He slumped against Osternak, and his body slid downward as far as the narrow chamber would permit. The door opened, and Osternak struggled to heave the inert form onto the floor outside. He stepped out behind and stooped over it. "That's what I was trying to tell you. . . ." But there was no point. Gorfmann was unconscious.

Osternak hurried through into the control room and scanned the instrument readouts. Through some fluke nobody seemed to be around, although it was still late in the working day. He thought back, replaying the events of the last several hours in his mind as accurately as he could. Yes, there was still time. He picked up the telephone handset from the hook on the side of the console and tapped in a number.

"Yes," a voice acknowledged at the other end.

"Professor Osternak?" he queried, just to check.

"This is Professor Osternak, yes. Who is this, please?"

"I am a version of your later self."

"Oh . . . Oh really? That is most interesting," the other Osternak's voice said.

"There isn't a lot of time. Now, if my guess is correct, Rudi Gorfmann is there with you at this moment, and you are having a rather disagreeable conversation about going public with the program. Am I right?"

"Yes, that is true, quite true." The other Osternak was doing a commendable job of managing to sound casual.

"And it is true, is it not, that you have been fearing that an illicit transfer will be made sooner or later?"

"Yes, that is so. But how do you—"

"I know what you think, because I am you, you see. But then again, I don't have to tell you, because you are me."

"Of course. Amazing! And so it happens."

"It has happened—a transfer. We have a problem."

"So, what can I do for you?"

"Not me, for yourself. I am you, from about five hours in the future. Five hours ago, I was you, sitting in that chair and taking this call."

"This is astounding. I—"

"Listen. Gorfmann is a lot worse than you think. He's insane."

"You are serious, yes?"

"Later this evening he is going to murder you."

"This is unbelievable. When does he intend to do this?"

"After eight, while his other self is at the banquet."

"Ach, so . . ."

"I haven't worked out all the details, but he seems to have set up another self as an alibi. He'll leave your office in a few more minutes, which will give us a couple of hours. I think we might be able to stop him."

"Can we get together and talk about this?"

"That's why I'm calling you."

"How?"

"Right now I am in the transfer control room. There is another version of Gorfmann here, too, but he is unconscious. He has gone through two transfers in too short a time, and I think the stress has deranged him completely—exactly what we have been worried about. There's no one else here at the moment, but I'm going to move him into the motor room in case anyone comes back. As soon as the one that's with you leaves the office, get over here as fast as you can and give me a hand to move him somewhere safer. Then we can talk about what to do."

"I shall be most interested to meet you."

*   *   *

The two Osternaks used a dolly from the materials store to cart the still lifeless Gorfmann across the compound and into the Keep, where they took him up to Professor Prandtl's office, since Prandtl was away for a week, and laid him out on the sofa by the window. They loosened his tie and made him comfortable with blankets and a pillow borrowed from the medical room on the floor below. As an afterthought, Osternak Two removed the car keys from Gorfmann's pocket. "I think as a precaution we'll hang on to these," he said. "It wouldn't do to let him go driving if he got out." Then they closed the door and went across the corridor to their own office to discuss what to do next.

The second Osternak—the one who had come back through the machine with Gorfmann—had a better idea of what was going on and assumed the initiative, taking the chair behind the desk. The other sat down opposite. "Fortunately, since we already share most of our thoughts, we don't have to waste a lot of time talking," Osternak Two said. In other words, Osternak One was already aware of the logical uncertainties surrounding this kind of situation. He didn't know if the events already established on a timeline could be altered; whether the situation involved parallel universes, branching universes, or heavens alone knew what; or what the complexities would be of skipping from one line to another. On the other hand, everything might be predetermined. That was precisely what the experiments currently in progress were designed to find out. Also, double passes through the process within too short a span of time caused disorientation of the central nervous system, and what the effects might be on somebody in Gorfmann's already unbalanced condition was anybody's guess.

"Agreed," Osternak One said. Which took care of the hours they could have spent debating things like that.

"I suggest that we play it safe until we're out of this wretched loop that Gorfmann has initiated," Osternak Two said. "Having two maniacs around is more than I know how to handle. So I say, let's play everything as it happened until the time that Gorfmann transferred back the first time to commit the murder. After that version of him goes back, there will only be one of him left, which will be a much simpler situation. We can worry about what to do next at that point.''

"What time was that—when he went back?" Osternak One asked.

"I don't know. I'm not even sure when he arrived. But since there have been people working in the transfer dome all day, I suspect he's already here somewhere. My guess is that he arrived last night or early this morning, and is holed up somewhere until the time he has picked.''

Osternak One nodded slowly. "Ah, I see . . . which will no doubt coincide with the time his other self is publicly visible at the banquet in Innsbruck.''

"Exactly," Osternak Two said.

"Hmm." Osternak One rubbed his chin. "Which one of us is going to get murdered?" he asked uncomfortably.

"Well, I've already been who you are right now, so it will have to be you.''

"Oh." Osternak One didn't sound overthrilled. Then his expression changed as the implication struck him. "Wait a minute, Osbert. If you were me, and you're not dead, then you can't have been killed.''

"Yes, I know you feel slightly stupid for having taken so long to see it, for I felt the same thing myself at this moment. So don't worry about it. The next question is, how are you going to stop him doing it?''

"You could tell me, of course.''

"Which is what I said, too, when I was you, of course. But I also know that you realized while you were saying it that it wouldn't do. It has to be your idea, to keep things the way they happened. We can experiment later with what happens when you deliberately change things—but let's get out of this situation first. Which I remember is what you are thinking yourself at this moment, anyway.''

"Well, if he is hiding in the building somewhere, we could search the place and . . . No, that wouldn't work, would it? That can't have happened with you.''

"You're catching on.''

"Why? Did you start to say the same thing?''

"Yes.''

"But I assume I must come up with something, since you evidently did.''

"I hope so. If not, God alone knows what happens."

Osternak One ran his fingers through his halo of white hair. "Well, the only thing I can think of is that we—I, that is—must fake it. Where do I get shot? Nothing gruesome, I hope."

"Twice, in the chest."

"Whose gun does he use?"

"Yours, from the desk. He makes it look as if an intruder was disturbed."

Osternak One thought for a moment, and then his expression lightened. "Ah, yes, well, in that case I could reload it with blanks. The sticky red solvent they use in the plating shop should make a passable blood substitute. . . . Er, does this happen in good light?"

Osternak Two beamed and nodded approvingly. "No, right here in the office. He lures you up to Hoetzer's lab for a few minutes with a bogus phone call, and when you get back he has fixed the lights. Complete darkness, apart from the light from the corridor."

"So a handful of the stuff carried in and smacked to the chest when he fires? . . ."

"Splendid, splendid!" Osternak Two said. He had a painful bruise on his hip from where he'd fallen over the chair, but saw no need to say anything about that. "Now, you have to stay here to take the phone call, which will come at about eight-thirty. Before then, I will have left a jar of red solvent from the plating shop on the table by the graphics printer in Hoetzer's office—you'll find out why when Gorfmann phones you. Also, I intend to install a hidden camera in the transfer-chamber room, running off a timer, to record when Gorfmann makes his first transfer back. Once that has occurred, we shall be out of the loop."

"He could have come back from several days ahead," Osternak One pointed out. "But of course, you are already aware of that."

"Yes. And that's why I'm going to set up a camera and not risk dying of cramp and cold trying to maintain a vigil there in person."

They stood up and regarded each other curiously. Finally Osternak One said, "Well, time is getting on. I have my preparations to make, and so do you. Is there anything useful I can do when I've cleaned up after being shot?"

"I'd just keep an eye on our sleeping friend across there," Osternak Two said, nodding his head in the direction of the door.

"Yes, well, I don't know if we're supposed to meet again, but in case not . . ." Osternak One held out a hand. The other shook it. "It's been . . . an interesting encounter." Osternak Two came around the desk, and walked toward the door. "One thing," Osternak One said. Osternak Two turned. "I don't know when I'm supposed to go back to become you."

"Oh, I think that will take care of itself," Osternak Two assured him. He turned away again and left through the door.

Outside in the corridor, Osternak Two looked briefly into Professor Prandtl's office to check on Gorfmann. The body was still out cold, but breathing more regularly now. Satisfied that there was no immediate call for medical help, he left the Keep through the rear entrance and went into the instrumentation lab to collect the things he needed to set up the camera. He carried the bits and pieces to the control room and found a suitable hiding place that commanded a good view of the transfer room and the door into the chamber. The camera and film were designed for extended-duration scientific work and would silently capture a frame every five seconds for twenty-four hours. There would be no trouble in coming back to change the magazine once a day if need be. He worked slowly and meticulously, his mind wandering over the peculiarities and apparent contradictions of the situation. How could the same object be physically present twice at the same time? What happened when somebody deliberately undid what had been done? Were memory patterns somehow altered to correlate with the changed circumstances? There were questions that he didn't have the beginnings of answers to yet. Time drifted on, and he became completely preoccupied with his thoughts. . . . And then his attention focused with the sudden realization that it was approaching eight-thirty . . . and his heart missed a beat. Oh God, the solvent!

He dropped what he was doing and hastened out into the

compound and over to the plating shop. There, he scooped a glob of the red goo from its container into an empty can, stuffed the can in a plastic bag, and hurried over to the Keep and in through the rear door. Just as he was about to ascend the rear stairs, he heard a voice coming from the passage leading through to the front lobby. Fearful that it was the other Osternak looking for him after failing to find the solvent— which would have meant that he'd missed his cue and ruined everything—he changed course and charged into the passage. But as he came closer to the lobby he recognized the voice as Gorfmann's and ducked hastily into a darkened doorway. Gorfmann was speaking under the canopy of the pay phone in the alcove at the end of the passage.

Gorfmann must have heard him come in, Osternak was certain. Yes, he could see Gorfmann's shadow form leaning out of the alcove to peer along the passageway toward the back door. Osternak froze in the doorway, not daring to move a muscle. And then, to his relief, Gorfmann moved back into the alcove again, and his voice resumed, "I'm sorry, but it is important . . . I wish to speak to somebody there called Gorfmann. A Dr. Rudi Gorfmann." Osternak frowned to himself in the darkness. He had guessed that Gorfmann must have made his call from somewhere nearby. The time was right, but the call wasn't. Why was Gorfmann calling himself? Was there a conspiracy being enacted between the two Gorfmanns, which he had never suspected? A sinking feeling of impending disaster came over him. From the alcove, Gorfmann's voice continued, "Just put me through, please . . . Thank you . . Just checking." Gorfmann sounded as if he was trying not to laugh. Then, "It doesn't matter. Let's just say that, as I know you'll be pleased to learn, you're even cleverer than you think." There was a click as Gorfmann hung up.

Osternak agonized in the darkness along the passage, wondering what to do. Then he realized that Gorfmann was making another call.

"Professor Osternak?" Gorfmann said, in a thick voice which the Osternak along the passage recognized instantly as something he had heard before. "Sorry to trouble you, Professor, but this is Security at the main gate . . . We've just had a call here from Dr. Hoetzer, in Innsbruck . . . Yes. He says that he was in a hurry to leave this evening, and . . .''

It was all still on track! He hadn't caused a disaster after all. Osternak drew in a deep breath to recover his wind after his rush across the compound and the tension he had experienced since, and then emerged from the doorway and backed quietly away along the passage. From the front of the building, he heard Gorfmann finish his call, leave the alcove, and go running up the front stairs. Osternak paused again for breath at the bottom of the rear stairs. Oh God, three flights.

When Osternak Two got to Hoetzer's office, Osternak One was already there, searching frantically under the table by the graphics printer and along the shelves above just as Osternak two had realized he would be. But Osternak Two was too breathless to explain, and besides there wasn't time. He opened the bag containing the can and held it while the other dipped his hand, and then waved weakly toward the door to send Osternak One on his way. Then he leaned against the printer for a while to regain his breath and composure. Just as he was coming back out onto the stairs, the sound of two shots in rapid succession came up the stairway from below.

When he was halfway back across the compound, it came to him that there were now not two, but three Gorfmanns loose: one at the banquet, one on Prandtl's couch, and the one who had just shot the other Osternak. So even when one of them made the transfer back through time, it would still leave two. The situation wouldn't simplify itself in the way he had imagined. He shook his head wearily, unable to grapple with any more of it and feeling like a piece of flotsam being carried along on a tide of events that was long past any ability of his to control. Resolved at least to complete what he had set out to do, he went back into the transfer dome to finish setting up the camera.

Professor Osternak One waited until he was sure that Gorfmann had left, then picked himself up slowly from the floor. His hip ached from the knock he had taken from the chair when he went down. Osternak Two could have warned him about that, he reflected huffily. Since he had no intention of lying there for the rest of the night, it followed that

Gorfmann would know anyway that the murder attempt had failed, should he choose to come back to the office for any reason. Therefore, Osternak reasoned, he might as well use some of the time he had to tidy things up. But first, he went to his lab to collect the spare shirt, tan sweater, and pants that he kept there in case of chemical spills and other accidents— the same clothes that Osternak Two had been wearing, he had noticed with curiosity, but it now made sense—and then proceeded to the washroom to change, and to sponge the worst of the stains from the clothes he had been wearing. Then he bundled up the wet clothes, returned to his office, and stowed them in a cupboard for sending to the cleaners the next day. That chore taken care of, he spent the next hour righting the furniture, returning the books to their places, and picking up and sorting through the papers that had been scattered all over the floor. It was a shame about the broken clock and the figurine, he reflected ruefully as he put them back in their places. Then he sat down and poured himself a brandy—he had just been murdered, after all. That deserved some compensation.

Only then did he remember that he was supposed to be keeping an eye on the Gorfmann in Prandtl's room across the corridor. Muttering a reproach to himself for his forgetfulness, he went out of the office, pushed open Prandtl's door, and looked in. And his jaw dropped in shock and dismay.

The couch and the room were empty. There was no trace of Gorfmann to be seen.

White-faced, Osternak One ran back into his own office and called the transfer-chamber room on an internal line. The ringing tone seemed to go on interminably, while all the time he tried frantically to think of the most likely places that Gorfmann might have gone. But with a madman, who could tell? Then the ringing stopped and his own voice answered cautiously, "Yes?"

"I'm in our office. He's gone. Gorfmann has gone. He's loose somewhere."

"I was just coming back. I've finished on the camera here. I'll be over there right away." Osternak Two hung up.

The car! Gorfmann mustn't be allowed to get to his car—in his state he could cause a massacre. He usually parked it in the executive area in front of the Keep, Osternak

knew. The first thing was to check if it was still there. He
went back into the corridor and along to the accounts office at
the front of the building, which overlooked the executive
parking area. He turned on a light, crossed the room to a
window, and peered down, shielding his eyes with a hand.
Gorfmann's car was still down there. That was something at
least. And then he remembered that Gorfmann couldn't use
the car anyway, because Osternak Two had taken his keys
when they put him in Prandtl's office. Silly of him to have
forgotten. Where, then— Keys! Gorfmann kept a spare set of
keys in his desk!

Osternak ran out of the accounts office and up the stairs
to the corridor where Gorfmann's office was situated. Sure
enough, there was a shadowy figure at the far end. He started
running toward it, expecting it to flee; it ran toward him,
evidently expecting the same thing. It was the other Osternak,
who, not surprisingly, had thought the same thing.

"His car's still there. I checked from the accounts office
window," Osternak One panted.

"I know it is," Osternak Two replied. "So did I."

The door of Gorfmann's office was open, the light was
on, and the top drawer of the desk had been pulled out. There
were no keys in it.

"He must be on his way down. We have to try and catch
him in the lobby," Osternak One cried. "You take the back
stairs. I'll take the front." He rushed out again to the end of
the building and scampered back down the front stairs. When
he was almost down to ground level, he saw a figure in a
topcoat and evening dress, its tie loosened, reeling drunkenly
some distance away from him in the open lounge area outside
the upper floor of the library. There could be no mistake this
time. He started in that direction, and in the same instant
Gorfmann saw him. "Rudi, stop," he called. But Gorfmann
vanished down a side staircase. Osternak followed as fast as
he could, but when he reached the bottom of the stairs,
Gorfmann had gone. There were several directions he could
have taken, but the two most probable, if he was going for
his car, were either through to the lobby or out the library
side door. Osternak picked the latter and followed the gravel
path outside around a corner of the building to the parking

area. Yes, there was a figure under the shrubs, near Gorfmann's car. Osternak started running toward it.

But instead of trying to escape, the figure stepped forward and called out, "Who are you? What do you want?"

Osternak halted in sudden confusion. It wasn't Gorfmann at all, in dinner dress, but somebody else in a black, single-piece garment that looked like a jumpsuit. The last thing that Osternak wanted now was further complication. He turned and ran back around the corner and in through the side door. Inside, he vacillated over which way to go and finally went through to the lobby and down the passage to the back door to check the compound.

As Osternak disappeared down the passage from the lobby, the crazed figure of Gorfmann came out of another opening behind him, staggered across the lobby, fumbling with his car keys, and disappeared out the front door.

Out in the compound, Osternak One halted uncertainly. Gorfmann, in evening dress, was approaching from the gate that opened through from the general staff parking area. But he was behaving in a suddenly very different manner, walking jauntily and whistling to himself. And although his tie was untied, all of a sudden he didn't have a topcoat. Aware that something odd was going on, Osternak faded back into the shadows by the rear door of the Keep. And then another figure appeared at the gate behind Gorfmann. "Hey, Rudi," it called. Gorfmann stopped and looked back. It was Hoetzer's voice. "You forgot your coat."

"Oh, silly of me." Gorfmann turned and retraced his steps to the gate.

And then it dawned on Osternak what was happening. This wasn't the Gorfmann he had been chasing at all, but the original one, back from Innsbruck. Osternak exhaled his breath slowly at the thought of the collision that had almost occurred, and let himself quietly back into the building. He walked quickly back along the passage to the front lobby, and just as he got there a car engine started up outside. A moment later, he saw headlamps through the lobby windows, then Gorfmann's car backing out of its parking slot and roaring away. He ran toward the door, although the gesture was already futile, but then stopped dead as he was about to open it. The figure in the black jumpsuit was still out there, standing in full view in the forecourt, now, looking up at the sky. Then the figure began crunching across the gravel toward the door. Osternak backed off and drew himself up into the darkness at the foot of the front stairs. The figure in the jump-suit came in through the door and then skidded on the tiles just inside the vestibule, almost falling over. Osternak heard him curse, and then watched him walk across to the passage at the back and go into the men's washroom a short distance along.

No sooner had that door closed when the sound of another door opening came from the far end of the passage, followed by footsteps approaching briskly. Osternak moved higher up the stairs, deeper into the darkness. It was the Gorfmann back from Innsbruck, no doubt going through to pick up his car. Hoetzer must have dropped him off in the general staff area for some reason instead of bringing him directly around to the front. Osternak was past trying to figure out what was happening now, or when, or with whom, or why. He waited in the stairway, totally bemused.

Gorfmann disappeared out through the front door. Osternak heard his footsteps come to a sudden halt outside on the gravel, then go stamping back and forth from one end of the parking area to the other. Finally they came back to the entrance, and Gorfmann burst through, slamming the door behind him. "What in hell's going on?" Osternak heard him muttering aloud to himself. "Oh God, this is too much. Not at a time like this, of all nights!" His voice faded away along the passage. The sound came of the back door opening, closing again with a bang, and then all was quiet.

Osternak waited a while longer, but everything remained still. He turned and went slowly up to his office, thinking that perhaps his other self might have gone there, too. But he found it deserted. He went over to his desk, sat down, took the flask from the cabinet below his terminal, and poured himself another large, straight brandy. He sat there for a long time, trying to make sense of it all, but he was too tired. Tomorrow he would write it all down. But for now . . . there was nothing more to be done for now. He replaced the flask, switched off the desk lamp, got up wearily, and walked over to the door. After one last look around and a final, baffled shake of his head, he turned out the light and walked the corridor to the front stairs. Just as he got there, a figure coming down the stairs fast almost ran into him. It was a Gorfmann. Osternak had no idea which one. He was wearing evening dress and a topcoat, but had his tie tied.

For a second Gorfmann just stood there, paralyzed with shock and looking as befuddled as Osternak felt. His eyes widened disbelievingly behind his spectacles, and his head shook protestingly. "It can't be," he whispered.

Suddenly the pieces fell together in Osternak's mind, and despite the circumstances he couldn't contain a thin smile. "Oh, but it can," he assured Gorfmann.

"How is this possible?"

"I don't understand it. You don't understand it. That's what I've been trying to tell you, Rudi, but you wouldn't listen. Do what you will. You can't win."

"Oh, but I can." Gorfmann drew out the gun. Osternak could have taken it, since it contained only blanks . . . but that would have spoiled everything.

As they walked away down the stairs, Osternak ahead and Gorfmann following a short distance behind with the gun, another figure who had been listening came down from the level above. He followed them at a safe distance across the compound and watched as they entered the transfer dome. He waited outside for a few minutes, and by the time he went inside, the control room was empty. He went over to the supervisory console, which had been activated, and read from the displays that the transfer countdown was just twenty seconds from zero. He moved quietly over to the door and peered around it into the transfer room just in time to see Gorfmann step into the chamber behind Osternak One and close the door. There was a brief humming noise, and then silence. Back in the control room the displays went through the posttransfer routine, and the system shut itself down.

Professor Osbert Osternak Two came back outside and stood looking around at the silhouettes of the Keep, the silent laboratory buildings, and the lights from the main gate area on the far side of the compound. He drew the set of Gorfmann's car keys from his pocket and stared at them for a long time, thinking to himself and wondering at the subtleties of the universe. Then he walked slowly back across the compound and into the Keep. Ten minutes later, wearing his overcoat and hat, he came out through the front entrance, climbed into his car, and left for home. It had been a long night in more ways than one. He had been awake an extra six hours, and his body was beginning to feel it. Tomorrow, for once, he would sleep in late, he decided. Very late.

Inspector Wenkle made a sweeping motion with his hand over the papers spread out on the desk in Professor Osternak's office. "The thing that puzzles me, Professor, is that the dentition of the victim matches Dr. Gorfmann's records perfectly. Also, we found traces of unburned hair that also matched samples from a comb found in Gorfmann's desk."

Osternak returned a what-am-I-supposed-to-say-to-that look. "Surely you're not suggesting that it was Gorfmann in the car, Inspector? How could it have been? You said that you interviewed him yourself the day after the accident happened."

"Also, they both had surgical pins in the same knee."

"Lots of people have surgical pins."

"But the dental records . . ."

"I'm afraid that's not my department, Inspector. Can't two people have similar dental histories?"

"Identical? I've never heard of it."

Osternak raised his eyebrows and held a prolonged shrug for a moment longer, and then placed his hands palms-down on his desk in a gesture of finality. "Well, all I can suggest, Inspector, is that you take a leaf from the practice of science," he said breezily.

"And what might that be, sir?"

"Hypotheses are built upon the best data available, but they are never inviolate. When incontrovertible facts are established which contradict the hypothesis, then the hypothesis must be revised. In this case, the hypothesis based on previous experience is that no two individuals have identical dentition. . . . I trust you take my point."

"I see." Wenkle rubbed his nose and seemed about to say something, then thought better of it. "This will cause quite a sensation among forensic circles," he remarked.

"Hmm? . . . Oh yes. Yes, I suppose it will."

"Well, I suppose there's no need to take up any more of your time, Professor."

"If you're sure I can be of no further help . . ."

"Oh, I think we've covered everything." Wenkle began collecting his papers together. "Where did you say Dr. Gorfmann went, again?"

"To Australia. He was a rather headstrong and unusually ambitious young man—very capable, mark you, but he thought he wasn't getting enough of an opportunity here. He resigned and went off to . . . oh, I forget the name of the place. One of those billabong-sounding, Aborigine words, out in the desert."

"A bit abrupt, wasn't it?"

"Remarkably so. It caused us a few headaches, I can tell you. But he was very temperamental. Terrible, the lack of consideration among young people these days. Terrible."

"It seems strange that he didn't wait to collect the insurance money."

"Didn't need it. His family's dripping with money. They own gold mines or something out in Australia. That's probably why he went there."

"Why would he have bought a new car so recently if he was going abroad?"

"Who knows? As I said, he was an extremely headstrong young man. It was probably an impulse that came out of the blue. He was like that. It doesn't surprise me at all. I only wish I had the money and freedom to be able to do things like that."

"I see." Wenkle zipped up his document holder and rose from his chair. "Just one more thing, Professor."

"Yes?"

"To enable us to close our file on the case, I suppose there'd be no objection to letting me have copies of the relevant documents—his resignation notice and termination papers?"

Osternak stared down at the desk for a moment. "You mean right now?"

"Well, if it wouldn't be any trouble, since I'm here anyway. . . ."

"Hmm . . ." Osternak sniffed and scratched his temple. "That might be difficult. I've just remembered that our secretary who handles all those things is off this afternoon."

"Well, maybe in the next couple of days?"

"Oh, in that case . . ." Osternak showed his palms in a

gesture of magnanimity. It would mean a long session with Hoetzer's high-resolution graphics printer, but he could survive another late night, he supposed. "Certainly, Inspector. Give me a couple of days, and I'll let you have all the documents you like."

"Very good, then. Good day, Professor Osternak. And thank you again for being so cooperative."

"Not at all. I like to do my best for another profession whose objective is uncovering the truth, eh? Good day to you, Inspector."

Osternak got up and escorted Wenkle to the door. Then he came back and stood for a long time staring at the equations on his chalkboard. The recent events demonstrated an even greater need for care than he'd imagined. But when he went over the things that had happened and examined them again in terms of symbolic relationships . . . yes, yes, he could see a strange kind of logic beginning to emerge. Intrigued, he moved nearer the board, picked up a piece of chalk, and began to write.

SOURCES

The original version of *"Silver Shoes for a Princess"* appeared in *Destinies* Vol. 1, No. 5, Ace Books, October-December 1979.

"Minds, Machines, and Evolution" is based on an article of the same name which appeared in *Destinies* Vol. 3, No. 1, Ace Books, Winter 1981.

"Till Death Us Do Part" was first published in *Stellar 6* anthology, Del Rey Books, January 1981.

The first edition of the novel *Code of the Lifemaker* was published in June 1983. Prologue reproduced by permission of Ballantine Books.

"Making Light" was first published in *Stellar 7* anthology, Del Rey Books, August 1981.

The original version of *"Assassin"* appeared in *Stellar 4* anthology, Del Rey Books, May 1978.

"Neander-tale" was first published in *Fantasy & Science Fiction*, December 1980.